LEGISLATING FOR

The Parliamenta

Human R...

LEGISLATING FOR HUMAN RIGHTS

The Parliamentary Debates on the Human Rights Bill

Edited by
JONATHAN COOPER
AND
ADRIAN MARSHALL-WILLIAMS

HART PUBLISHING
OXFORD AND PORTLAND OREGON
2000

Hart Publishing
Oxford and Portland, Oregon

Published in North America (US and Canada) by
Hart Publishing
c/o International Specialized Book Services
5804 NE Hassalo Street
Portland, Oregon
97213-3644
USA

Distributed in Netherlands, Belgium and Luxembourg by
Intersentia, Churchillaan 108
B2900 Schoten
Antwerpen
Belgium

© JUSTICE 2000

The editors have asserted their rights under the Copyright,
Designs and Patents Act 1988, to be identified as the
authors of this work.

Hart Publishing is a specialist legal publisher
based in Oxford, England.
To order further copies of this book or to request a list of
other publications please write to:

Hart Publishing,
Salters Boatyard, Folly Bridge,
Abingdon Rd, Oxford, OX1 4LB
Telephone: +44 (0)1865 245533
Fax: +44 (0) 1865 794882
email: mail@hartpub.co.uk

British Library Cataloguing in Publication Data
Data Available

ISBN 1-84113-098-2

Typeset by
John Saunders Design and Production, Reading
Printed and bound in Great Britain
by Biddles Ltd. www.biddles.co.uk

Contents

Foreword Anne Owers, Director of JUSTICE ... ix
About the Editors ... xv
Speakers in the debates featured in this book ... xvii
Note on Referencing ... xix

Part 1: General Statements on the Human Rights Act

Opening speeches at Second Reading ... 1
Ministerial Replies at Second Reading ... 8
General Contribution During Second Reading ... 11
Opening Speech at Third Reading ... 13

Part 2: The Human Rights Act Section by Section

Long title ... 19
    Absence of Purpose Clause ... 21

Section 1: The Convention Rights ... 24
    Protocols 4, 6 and 7 to the European Convention on Human Rights ... 25
    Addition of Protocol 6 ... 26

Section 2: Interpretation of Convention Rights ... 35
    Section 2(1) ... 36

Section 3: Interpretation of Legislation ... 45
    Doctrine of implied repeal ... 57

Section 4: Declaration of Incompatibility ... 64
    'A Convention right' in section 4(1) and (2) ... 69

Section 5: right of the Crown to intervene ... 71
    Subsection 5(2) ... 72
    Costs ... 76

Contents

Section 6: Acts of Public Authorities — 80
  Section 6(1) — 95
  Definition of persons for clause 6(3) — 96
  Public authorities covered — 98
  Position of the Churches — 101
  Position of the Armed Forces — 101
  Position of 'hybrid bodies' — 102
  Position of prosecutors — 103
  Section 6(6) — 107

Section 7: Proceedings — 109
  Section 7(1) — 111
  Section 7(3): Standing for public interest groups — 114
  Section 7(5): Limitation periods for section 7 actions — 121
  Section 7(8) — 125
  Section 7(11) — 126

Section 8: Judicial remedies — 130
  Section 8(1) — 131
  Relationship with Article 13 — 132
  Damages in judicial review proceedings — 136
  Effect of section 8 on fair trial guarantees — 138

Section 9: Judicial acts — 142
  Section 9(1) and Article 5(5) of the European Convention on Human Rights — 143

Section 10: Power to take remedial action — 147
  Section 10(1)(a) — 159
  Section 10(6) — 161

Section 11: Safeguard for existing human rights — 164

Section 12: Freedom of expression — 168

Section 13: Freedom of thought, conscience and religion — 177
  Background: Position of the Churches — 184

Sections 14 to 17: Derogations and reservations — 189

Section 18: Appointment to European Court of Human Rights — 193

Section 19: Statements of Compatibility — 195

Section 20: orders etc. under this act	202
Section 21: Interpretation	203
Section 22: Short title, commencement, application and extent	206
Schedule 2: remedial orders	208
Procedure	212

Part 3: Specific Issues Arising out of the Human Rights Act

Articles 8 & 10: Press freedom, self regulation, and the right to respect for private life	217
Article 13: The absence of a right to an effective remedy	231
Margin of Appreciation	248
Human Rights Commission	250
Parliamentary Committee	255
Article 14: Protecting against discrimination	257
Scotland	259
Section 2	260
Section 4	260
Church of Scotland's position	262
Channel Islands and the Isle of Man	275
Duties on Counsel	279

Foreword: Legislating for Rights

The Human Rights Act, which for the first time incorporated positive rights into United Kingdom (UK) law, is one of the most important legislative reforms of this century. Together with devolution and the proposed reform of the House of Lords, it was part of a new constitutional platform, changing the legal and political landscape of the UK. This book provides a fascinating insight into the process by which this was achieved, and the underlying principles and motives which impelled the Government and Parliament to enact it.

The background

The Labour Party's 1997 election manifesto included a commitment to incorporate the European Convention on Human Rights (ECHR) into UK law. This followed a party consultation paper, *Bringing Rights Home*, published in November 1996. The Labour Party, and those on the left in politics, had not always been in favour of justiciable rights; the turning point came in 1993 when John Smith, then party leader, pledged himself and the party to the principle of incorporating the ECHR. Incorporation was seen to be necessary in order to remedy the failings of the existing system for enforcing human rights within the UK and the fact that a remedy for a human rights breach was only available to those who were able to take the long, slow road to Strasbourg. It was seen to be absurd that the UK courts were unable to adjudicate on human rights issues.

Incorporation of the ECHR was announced in the new Government's first Queen's Speech in May 1997. The Human Rights Bill was published in October 1997, together with a Home Office consultation paper, *Rights Brought Home*, explaining the mechanism of incorporation. That mechanism was unique, and much-praised. It located the newly justiciable Convention rights (as set out in the Bill) within the framework of parliamentary sovereignty, placing duties and responsibilities on the courts, Parliament and all public authorities, including government. Courts would have a duty to protect and enforce human rights, with a strong duty to interpret common and statute law compatibly; but they could not strike down primary legislation. The

High Court could, however, declare a statute to be incompatible with the Convention rights; and if so, the Bill provided for a fast-track mechanism by which the defect could be remedied, if Parliament chose. At the same time, new legislation coming before Parliament would need to state on its face whether it was considered compatible with Convention rights. In addition, a wide range of public bodies, including all those carrying out a public function, would be challengeable, directly or in the context of other legal proceedings, if their acts or omissions breached the Convention rights.

The debates

This publication follows the Human Rights Bill, the vehicle for incorporation, through all its parliamentary stages: from its Second Reading in the House of Lords on 3rd November 1997, to Royal Assent on 9 November 1998. This edited text of the Parliamentary debates will therefore provide an invaluable insight into understanding Parliament's intention and motives for incorporation. It also sets out any concerns expressed, and how these were addressed. As such it will be required reading for all those responsible for implementing the Human Rights Act 1998 (HRA). Clearly, lawyers and judges will find this text useful when seeking to establish Parliament's intention under the doctrine of *Pepper v Hart*, and the cross-referencing should help to clarify the Minister's statements on a particular subject.

However, the debates on the Human Rights Bill are also of great interest to historians and political scientists. They capture history in motion, as the UK's constitutional framework was fundamentally and definitively altered, and underpinned by the assertion of positive, prescribed and enforceable human rights standards. These debates are therefore part of an ongoing debate, since at least the eighteenth century, on the relationship between the state and the individual, and between democracy and the courts, which led to the adoption of constitutionally protected rights in the United States and many European countries.

The debates are also fascinating for the general reader. They show Ministers defining and enthusiastically defending the new and finely-balanced constitutional arrangement, which would set limits to their own powers; and opposition parties teasing out the precise meaning of these novel provisions in order to refine and clarify them, rather than engaging in pure adversarial politics. As the scheme and scope of the

Bill unfolds in debate and explanation, the reader is caught up in the reality, the importance and indeed the excitement of implementing human rights standards within a parliamentary process.

The debates are distinguished by some extremely high quality and informed cross-party discussion of human rights principles and practice. Ministers steered a careful course, designed to put into effect a key manifesto commitment with as much all-party agreement as possible. Because of the wide-ranging constitutional implications of the Bill, the House of Commons during Committee stage sat as a Committee of the whole house. As a consequence, all MPs were able to participate in detailed discussion of the Bill's 22 clauses.

This process of detailed scrutiny allowed the opposition parties in both Houses to tease out the implications of the Bill. The Conservative opposition did not oppose incorporation in principle: but they did force the Government to defend the charge that it would increase the power of the executive, diminish the authority of Parliament and politicise the judiciary; and to show that the chosen method of incorporation was workable and justifiable. The Liberal Democrats fought valiantly, though unsuccessfully, for the inclusion of a UK Human Rights Commission in the Bill's provisions, concentrating minds on the large task involved in ensuring successful implementation of such a profound change. The opposition parties secured significant changes and safeguards in the arrangements for remedial orders (introduced where legislation has been held to be incompatible by the courts). Later, the concerns of the press and some of the churches led to clauses clarifying the Bill's implications for freedom of expression and religion.

The consequences

The ECHR is the foundation document of post-war Europe; ratification is a condition of membership of the Council of Europe, which now stretches across the whole continent. It is curious that the UK, which has strongly promoted the ECHR and its values, and whose lawyers were instrumental in drafting it, has been among the last Council of Europe country to give it domestic and practical effect. As a result, though the ECHR was binding on the UK as a matter of public international law, its provisions could not be directly enforced on public authorities or relied upon in courts. The 'ECHR gap' was perhaps most clearly visible in the challenges mounted to the blanket ban on lesbians and gay men serving in the armed forces. The English courts, applying the Wednesbury judicial review test, were unable to find the ban irrational or perverse; but were also unable to determine whether it breached the applicants' human rights. They could only act as a staging post for the decision of the Strasbourg court, which was in effect the court of first instance for determining human rights within the UK. The Strasbourg court duly, and unanimously, found the ban to be in breach of the ECHR.

The Human Rights Act remedies this. It places universal, indivisible human rights principles within the UK's legal and political systems. All UK courts and tribunals will now be able to adjudicate on Convention rights; one of the Act's key features is that it roots the protection of rights firmly within the existing legal system rather than creating a separate and distinct procedure for asserting human rights claims. The Strasbourg court will therefore assume its appropriate function as a public international law tribunal of last resort which sets down the minimum standard of human rights protection.

However, the Act's impact is not only that it domesticates Convention proceedings. It also fundamentally alters the nature of accountability within the UK's constitutional arrangements. Under the Act, the courts, Parliament and the Government are now accountable individually and to each other. Parliament remains the highest source of law, but its actions can be challenged and if necessary amended. The policies and decisions of Government (and all public bodies) can and will be measured against the minimum standards set down in the Act. The courts have to engage in the promotion and protection of human rights, even if that puts them at variance with Parliament.

This will not only change relationships at the centre of government and law; it will also require greater accountability and transparency in decisions which affect ordinary people's lives. The debates in Parliament recognise these changes in the nature and quality of accountability. Much of the language is framed in terms of a new culture of rights and responsibilities. That responsibilities flow from the exercise of rights is explicit in the structure of the ECHR, and the effective application of human rights is based on that principle. Where rights require a balance to be struck between the rights of an individual and the community, or between competing rights, there is a transparent procedure to be followed. Once a Convention right is engaged, it is for the public authority to show that any interference can be justified in Convention terms: on grounds that it is lawful, necessary and proportionate.

Though the 'horizontal effect' of the Act – its application in regulating conduct between private individuals or bodies – is the subject of considerable debate and some disagreement, it can clearly have application in matters that are essentially private (such as family law issues), and its principles will infuse the making, development and interpretation of all law.

The aim of this book is to bring the process of incorporation alive. As well as being instructive, the debates are also interesting and enjoyable reading. It is only regrettable that, due to constraints of space, many interventions from individual Members could not be included. The changes in the UK system of government which the Act will bring about give it constitutional significance. Like the process of securing universal franchise between 1832 and 1928, the Parliament Acts of 1911 and 1949 and the European Communities Act 1972, the HRA will become an essential element of the legal and administrative framework. This edited text shows how its implications were anticipated and how Parliament responded to such profound constitutional reform.

Anne Owers
Director, JUSTICE
July 2000

About the editors

Jonathan Cooper is the Director of the Human Rights Project at JUSTICE. He has taken several cases to the European Court of Human Rights and has written many articles and spoken extensively on the Human Rights Act and the European Convention on Human Rights. He is book review editor for the European Human Rights Law Review (Sweet & Maxwell).

Adrian Marshall-Williams is a barrister at 2 Garden Court.

Speakers in the debates featured in this book

The Secretary of State for the Home Department (Mr Jack Straw)
The Parliamentary Under-Secretary of State for the Home Department (Mr Mike O'Brien)
The Parliamentary Under-Secretary of State for the Home Department (Lord Williams of Mostyn)
The Lord Chancellor (Lord Irvine of Lairg)
The Parliamentary Secretary, Lord Chancellor's Department (Mr Geoffrey Hoon)
The Lord Advocate (Lord Hardie)

Mr Kevin McNamara (Labour, Hull North)
Mr Terry Davis (Labour, Birmingham, Hodge Hill)
Mr Paul Stinchcombe (Labour, Wellingborough)
Mr Gerald Kaufman (Labour, Manchester, Gorton)
Mr Martin Linton (Labour, Battersea)
Mr Denzil Davies (Labour, Llanelli)

Sir Brian Mawhinney (Shadow Home Secretary (to June 1998); Conservative, Cambridgeshire North West)
Sir Norman Fowler (Shadow Home Secretary (from June 1998) Conservative, Sutton Coldfield)
Lord Kingsland (Shadow Lord Chancellor, Conservative)
Sir Nicholas Lyell (Shadow Attorney General; Conservative, Bedfordshire North East)
Lord Mackay of Drumadoon (Shadow Lord Advocate; Conservative)
Mr James Clappison (Front Bench Spokesman, Home Affairs; Conservative, Hertsmere)
Mr Edward Garnier (Front Bench Spokesman, Lord Chancellor's Department; Conservative, Harborough)
Mr Dominic Grieve (Conservative, Beaconsfield)
Mr John Bercow (Conservative, Buckingham)
Mr Douglas Hogg (Conservative, Sleaford and North Hykeham)

Lord Henley (Conservative)
Mr Andrew Rowe (Conservative, Faversham and Kent Mid)
Mr David Ruffley (Conservative, Bury St Edmunds)
Mr Andrew David Lansley (Conservative, Cambridgeshire South)
Mr Peter Bottomley (Conservative, Worthing, West)
Miss Ann Widdecombe (Conservative, Maidstone and the Weald)
Mr Gerald Howarth (Conservative, Aldershot)
Lord Wakeham (Conservative)
Lord Renton (Conservative)
Lord Campbell of Alloway (Conservative)
Lord Mackay of Clashfern (Conservative)

Mr Robert Maclennan (Front Bench Spokesman, Constitutional Affairs; Liberal Democrat, Caithness Sutherland and Easter Ross)
Mr Simon Hughes (Liberal Democrats, Southwark, North and Bermondsey)
Lord Lester of Herne Hill (Liberal Democrats)
Lord Meston (Liberal Democrats)
Baroness Williams of Crosby (Liberal Democrats)
Lord Goodhart (Liberal Democrats)

Rev Martin Smyth (Shadow Leader of the House; Ulster Unionist Party, Belfast, South)

Lord Cooke of Thorndon (Cross Bench)
Lord Simon of Glaisdale (Cross Bench)
Lord Browne-Wilkinson (Cross Bench)
Lord Ackner (Cross Bench)
Lord Donaldson of Lymington (Cross Bench)
Lord Hylton (Cross Bench)

Note on Referencing

The bulk of this book consists of the statements and contributions made during the parliamentary debates on the Human Rights Act 1998. The reference materials are given in the following format:

[Place], [Stage]

[Hansard Reference]

[Speaker]:...[text]

So, for example:

House of Commons, Committee Stage

Official Report, House of Commons, 20 May 1998, vol. 312, col. 981

The Secretary of State for the Home Department (Mr. Jack Straw):...I wish future Judicial Committees of the House of Lords luck in working through these debates. One sometimes wonders about the wisdom of the Pepper *v.* Hart judgment in terms of the work that it has given the higher judiciary.

Part 1: General Statements on the Human Rights Act

OPENING SPEECHES AT SECOND READING

Need for Act – Act crafted to respect the traditional doctrine of separation of powers and to respect 'parliamentary sovereignty' – Conflict between Acts of Parliament and Human Rights Act resolved by declaration of incompatibility then for Parliament to decide

House of Lords, Second Reading
Official Report, House of Lords, 3 November 1997, vol. 582, col. 1227

The Lord Chancellor (Lord Irvine of Lairg): . . . [This Bill]occupies a central position in our integrated programme for constitutional change. It will allow British judges for the first time to make their own distinctive contribution to the development of human rights in Europe. It is today a happy reflection that British jurisprudence will shortly flow into...the European Court of Human Rights in Strasbourg. [. . .] [c. 1228] . . . Our legal system has been unable to protect people in the 50 cases in which the European Court has found a violation of the Convention by the United Kingdom. That is more than any other country except Italy. The trend has been upwards. Over half the violations have been found since 1990. [. . .]This Bill will bring human rights home. People will be able to argue for their rights and claim their remedies under the Convention in any court or tribunal in the United Kingdom. Our courts will develop human rights throughout society. A culture of awareness of human rights will develop. Before Second Reading of any Bill the responsible Minister will make a statement that the Bill is or is not compatible with Convention rights. So there will have to be close scrutiny of the human rights implications of all legislation before it goes forward. Our standing will rise internationally. The protection of human rights at home gives credibility to our foreign policy to advance the cause of human rights around the world.

Our critics say the Bill will cede powers to Europe, will politicise the judiciary and will diminish parliamentary sovereignty. We are not ceding new powers to Europe. The United Kingdom already accepts that Strasbourg rulings bind. Next, the Bill is carefully drafted and designed to respect our traditional understanding of the separation of powers. It does so intellectually convincingly and, if I may express my high regard for the parliamentary draftsman, elegantly.

The design of the Bill is to give the courts as much space as possible to protect human rights, short of a power to set aside or ignore Acts of Parliament. In the very rare cases where the higher courts will find it impossible to read and give effect to any statute in a way which is compatible with Convention rights, they [c. 1229] will be able to make a declaration of incompatibility. Then it is for Parliament to decide whether there should be remedial legislation. Parliament may, not must, and generally will, legislate. If a Minister's prior assessment of compatibility (under Clause 19) is subsequently found by declaration of incompatibility by the courts to have been mistaken, it is hard to see how a Minister could withhold remedial action. There is a fast-track route for Ministers to take remedial action by order. But the remedial action will not retrospectively make unlawful an act which was a lawful act—lawful since sanctioned by statute. This is the logic of the design of the Bill. It maximises the protection of human rights without trespassing on parliamentary sovereignty.

[. . .][c. 1234]I am convinced that incorporation of the European Convention into our domestic law will deliver a modern reconciliation of the inevitable tension between the democratic right of the majority to exercise political power and the democratic need of individuals and minorities to have their human rights secured.

Importance of Act – Britain committed to the European Convention from beginning – Effects of non-incorporation – Benefits of incorporation – Act to set minimum standards of treatment by local authorities –British judges to make contribution to rights jurisprudence- preservation of parliamentary sovereignty 'fundamental' to method of incorporation[1] *– but incorporation to have effect on process of legislating*

---

[1] See also comments below under clause 6

House of Commons, Second Reading
Official Report, House of Commons, 16 February 1998, vol. 307, col. 769

The Secretary of State for the Home Department (Mr. Jack Straw): . . . This is the first major Bill on human rights for more than 300 years. It will strengthen representative and democratic government. It does so by enabling citizens to challenge more easily actions of the state if they fail to match the standards set by the European Convention. The Bill will thus create a new and better relationship between the Government and the people.

Nothing in the Bill will take away the freedoms that our citizens already enjoy. However, those freedoms alone are not enough: they need to be complemented by positive rights that individuals can assert when they believe that they have been treated unfairly by the state, or that the state and its institutions have failed properly to protect them. The Bill will guarantee to everyone the means to enforce a set of basic civil and political rights, establishing a floor below which standards will not be allowed to fall. The Bill will achieve that by giving further effect in our domestic law to the fundamental rights and freedoms contained in the European Convention on Human Rights.

The Convention is a treaty of the Council of Europe, now a body of some 40 countries. The Council was established at the end of the second world war as part of the allies' programme to reconstruct civilisation on the mainland of Europe. The United Kingdom was a prime mover in the Convention and played a major and dignified part in its drafting. One of its draftsmen, David Maxwell Fyfe, later became, as Lord Kilmuir, a distinguished Lord Chancellor in the Conservative Government from 1954 to 1962. The United Kingdom was also among the first countries to sign the Convention, which we did on the first available day. We were the first to ratify it, in March 1951.

The United Kingdom's international commitment to the Convention has continued ever since. In 1966, we accepted the right of individuals to bring cases against the United Kingdom. The United Kingdom has also set a [c. 770] good example in responding to any adverse findings of the European Court of Human Rights in Strasbourg. For nearly 50 years, there has been broad political support for what the Convention does and what it stands for, with a fundamental recognition that, in practice, decisions of the Strasbourg court must be implemented.

[...]

Since the Convention's drafting nearly 50 years ago, almost all the states that are party to it have gradually incorporated it into their domestic law. Ireland and Norway have not done so, but Ireland has a Bill of Rights which guarantees rights similar to those of the Convention, and Norway is in the process of incorporating the Convention. Several other countries with which we share our common law tradition, such as Canada and New Zealand, have provided similar protection for human rights in their legal systems.

The effect of non-incorporation on the British people is a practical one. The rights, originally developed by Britain, are no longer seen as British, and enforcing them takes far too long and costs far too much—on average five years and £30,000 to get an action into the European Court at Strasbourg once all domestic remedies have been exhausted. Bringing these rights home will mean that the British people will be able to argue for their rights in the British courts, without inordinate delay and cost. It will also mean that the rights will be brought much more fully into the jurisprudence of the courts throughout the United Kingdom, and their interpretation will thus be far more woven into our common law.

There will be another benefit: British judges will be enabled to make a distinctively British contribution to the development of the jurisprudence of human rights across Europe. It is also now plain that the approach that the United Kingdom has so far adopted towards the Convention has not stood the test of time. The most obvious proof of that lies in the number of cases in which the European Court has found that there have been violations of Convention rights in the United Kingdom. It is only natural that people of all political persuasions have asked, "Why do individuals in the United Kingdom have to go to Strasbourg to enforce their British rights? Why can they not rely on them before our domestic courts?"

[c. 771] [...]

Alongside the Bill . . . I published a White Paper entitled "Rights Brought Home", setting out the case for the Bill and how it would work. The Bill does not create new substantive rights, but it makes the existing Convention rights more immediate and relevant. Under the Bill, all courts and tribunals will be required to have regard to these rights.

Having decided that we should incorporate the Convention, the most fundamental question that we faced was how to do that in a manner that strengthened, and did not undermine, the sovereignty of Parliament. Some had argued that the courts should have power to set aside primary legislation, whether past or future, on the ground of incompatibility with the Convention. That is a feature of many, though by no means all, government systems with a basic law enshrined in a written constitution. It is also true that, under the European Communities Act 1972, enacted by the then Conservative Government, European law with direct effect automatically takes precedence over our domestic law and Parliament, whatever Parliament wants to do otherwise. [**c.** 772] That is not the road that we are going down. The Bill, important though it is, has the limited function of bringing the British people's rights home. It is no part of the project to call into question constitutional arrangements that have evolved in this country to make us one of the world's most stable democracies.

The sovereignty of Parliament must be paramount. By that, I mean that Parliament must be competent to make any law on any matter of its choosing. In enacting legislation, Parliament is making decisions about important matters of public policy. The authority to make those decisions derives from a democratic mandate. Members of this place possess such a mandate because they are elected, accountable and representative.

To allow the courts to set aside Acts of Parliament would confer on the judiciary a power that it does not possess, and which could draw it into serious conflict with Parliament. As the Lord Chief Justice said on Second Reading in another place, the courts and the senior judiciary do not want such a power, and we believe that the people do not wish the judiciary to have it.

Although the Bill does not allow the courts to set aside Acts of Parliament, it will nevertheless have an impact on the way in which legislation is drafted, interpreted and applied, and it will put the issues squarely to the Government and Parliament for future consideration. It is important to ensure that, for their part, the Government and Parliament can respond quickly.

In the normal way, primary legislation can be amended only by further primary legislation. As we all know—in normal circumstances, this is entirely correct—that can take a long time. One of the consequences of not having a special procedure to remedy defects in legislation is a degree of paralysis. Until now, the remedy has been through the Strasbourg Court.

Mr. Simon Hughes (Southwark, North and Bermondsey): The Home Secretary will know that I fully [c. 774] support the Government's incorporation of the Convention into domestic law, and that I have worked towards that end in the Council of Europe. May I, however, ask him to test the central point that he is making against the example that I am about to give?

If a Government introduced legislation or other rules banning members of an organisation such as Government communications headquarters—GCHQ—from belonging to a trade union, would they be able to go to a British court immediately for a remedy that would give them the right to union membership, freedom of expression and freedom of association? If Parliament voted by a majority to prevent those people from having that right, would it be able to maintain the denial of liberties that the Convention requires them to have?

The Secretary of State for the Home Department (Mr. Jack Straw): The Bill makes the position clear, in clause 4(6) and elsewhere. Clause 6 excludes the Houses of Parliament from the category of public authorities, for very good reasons. What the Bill makes clear is that Parliament is supreme, and that if Parliament wishes to maintain the position enshrined in an Act that it has passed, but which is incompatible with the Convention in the eyes of a British court, it is that Act which will remain in force.

There is, however, a separate question, which is why, in most instances, Parliament and Government will wish to recognise the force of a declaration of incompatibility by the High Court. Let us suppose that a case goes to Strasbourg, where the European Court decides that an action by the British Government, or the British Parliament, is outwith the Convention. According to 50 years of practice on both sides, we always put the action right, and bring it into line with the Convention. One of the questions that will always be before Government, in practice, will be, "Is it sensible to wait for a further challenge to Strasbourg, when the British courts have declared the provision to be outwith the Convention?"

[. . .] [c. 781]

The Opposition amendment seeks to block the Bill's Second Reading on three main grounds: that it will further increase the power of the Executive; that it will diminish Parliament; and that it will politicise the judiciary. As I hope I have shown, none of them has any serious foundation. [c. 782] The power of the Executive will be reduced by the Bill because the state will be made far more accountable for its acts and omissions to its citizens. The Bill enhances parliamentary sovereignty in practice, and the scheme that we have chosen ensures that the judiciary will not be involved in politics.

It is interesting that none of those concerns cut any ice with the then Conservative Chairman of the Home Affairs Committee, Sir Edward Gardner, when he introduced his Bill on incorporation 11 years ago. More than 50 Conservative Members voted for it, with four members of the present Conservative Front-Bench team, including the shadow Health Secretary. The only difference between the two Bills is that this one gives far greater protection to the sovereignty of Parliament.

There is another matter that the Opposition may have forgotten in tabling their amendment. In 1977, the architect of modern Conservatism, Lady Thatcher, supported the incorporation of the European Convention on Human Rights. She had the then Mr. Leon Brittan move amendments to the Scotland Bill to do that.

If the Conservatives were correct then, why are they wrong now? We not only have the benefit of Lady Thatcher's views on incorporation 20 years ago, but, just four months ago, we had the view of the shadow Lord Chancellor, Lord Kingsland. On the day that the Bill was published, he said in a radio interview that he was "satisfied" with it. He added:

> "From my vantage point we are not in principle against incorporation. The two concerns that we have about it, first of all, parliamentary sovereignty, and secondly, too big a shift of power from Parliament to judges. These concerns do not appear to be serious ones in the context of this Bill."

MINISTERIAL REPLIES AT SECOND READING

United Kingdom Parliament remains sovereign – Point of bill is which judges exercise what powers – All public authorities will have to adapt to culture of rights – general description of rights more appropriate

House of Lords, Second Reading
Official Report, House of Lords, 3 November 1997, vol. 582, col. 1307
The Parliamentary Under-Secretary of State, Home Office (Lord Williams of Mostyn): . . . The United Kingdom Parliament remains sovereign. We have therefore opted, I believe prudently, rightly and in accordance with United Kingdom tradition, to limit the power of the judges to the declaration of incompatibility. It really is as simple as that.

. . . It is suggested that perhaps this is an unconscious and unknowing conspiracy by the judiciary to take over power from the legislature. Nothing could be further from the truth. A number of noble Lords who have spoken have said that the judges will have powers. Indeed, yes: which judges, what powers and exercised where, is the whole point. . . . [. . .] [**c. 1308**] . . .

Our courts will have the opportunity to develop our jurisprudence. That is not, as the Lord Chancellor pointed out, simply, "You will be able to get your rights enforced quickly and cheaply because you will not have to make the journey to Strasbourg". It is much more important than that. Every public authority will know that its behaviour, its structures, its conclusions and its executive actions will be subject to this culture.

It is exactly the same as what necessarily occurred following the introduction of, for example, race relations legislation and equal opportunities legislation. Every significant body, public or private, thereafter had to ask itself, with great seriousness and concern, "Have we equipped ourselves to meet our legal obligations?" That has caused, as the noble Baroness, Lady Williams, said, a transformation in certain areas of human rights. The same is likely to follow when this Bill becomes law. . . . [**c. 1309**]

The right reverend Prelate[2] asked whether some of the rights or qualifications were not dangerously general. I am bound to say—this has

---

[2] The Lord Bishop of Lichfield at *ibid.*, c. 1249

been said many times—that a general description of rights is in many ways much more appropriate than an attempted description or prescription of rights which is not capable of being flexible with changing social conditions. Perhaps I may give one example. The noble Baroness, Lady Williams of Crosby, referred to electronic surveillance. Of course, that was not known 50 years ago in its present subtlety and sophistication, but the matter is still well covered by Article 8. We do not need over-prescription in this delicate area.

Parliamentary sovereignty preserved, Bill's purpose to 'bring rights home' – Bill to improve people's access to their rights – courts enabled to take account of Convention – present situation unsatisfactory

House of Commons, Second Reading
Official Report, House of Commons, 16 February 1998, vol. 307, col. 858

The Parliamentary Under-Secretary of State for the Home Department (Mr. Mike O'Brien): The purpose of the Bill is simple: it is to bring rights home. It is to reclaim, for people in this country, the rights to which they are entitled under the Convention. The purpose may be simple, but the effects will be profound. The Bill will benefit individuals, Government and the whole of society.

First and most obviously, the Bill will improve people's access to their rights. . . . At present, those who feel that their Convention rights have been infringed cannot, save in very limited circumstances, obtain redress in this country. They must take their grievances to Strasbourg. That is not a road to be taken by the faint-hearted. It takes about five years for a case to be resolved. Only those with time, patience, considerable willpower and, sometimes, considerable money are likely to stay the course. It cannot be right to ration rights so that only the dogged few can hope to benefit from them.

Enabling our courts to take account of the Convention is about more than reaching quicker decisions. It will mean that the judges of a domestic court can consider all the issues relevant to the case before them. They will no longer have to put out of their mind Convention arguments that might be relevant to the case, but which they are currently debarred from considering. Therefore, the Bill will change the approach that the courts adopt to Convention cases.

The present situation is wholly unsatisfactory for the courts and for individuals. It is artificial to cordon off a set of rights and make them the exclusive preserve of the Court in Strasbourg. It leads to frustration and it impedes effective justice. [c. 859] The right hon. Member for North-West Cambridgeshire (Sir B. Mawhinney) was worried about politicisation. I consider that our judges must be able to bring their knowledge of the United Kingdom's traditions and practices to bear on the cases that come before them. They will be able to interpret the Convention rights in ways sensitive to the specific circumstances that will apply in this country. The rights under the Convention will become interwoven with our laws.

The Strasbourg Court recognises that domestic courts have the primary role to play in protecting individuals' rights under the Convention. The proper role of the Strasbourg Court is to act as a backstop but, at present, the Strasbourg institutions are often placed in the front line, as the first bodies to consider issues arising under the Convention. That serves no one's interest.

Opponents of the Bill seem to exhibit a touch of schizophrenia. Human rights are, it seems, to be supported abroad, but ignored at home. On one hand, we have an exemplary approach to fulfilling our international obligations under the Convention—I have praised the previous Government's method of doing so—but on the other, we have been almost alone in denying our people domestic access to their rights.

Half in, half out—the hokey-cokey approach will not work. [. . .] We need an end to these mixed messages. Our citizens need a clear lead. The Government will give it. We are firmly committed to protecting the rights of our people, and the Bill is one demonstration of that. [. . .] [c. 861]

The Bill is part of the Government's modernisation of British politics. It is about giving people new rights in their dealings with the state. It is part of a comprehensive package of constitutional reforms which will increase individual rights, decentralise power, open up government and reform Parliament. We have moved to create a Scottish Parliament and a Welsh Assembly. There is to be a Freedom of Information Act, a referendum on the voting system for the House of Commons, a long-overdue reform of the House of Lords, the abolition of the law-making powers of hereditary peers and, by means of the Bill, the introduction of the European Convention on Human Rights into UK law. That will enable our people to access their rights in our domestic courts without having to go to Europe. The Bill empowers our people and I commend it to the House.

GENERAL CONTRIBUTION DURING SECOND READING

Bill's international significance – Problems with Bill outweighed by benefits, in particular declaration of incompatibility in comparison to New Zealand - (Lord Cooke of Thorndon)

House of Lords, Second Reading

Official Report, House of Lords, 3 November 1997, vol. 582, col. 1272

Lord Cooke of Thorndon: It is a Bill whose significance extends even beyond the United Kingdom and Europe, for it signifies the adherence of the United Kingdom to the international movement towards the national codification of human rights: a movement which answers the aspirations of peoples and takes its origins from the aspirations of peoples. The very existence of such a movement may be seen to refute the arguments about handing political power to the judges, vague generalities and so forth, which a number of noble Lords have with no little vigour and even charm put to your Lordships today. When the Bill is enacted, it is significant that, of the older Commonwealth countries, only Australia will be without some general enforceable affirmation of state guaranteed human rights.

[. . .] [c. 1272]

The United Kingdom Bill has limited aims. For instance, it is tied to the rather elderly European Convention, taking no notice of international developments since. Again, it does not itself lay claim to comply with Article 13 of that Convention, which guarantees to everyone an effective remedy before a national authority. That omission is perhaps to be explained as a matter of drafting technique, but it may not be clear that even the Government are making that claim. [. . .]

I believe, however, that the shortcomings of the Bill—and there are some—are far outweighed by its merits and that it may well prove to have real bite. I believe this for two reasons. The first is the express empowerment of the higher courts to make a declaration of incompatibility. Such express power is not given in the New Zealand Bill of Rights, under which, as was accurately summarised by the noble Lord, Lord Kingsland, sufficiently clear legislation overrides the affirmed rights. As a judge, I feared that the courts might seem to come into

conflict with Parliament if they declared that an Act was clear and overriding but nonetheless a violation. Happily, that fear will not exist in the United Kingdom because of Parliament's authorisation of such declarations. Nor does it seem likely that a declaration will be a mere brutum fulmen, if one from the Antipodes may be forgiven what has been called "the worst type of Latinism in the law". It is true that the power of a Minister to make remedial orders is neither expressed as a duty nor restricted in time; nor of course is the power of Parliament—but reasonable expedition would appear to be the essence of the concept in Clauses 10, 11 and 12; they breathe it. And if a national court has made a declaration of incompatibility and expeditious remedial steps have not followed, will not that state of affairs amount to a plain invitation to a journey to Strasbourg? After all, as was pointed out, the European Court of Human Rights retains all its power and can always have the last word. That in itself may well be a strong incentive towards adopting compatible interpretations in this jurisdiction.
[...] [c. 1273]

OPENING SPEECH AT THIRD READING

Changes made to the Act: some technical changes, some substantive changes to (i) remedial orders (ii) the position of the Churches (iii) the press – Bill will have 'significant ramifications' – need to prepare the judiciary and lay magistrates – task force to assist implementation

House of Commons, Third Reading

Official Report, House of Commons,21 October 1998, vol. 317, col.1357

Mr. Straw: . . . Three sets of changes have been made as a result of concerns expressed here and in the other place. The first concerns remedial orders. We continue to believe that it should be possible to amend Acts of Parliament by a remedial order so as to bring them into line with the Convention rights, but we have, after listening carefully to the debates, considerably restricted the circumstances in which they can be made, and we have significantly enhanced the parliamentary opportunities for scrutiny of those orders. [c. 1358] We have explained that any response to a declaration of incompatibility by the courts, whether by fresh primary legislation or by a remedial order, is a matter on which the Government will propose, but it is for Parliament to dispose. One of the Bill's many strengths is that it promotes human rights while maintaining the sovereignty of Parliament and the separation of powers which underpins our constitutional arrangements.

Secondly, there is the issue of the Churches, on which we had an interesting debate some minutes ago, including an entertaining excursion into the history of the Church of Scotland. We were, for reasons that I explained, unable to accept the amendments made by the other place which would have exempted Churches from the Bill's public authority provisions in the few circumstances where they would otherwise have been regarded as public authorities. At the same time, we recognised their concern about what they saw as the Bill's potential impact on such matters as faith and doctrine. In that regard, I tabled an amendment in Committee requiring the courts to have particular regard to the rights of religious organisations to freedom of thought, conscience and religion, and in so doing I believe that the Government and the House were able to go a long way towards meeting their concerns.

The third issue is that of the press. We never believed that the Bill would undermine the freedom of the press. The Strasbourg institutions attach a high value to freedom of expression, as is clear from a series of cases, including the Spycatcher case. Our courts will take that case law into account. But as with the Churches, we sought to meet the concerns of the press in a way which is consistent with the principles on which the Bill is based.

We did so with an amendment in Committee requiring the courts, among other things, to have particular regard to freedom of expression when they are considering granting any relief which might affect it. The amendment followed detailed discussions with the chairman of the Press Complaints Commission, Lord Wakeham, and with media representatives. I think that the amendment was well received in the House and outside.

I have commented on three particular issues that have arisen from the Bill. More generally, it is clear to everyone that the Bill has significant ramifications. Its provisions will have profound implications for the conduct of all public authorities, for the interpretation of legislation and for the operation of the court system at all levels. It will be much easier for individuals to rely on their Convention rights against public authorities, and I believe that they will take that opportunity.

Over time, the Bill will bring about the creation of a human rights culture in Britain. In future years, historians may regard the Bill as one of the most important measures of this Parliament. I talk about a human rights culture. One of the problems which has arisen in Britain in recent years is that people have failed to understand from where rights come. The philosopher David Selbourne has commented on the generation of an idea of dutiless rights, where people see rights as consumer products which they can take, but for nothing. The truth is that rights have to be offset by responsibilities and obligations. There can and should be no rights without responsibilities, and our responsibilities should precede our rights. [c. 1359] In developing that human rights culture, I want to see developed a much clearer understanding among Britain's people and institutions that rights and responsibilities have properly to be balanced—freedoms by obligations and duties. [. . .]

As the Bill nears the end of its parliamentary passage, it is right to look ahead to its implementation. Precisely because the Bill will have such a fundamental effect, we need to prepare for it thoroughly. We are providing training through the Judicial Studies Board for all courts and tribunals to enable them to deal adequately with the Convention points that will come before them in case after case. We have allocated just under £5 million in addition to the normal budget of the Judicial Studies Board and associated bodies for this judicial training.

We are also ensuring that Government Departments and other public authorities are properly prepared for the obligations that the Bill places on them. They will need not only to review their legislation and practices for compatibility with the Convention but to ensure that their staff are trained in an awareness of the Convention rights so that those rights permeate all the decisions that they make. We need to work out how the criminal justice system can best accommodate the additional pressures that are likely to follow from the Bill.

To answer directly the point made by the right hon. and learned Member for North-East Bedfordshire(Sir N. Lyell), that means that there is a great deal of work to do before the Bill can be implemented. We need to carry that out in a fair, systematic, balanced and positive way. The right hon. and learned Gentleman asked me to give a precise date for implementation. It cannot happen in the near future, and I hope that he will forgive me for being unable to give a precise date. We want to implement the Bill as soon as is feasible but we must all recognise that we cannot do so straight away.

One exception is clause 19, which requires ministerial statements of compatibility. The clause, which is important for the presentation of Bills before the House, does not form part of the main scheme of the Bill, and could be brought into force well in advance of the main provisions. I am considering the options for implementing clause 19 with my right hon. Friend the President of the Council and others, and I hope to make an announcement as soon as possible.

Mr. Maclennan: Before the Home Secretary leaves the matter of the date of the Bill's effective operation, will he tell us more about the criteria that he will apply in determining the practicality of proceeding? I understand that there is a need for judicial training, and the Home Secretary has spoken of the Government's efforts on that, but are there any other hidden obstacles to proceeding with implementation that he might want to disclose?

Mr. Straw: I do not think that there are any other hidden obstacles—I was trying to search my brain for [c. 1360] secrets but there are none.

We are bringing into Scots law and English law—by which, for the avoidance of doubt, I mean also the law that applies in Wales and Northern Ireland—not only the Convention, which is easily stated, as it is in the Bill, but its jurisprudence. It is crucial that we properly prepare our judicial system, including senior judges who have in many ways been living with the Convention for a long time.

Often when the law is ambiguous, the courts use the Convention and its jurisprudence as an aid to interpretation. However, the Convention has not reached many crown courts or county courts, and it has certainly not reached magistrates courts—it is outwith their experience. If we are not prepared and if we do not prepare those who serve in a judicial capacity, including 30,000 lay magistrates, we will find that sharp lawyers will seek to make disruptive points. We must be aware of that—we have always acknowledged it—and we must be prepared for it.

The Bill not only concerns the rights of individuals in a narrow sense but will change our society's culture. For example, those who are charged with criminal offences have rights and we must recognise and protect those rights, but others in society also have rights. It would be wrong to set sharp lawyers who have examined the jurisprudence against lay magistrates, justices clerks, busy county court and crown court judges who have not had the opportunity to do so. That would bring the Bill's implementation into disrepute. I want the process to succeed, so we need time to prepare for it.

I do not want to implicate the right hon. Member for Caithness, Sutherland and Easter Ross (Mr. Maclennan) in the process, but he has been closely associated with the project, both in opposition and in government. I thank him for that contribution. He knows that the Bill is an important priority for the Government and that there was considerable discussion about it in the joint consultative committee—of which he was a joint chairman—of the Liberal Democrat party and the Labour party. He will recognise that we must get on with the project—I know that he is on the case—but we must balance that against the need for preparation. [. . .]

The work of preparing for the Bill's implementation is not for the Government alone. We recognise that many outside the Government have a keen interest in how the Bill is implemented and want to contribute to its success. We draw on their expertise, as we did in opposition, and we take account of their concerns.

As the Under—Secretary of State for the Home Department, my hon. Friend the Member for North Warwickshire (Mr. O'Brien), said earlier, I have decided to establish a task force to assist the Government in the preparations for implementation.

The task force will be chaired by my noble Friend the Lord Williams of Mostyn and will include my hon. Friends the Solicitor-General and the Minister of State, Lord Chancellor's Department. The membership will also include those non-governmental organisations which have made extremely valuable contributions to the project and have continued to offer their advice as the Bill has proceeded through Parliament. They will include Francesca Klug, from the Human Rights Incorporation [c. 1361] Project; Anne Owers, from Justice; Andrew Puddephatt, from Charter 88; Sarah Spencer, from the Institute for Public Policy Research; Veena Vasista, from the 1990 Trust and John Wadham from Liberty.

The task force will help us to create the human rights culture to which I referred. Its tasks will include maintaining a dialogue between the Government and non-governmental organisations on the readiness of Departments, other public authorities and the legal profession for implementation and on its timing; working together to heighten public awareness of the Bill relating to responsibilities as well as rights; providing training opportunities for public authorities outside Government, and co-operating with other organisations in disseminating awareness, particularly among young people, of the rights and responsibilities inherent in the Convention.

We are preparing guidance on the Bill which is designed to assist Government Departments and others, and I expect the task force to take a keen interest in that.

House of Lords, Third Reading

Official Report, House of Lords, 5 February 1998, vol 585, col. 839

The Lord Chancellor (Lord Irvine of Lairg): My Lords, it is right that this Bill occupies a central position in our programme of constitutional reform. By bringing rights home it will enable people in this country to enforce their Convention rights against public authorities before our domestic courts. I believe that this will have a profound and beneficial effect on our system of law and government and will develop over the years a strong culture of human rights in our country.
[. . .]

The Bill is based on a number of important principles. Legislation should be construed compatibly with the Convention as far as possible. The sovereignty of Parliament should not be disturbed. Where the courts cannot reconcile legislation with Convention rights, Parliament should be able to do so—and more quickly, if thought appropriate, than by enacting primary legislation. Public authorities should comply with Convention rights or face the prospect of legal challenge. Remedies should be available for a breach of Convention rights by a public authority. We have brought these principles together into what your Lordships have, I think, generally agreed is a carefully constructed Bill.

[. . .]

The Bill provides for all legislation, past and future, to be interpreted as far as possible in a way which is compatible with the Convention rights. The Convention rights are the magnetic north and the needle of judicial interpretation will swing towards them.

The noble Lord knows, and I am sure accepts, that the courts are not to set aside primary legislation under the Bill, but the principle of statutory construction is a strong alternative. It will be unlawful for public authorities to act in a way which is incompatible with the Convention rights and that also is a strong and far-reaching provision. Taken together, those measures provide for the Convention rights to have a great effect in our domestic law. I go further; in 99 per cent. of the cases that will arise, there will be no need for judicial declarations of incompatibility.

What the Bill does not do is make the Convention rights themselves directly a part of our domestic law in the same way that, for example, the civil wrongs of negligence, trespass or libel are part of our domestic law. Claims in those areas are all actionable in tort in cases between private individuals. But, as the noble Lord knows, we have not provided for the Convention rights to be directly justiciable in actions between private individuals. We have sought to protect the human rights of individuals against the abuse of power by the state, broadly defined, rather than to protect them against each other. That is the only practical difference between the full incorporation of the Convention rights into our domestic law and the actual effect of the Bill. I hope that we can put to one side what is really a theological dispute in relation to the meaning of the word "incorporation" and concentrate on what the Bill was designed to achieve, which is a real enhancement of the human rights of people in this country.

Part 2: The Human Rights Act Section by Section

LONG TITLE

An Act to give further effect to rights and freedoms guaranteed under the European Convention on Human Rights; to make provision with respect to holders of certain judicial offices who become judges of the European Court of Human Rights; and for connected purposes.

Bill does not make European Convention 'part of our law' - Meaning of 'give further effect'

House of Lords, Committee Stage
Official Report, House of Lords, 18 November 1997, vol. 583, col. 478
The Lord Chancellor (Lord Irvine of Lairg): . . . I believe that the Long Title to the Bill is admirably clear to a layman and to lawyers. The reason the Long Title uses the word "further" is that our courts already apply the Convention in many different circumstances. For example—and the courts are well familiar with these examples—where a statute is capable of two interpretations, one consistent and one inconsistent with the Convention, the courts will presume that Parliament intended to legislate in accordance with the Convention. If the common law is uncertain, unclear or incomplete, the courts will rule wherever possible in a manner which conforms with the Convention. That is English law today.

House of Lords, Report Stage
Official Report, House of Lords, 29 January 1998, vol. 585, col. 419
Lord Simon of Glaisdale: . . . In the absence . . . of a purpose clause . . . the Long Title . . . [a]t present, . . . reads:

> "An Act to give further effect to rights and freedoms guaranteed under the European Convention."

My noble and learned friend the Lord Chancellor said quite correctly that that was perfectly true. . . . There are two directions in which the Bill gives further force to the Convention. One is that it amplifies rights already given by our common law and contributes to the European Convention. The other is that it makes the Convention rights enforceable against public authorities in our own courts. But that is clear from the contents of the Bill.

What a court of construction wants to know is whether it is intended that the Convention rights should apply in domestic law. That is precisely what the White Paper said and what my noble and learned friend has said on many occasions. So all I suggest is that in place of "further effect", the Long Title should read "domestic effect". That will mean something to a court of construction, whereas the Long Title at the moment means nothing at all. [. . .] [c. 421]

The Lord Chancellor (Lord Irvine of Lairg): . . . I do not believe that there is much that I can add to what I said . . . at Committee stage. The word "further" is included in the Long Title because, in our national arrangements, the Convention can, and is, already applied in a variety of different circumstances and is relied on in a range of ways by our own courts.

The Bill will greatly increase the ability of our courts to enforce Convention rights, but it is not introducing a wholly new concept. As I have said before, the Bill as such does not incorporate Convention rights into domestic law but, in accordance with the language of the Long Title, it gives further effect in the United Kingdom to Convention rights by requiring the courts in Clause 3(1),

"So far as it is possible to do so"

to construe—in the language of the statute, to read and give effect to—primary legislation and subordinate legislation in a way which is compatible with the Convention rights. That is an interpretative principle. [. . .]

I have to make this point absolutely plain. The European Convention on Human Rights under this Bill is not made part of our law. The Bill gives the European Convention on Human Rights a special relationship which will mean that the courts will give effect to the interpretative provisions to which I have already referred, but it does not make the Convention directly justiciable as it would be if it were expressly made part of our law. I want there to be no ambiguity about that.

Lord Lester of Herne Hill: My Lords, I am extremely grateful to the Lord Chancellor; but I wonder whether he would mind explaining the difference [c. 422] between requiring our courts (as a public authority) to give effect to the Convention; requiring our courts where possible to interpret Acts of Parliament to comply with the Convention; requiring our courts in developing the common law to have regard to the Convention rights, and requiring our courts to give effective remedies where there is a breach of those rights. What is the difference between all of that and incorporating the Convention? What else would be needed over and above all that in order to incorporate the Convention?

The Lord Chancellor: My Lords, this is fast becoming something of a theological dispute and I should like to bring it to a conclusion as quickly as I may. The short point is that if the Convention rights were incorporated into our law, they would be directly justiciable and would be enforced by our courts. That is not the scheme of this Bill. If the courts find it impossible to construe primary legislation in a way which is compatible with the Convention rights, the primary legislation remains in full force and effect. All that the courts may do is to make a declaration of incompatibility.

I have a feeling that in these dying moments of Report stage we are behaving in a way in which judges sometimes behave at the end of a very long case. It is almost as if they cannot bring themselves to depart from the case and to be left to consider it themselves, and question after question continues. I have given the best argument that I may.

Absence of Purpose Clause

Purpose clause not necessary, doubts about whether Bill to 'incorporate' Convention not resolved

House of Lords, Report Stage
Official Report, House of Lords, 19 January 1998, vol. 584, col.1257

Lord Lester of Herne Hill: The [Renton] report stated that there is one circumstance in which a purpose clause should be used; namely, where a Bill seeks to give effect to an international treaty obligation. That is exemplified by the present Bill.

Why is that the case? It is because there is a discrepancy between what was stated in the White Paper both by the Prime Minister, on behalf of the Government as a whole, and statements by the noble and learned Lord the Lord Chancellor in the course of debate, which need to be clarified. It may be that they can be clarified when the noble and learned Lord the Lord Chancellor replies, in which case the need for this clause may be reconsidered.

Perhaps I may explain the discrepancy. In his preface to the White Paper the Prime Minister said:

> "We are committed to a comprehensive programme of constitutional reform . . . The elements are well-known . . . new rights based on bringing the European Convention . . . into United Kingdom law".

The introduction and summary stated:

> "The Government has a Manifesto commitment to introduce legislation to incorporate"—

I emphasise the word "incorporate"—

> "the European Human Rights Convention into United Kingdom law. The Queen's speech . . . announced that the Government would bring forward a Bill for this purpose",

that is to say, for the purpose of incorporating Convention rights into domestic law.

Paragraph 1.19 of the White Paper states:

> "to make more directly accessible the rights which the British people already enjoy under the Convention. In other words, to bring those rights home".

All that is very plain—although not plainly stated on the face of the Bill.

In Committee, however, the noble and learned Lord the Lord Chancellor stated:

> "Convention rights will not . . . in themselves become part of . . . substantive domestic law".—Official Report, 18/11/97; col. 508.]

It is very important to assist the courts and members of the public to know whether, as the White Paper states, the purpose of the Bill is to provide effective remedies to the violation of Convention rights by incorporating Convention rights into domestic law. I hope, and believe, [c. 1258] that the noble and learned Lord the Lord Chancellor will be able to confirm that the main purpose is indeed to provide effective remedies for violation of Convention rights. That is what is meant by bringing Convention rights home.

Article [1] of the Convention obliges the United Kingdom to secure Convention rights for everyone within the jurisdiction of this country; and Article 13 obliges the UK to provide effective domestic remedies. It has not been argued in previous debates either by the noble and learned Lord the Lord Chancellor or the noble Lord, Lord Williams of Mostyn, that there is any practical objection to a purpose clause of this kind. [...] [c. 1261]

The Lord Chancellor (Lord Irvine of Lairg): . . . [T]he Government have reflected carefully on this matter since Committee stage but continue to believe that there is nothing to be gained by including a statement of purpose in the Bill . . . We believe that the purpose of the Bill can be readily understood from the scheme of the Bill, which is well understood, as was demonstrated in Committee. The Bill provides a clear and coherent scheme by which the Convention rights are to be given further effect in our domestic law. The purpose of the Bill is obvious: it is to enable Convention rights to be asserted directly in our domestic courts. The medium of achieving that is, among others, Clause 3, the interpretative principle that, so far as possible, the courts are to construe primary legislation and subordinate legislation compatibly with Convention rights.

SECTION 1: THE CONVENTION RIGHTS

The Convention Rights.

1. - (1) In this Act "the Convention rights" means the rights and fundamental freedoms set out in-

> (a) Articles 2 to 12 and 14 of the Convention,
> (b) Articles 1 to 3 of the First Protocol, and
> (c) Articles 1 and 2 of the Sixth Protocol, as read with Articles 16 to 18 of the Convention.

(2) Those Articles are to have effect for the purposes of this Act subject to any designated derogation or reservation (as to which see sections 14 and 15).

(3) The Articles are set out in Schedule 1.

(4) The Secretary of State may by order make such amendments to this Act as he considers appropriate to reflect the effect, in relation to the United Kingdom, of a protocol.

(5) In subsection (4) "protocol" means a protocol to the Convention-

> (a) which the United Kingdom has ratified; or
> (b) which the United Kingdom has signed with a view to ratification.

(6) No amendment may be made by an order under subsection (4) so as to come into force before the protocol concerned is in force in relation to the United Kingdom.

Effect of section 1

House Of Lords, Second Reading
Official Report, House of Lords, 3 November 1997, vol. 582, col. 1230
The Lord Chancellor (Lord Irvine of Lairg): . . . Clause 1 lists the Convention rights that are to be given further effect in the United Kingdom by the Bill. . . . Also, Clause 1 makes it possible for the rights

contained in other protocols to be added to the Bill if the United Kingdom becomes a party to them in future.

House of Commons, Second Reading
Official Report, House of Commons, 16 February 1998, vol. 307, col. 780
The Secretary of State for the Home Department (Mr. Jack Straw): . . . Clause 1 lists the Convention rights to which the Bill will give further effect in our domestic law.

Protocols 4, 6 and 7 to the European Convention on Human Rights

Protocols 4 and 7

Protocol to be ratified once inconsistency with domestic law removed – Not possible to ratify Protocol 4 – Protocol 6 a matter for free vote in Parliament

House of Lords, Committee Stage
Official Report, House of Lords, 18 November 1997, vol. 583, col. 504
The Parliamentary Under-Secretary of State, Home Office (Lord Williams of Mostyn): . . . Before we introduced this Bill the Government did conduct a review of the United Kingdom's position on the three protocols to the Convention which contain substantive rights which we have not ratified. That is Protocols 4, 6 and 7.

I am obliged for the support of the noble Lord, Lord Henley. We explained very clearly in the White Paper that we intend to sign and ratify Protocol 7 once an opportunity arises to legislate to remove some inconsistencies between what is in our domestic law and the provisions of that protocol. Following that review, we have concluded that it is not presently possible to ratify either Protocol 4 or Protocol 6.

Protocol 4 contains important rights. They reaffirm the statement in the White Paper that the Government would like to see them given formal recognition in our international legal obligations. But that would be possible only if potential conflicts with our domestic laws could be resolved. As was foreseen by the noble and learned Lord, Lord Archer of Sandwell, there were particular concerns about Article 3(2) of the protocol which protects the right of nationals not to be excluded from their home state.

Our calculation is that that could possibly be relevant to the position of about 5.5. million people, which is a larger figure than that contended by the noble and learned Lord, Lord Archer of Sandwell. It would relate to various categories of British nationals: British dependent territory citizens, British overseas citizens, British subjects and British nationals overseas who do not presently have that right. These matters need careful consideration and therefore we have no plans at present to ratify the protocol.
[. . .]

The purpose of the Bill is to give effect to those rights and freedoms which we have an obligation to secure to individuals in our jurisdiction as a result of our being a party to the Convention . . . it is not to make provision for other rights. In due time, if we decide to ratify Protocols 6 or 4 (or any other protocol), your Lordships will have noted that Clause 1 provides the power for rights in Protocols 4, 6 or 7 (or, indeed, in any other) to be added by order to Convention rights. That is the scheme that we have set. It seems to be workable, practicable and attainable.

Addition of Protocol 6

Addition of Sixth Protocol on the abolition of the Death Penalty

House of Commons, Committee Stage

Official Report, House of Commons, 20 May 1998, vol. 312, col. 987

Mr. Kevin McNamara (Hull, North): I beg to move amendment No. 111, in page 1, line 9, at end insert 'and—

(c) Articles One and Two of Protocol Number 6,'.

The Chairman: With this, it will be convenient to discuss amendment No. 112, in schedule 1, schedule 1, page 19, line 23, at end insert—
'PROTOCOL No. 6—

Article 1
The death penalty shall be abolished
Article 2

A State may make provision in its law for the death penalty in respect of acts committed in time of war or of imminent threat of war; such penalty shall be applied only in the instances laid down in the law and in accordance with its provisions. The State shall communicate to the

Secretary General of the Council of Europe the relevant provisions of that law.'.

Mr. McNamara: The amendment would insert in the Bill the sixth protocol of the European Convention on Human Rights and, in particular, its first two articles. [. . .]

The Committee knows that, as a House, we abolished the death penalty for a trial period in 1965. That was made permanent in 1969 for this island and in 1973 for Northern Ireland.

There remained on the statute book two crimes which carried the death penalty: treason and piracy. However, as a result of an amendment, tabled in another place by Lord Archer of Sandwell, to clause 33 of the Crime and Disorder Bill, those crimes were removed from the statute book. That clause has passed through the Committee of the House of Commons and, although challenged, [c. **988**] remains. By free vote of the House, we have taken a matter which everyone has regarded as a matter of conscience—the death penalty—out of our normal civil law.

[. . .]

Following last year's general election, our new Government reviewed the United Kingdom's position on the death penalty, in preparation for the summit of the Council of Europe at Strasbourg in October 1997. As a result of that review, the Government supported the final declaration, which called for universal abolition of the death penalty. In a written answer to me on 19 January, the Prime Minister said:

> "The Government have supported international calls for the abolition of the death penalty because Parliament has consistently voted against re-introduction of capital punishment for murder."—[*Official Report*, 19 January 1998; Vol. 304, c. *401*.] [c. **989**]

In a letter to David Bull, director of Amnesty International UK, dated 28 November, my right hon. Friend the Foreign Secretary said:

> "Our new stance will make a real difference in allowing us to make demarches on the death penalty to other countries, either alone or with our EU partners".

However, he went on to say:

> "The Government continues to believe that the issue of whether the death penalty should be reintroduced for murder is a matter for

Parliament on a free vote and has no plans to change that approach. We have no plans, therefore, to accede to the 6th Protocol to the ECHR, or the 2nd Optional Protocol to the ICCPR."

[. . .]

Mr. Grieve: I am much obliged to the hon. Gentleman for giving way, because I have been trying to follow his argument. At the outset he said, properly, that the issue of capital punishment is one for conscience and a free vote, and at any time it chooses the House can debate that issue as it relates to individual instances—whether it be treason or piracy or whether the death penalty should apply in wartime—but would not the effect of what he proposes be to fetter the ability of Parliament to express its conscience? If we accept the Protocol as the hon. Gentleman seeks to admit it, it would no longer be open to Parliament to debate that issue without, effectively, throwing out the whole European Convention, lock, stock and barrel, or at least changing it. Acceptance of the Protocol would introduce an extra hurdle, which fetters Parliament's ability to express its conscience on a matter which, I am sure that he will agree, is of widespread public importance, and often discussed.

[. . .]

Mr. McNamara: [. . .][**c. 990**] Responding to a similar amendment moved by Lord Archer of Sandwell in another place, the Minister, Lord Williams of Mostyn, said:

> "The Government's view has been that the issue of the death penalty . . . is a matter of judgment and conscience to be decided by Members of Parliament as they see fit. I believe that all political parties have taken a view on that particular aspect which is different from other human civil rights. Therefore, if we ratified Protocol 6, we could not reintroduce the death penalty for murder short, of renouncing the Convention."—
> [*Official Report, House of Lords*, 18 November 1997; Vol. 583, c. 504-05.]

That is splendid. I suppose that every conscience will flick over just like that, to change its position.

That is particularly interesting on the basis of the point made by the hon. Member for Beaconsfield (Mr. Grieve) about the constitutional principle. Paragraph 4.13 of the excellent White Paper, "Rights Brought Home: The Human Rights Bill", states:

> "The view taken so far is that the issue is not one of basic constitutional principle but is a matter of judgement and conscience to be decided by Members of Parliament as they see fit."

Suddenly, out of the air, a strange constitutional principle that one Parliament cannot bind another is produced. That is what we all accept, except that we also say that we are not bound by what went before and can change it if we will.

The hon. Gentleman said that that goes in favour of future Parliaments, but that is not the case. A future Parliament can, if it wishes, change precisely what we are seeking to do today, and that will have ramifications. It can be debated in the House. That can be applied to any international agreement that we have made. It applies directly to the EU and other matters that we have conceded. We could vote tomorrow—I am sure my right hon. Friend the Member for Llanelli (Mr. Davies) would want us to do so—to take back many of the powers that we have given to the Commission, such as the powers that we have surrendered with regard to majority voting. We could pass that legislation tomorrow. We can, if we wish, bring back the European Communities Act 1972. It would have profound and difficult ramifications and the hon. Gentleman is entering deep waters, but his argument does not stand up.

Mr. Grieve: Surely that is precisely the point. As is generally well known, I favour incorporation of the Convention. However, the hon. Gentleman may agree that he is making life complicated for himself quite unnecessarily. He may agree that the subject commands much emotion and diverse views, but he is seeking by the amendment to entrench the matter in a way that will fetter Parliament when there is no necessity to do so.

Mr. McNamara: With the greatest respect, we are not fettering Parliament. We are saying that this is a decision of this Parliament. We are not saying that a future Parliament cannot change it. It will do that in the knowledge of the necessary consequences of what it does.

Mr. John Bercow (Buckingham): I have been following closely the logic of the hon. Gentleman's argument, bizarre though it seems to me. If the hon. Gentleman is confident that a future Parliament would not seek to reinstate the death penalty, of what precisely in the present arrangement is he afraid? If, on the other hand, he fears that a future Parliament might seek to re-establish [c. **991**] the death penalty, is not his effort today designed to prevent a future House of Commons doing just that? Therefore, is not my hon. Friend the Member for Beaconsfield (Mr. Grieve) right when he says that the hon. Gentleman is seeking to fetter and circumscribe the sovereign omnicompetence of the House of Commons?

Mr. McNamara: In the House, sovereignty has long since slipped away on many issues. One must recognise that. Whether one is happy about it or not, it has happened on a range of issues. I shall not bore the Committee with examples. I do not object to what has happened in that regard—it is not a problem for me—but why can all the other members of the EU happily sign Protocol 6 without finding the argument advanced by the hon. Member for Beaconsfield and others particularly onerous? To me as an abolitionist, and I should have thought to other abolitionists, what the hon. Gentleman says is a powerful argument for incorporating the protocol. Bearing in mind those crimes that were subject to capital punishment before 1965, and all those miscarriages of justice of which we have had a calendar in the past two decades, it would be just as well if we were fettered in that way.
[. . .]

The Government's position is inconsistent and contradictory. We welcome other countries' ratification of death penalty protocols and we urge them to do so, we call for the universal abolition of the death penalty, but we refuse to accede to the death penalty protocol itself. We do that so that Parliament can reintroduce the death penalty. That is the nature of the argument. [c. 992] Therefore, in the interests of our international standing and consistency, I urge the Committee to take on board what the Home Secretary said in the White Paper—that this is a matter of conscience to be decided by Members of Parliament as they see fit. I reiterate the point that I made earlier that the view taken so far is that this issue is not a matter of basic constitutional principle.

Mr. Maclennan: . . . I have great sympathy with the objectives of those who support the amendment, but I have some doubt about whether it is appropriate as a means of ratifying the protocol. I would have preferred the Executive to announce their intention to ratify the protocol and, as a consequence of that decision, to include it in the Bill. I agree with the hon. Member for Hull, North. To say that it is simply a matter of judgment and conscience to be decided by Members of Parliament as they see fit is to misunderstand the concerns of constitutional law and is inconsistent with our acceptance of Article 3 of the European Convention.

Mr. Grieve: . . . My complaint about the manner in which the amendment is being introduced goes not to the right of the House to legislate on the issue, but to the fact that[**c. 993**] I—although not necessarily all members of my party—have been a proponent of incorporation, based on our obligations under the European Convention as it now stands and to which we have signed up.

If the consequence of the amendment is that the scope of the Convention is altered without the opportunity for adequate public debate, I fear that we shall forfeit the regard of the public in respect of this proposal. Because I am in favour of the proposal and have made no secret of it, that particularly disappoints me.

There is ample scope for those who share the hon. Gentleman's view to raise an Adjournment debate and to lobby Ministers to sign up to Protocol 6. That should be the subject of legitimate public debate, because it has a knock-on effect on the ability of the House to review the position, as it has traditionally done, once every Parliament. I fear that, if we start to go down that road when there is no necessity to do so, the public will ask what Parliament has done.

Mr. McNamara: On the matter of lobbying, on Second Reading of the Crime and Disorder Bill, I intervened and asked my hon. Friend the Minister of State about that. He replied:

> "As my hon. Friend is well aware, that is covered by the Human Rights Bill rather than this Bill."—[*Official Report*, 8 April 1998; Vol. 310, c. 451.]

As urged by my hon. Friend, I have raised the matter now.

Mr. Grieve: . . . If we accept the amendment, we are usurping the right of the citizens of this country to pronounce on the issue, and we are doing so for no good reason. It will vitiate the effect of the Bill, which is in other ways so desirable. I understand why the amendment was tabled, but I ask the hon. Member for Hull, North to reconsider, and I ask all hon. Members to consider carefully whether, even if they support the intention behind the amendment, this is the proper way to achieve it.

[. . .] [**c. 1003**]

Mr. Mike O'Brien: Let me make it clear that, as far as the Government are concerned, this is a free vote. I shall express the personal view of myself and of the Home Secretary, but no Government Whip has been asked by us to act as a Teller. This is a matter of conscience for hon. Members.

The Government's position was set out clearly in the White Paper:

> "The view taken so far is that the issue is not one of basic constitutional principle but is a matter of judgement and conscience to be decided by Members of Parliament as they see fit. For these reasons, we do not propose to ratify Protocol 6 at present."

The amendments would add the two substantive articles of Protocol 6, involving the abolition of the death penalty, except for acts committed in time of war or imminent threat of war, to the Convention rights. The right hon. and learned Member for Sleaford and North Hykeham (Mr. Hogg) said that the argument was finely balanced, and I agree. The issue is not just whether we agree with the death penalty. The tendency is often to discuss these issues emotively because, obviously, hon. Members feel strongly about them, but there is a need to examine the proposal with great consideration. [c. 1004] Before introducing the Bill, Ministers conducted a review of the United Kingdom's position on the three protocols to the Convention that contain substantive rights that we had not ratified. Those are Protocols 4, 6 and 7. We explained in the White Paper "Rights Brought Home: The Human Rights Bill" that we intended to sign and to ratify Protocol 7 once an opportunity arose to remove some inconsistencies between our domestic law and the protocol's provisions. However, we judged that we should not ratify Protocols 4 or 6 at this time or to include them in the Bill.

In the past three decades, the House has repeatedly opposed the death penalty. Indeed, in the previous substantial debate in the previous Parliament, I spoke strongly against it. Neither the Home Secretary nor I believes that the House will restore it, but we also take the view that this is not the time to block the rights of Members of Parliament in all conscience to debate and to vote on restoring it.

My personal view and that of the Home Secretary is that Parliament should be free to decide on death penalty matters on a free vote and that Protocol 6 would make a free vote difficult. Ratification of the protocol, from which no derogation or reservation is permitted, would interfere with the ability of a United Kingdom Parliament to consider the issue in future, short of effectively denouncing the Convention.

Our constituents widely engage in the debate about the death penalty. Should Parliament prevent itself from debating issues that the public debate? That would be the effect if we embraced Protocol 6. We would restrict and put a block on our ability to debate the issue. Assuming that the Convention would remain law, if we embraced Protocol 6, we would remove the decision on the death penalty from Members of Parliament for all time and place it in the realm of international law.

The death penalty is a sensitive and difficult issue. This is not the time, nor is this the Bill, to implement the amendment. The issue is not about supporting or opposing the death penalty, but about the procedure for doing so: is a new procedural hurdle to be placed in the way of those hon. Members who wish to bring this matter before the House?

Mr. Maclennan: In the light of the Minister's helpful indication that the Government do not propose to put on a Whip tonight, can he say how the Government would view the passing of the amendment? Would they take it as an instruction of the House and proceed, notwithstanding the view that he has expressed on behalf of himself and the Home Secretary, to ratify the protocol?

Mr. O'Brien: The answer to that is yes. May I make it clear, if the right hon. Gentleman is in any doubt, that, on this issue, we are not putting in Whips, but that, on other issues tonight, we may decide to do so. [. . .] I accept that it would be possible for the death penalty to be reintroduced by a future vote of Parliament, but only by way of an amendment to what would then be the Human Rights Act, if Parliament wills it. However, it would be contrary to the principles of the Bill and of the Convention.

The Bill's purpose is to give further effect in domestic law to those rights that the United Kingdom has an obligation under the Convention to secure to individuals [c. 1005] in its jurisdiction. The inclusion of Articles 1 and 2 of Protocol 6 within the Bill's definition of the Convention rights would grant rights in this country that we are not, at present, internationally bound to secure. It appears to be an academic point and I do not want to go into angels dancing on pinheads, but it is an important part of the Government's view that the Bill is about giving access to rights, rather than creating new areas of law.
[. . .]

Parliament could certainly debate that issue, but let us be clear: if we agree to the amendment, we will have a hurdle, a block on making a decision to restore the death penalty. Hon. Members will have to decide

whether they wish at this stage to put that hurdle or block in the way of the House.
[...]
Some concerns have been expressed that if we do not ratify Protocol 6, the UK will be unable to campaign effectively against the use of the death penalty in other countries. We do not see that as a serious difficulty. We are able to support international calls for the abolition of the death penalty because Parliament has repeatedly voted against capital punishment. In the current Parliament, any motion to reintroduce capital punishment is likely to be defeated by a large majority. [c. 1006] On 11 October 1997, at the summit of the Council of Europe, the Prime Minister signed the Council of Europe declaration calling for the universal abolition of the death penalty. That demonstrates that we are able to take a positive stand on this issue and encourage others to do so, but it does not require the inclusion of Article 6.
[...]
I repeat—this is a free vote, as all hon. Members are aware. The Home Secretary and I have expressed our advice, but each Member can exercise his or her own conscience on this matter.
[...] [c. 1008]

Mr. Davis: With great respect, I tell the Under-Secretary that, from my experience—regardless of whether we sign Protocol 6; even if we do not sign it—if at some time in the future the House votes for restoration of the death penalty, the United Kingdom will be expected to withdraw from the Council of Europe—[Hon. Members: "No."] Oh, yes. My colleagues from the delegation will agree that, internationally, feeling on the issue is so strong that we would risk being suspended from membership of the Council of Europe—*[Interruption.]* Yes, that is my view. I am entitled to my view, which is based on some experience of the Council of Europe, and I was one of those who criticised Ukraine for not fulfilling its obligations.
[...] [c. 1009]
Human rights are at the centre of our foreign policy. Protocol 6 has tremendous symbolic importance. If we vote against the amendment, it will be impossible for many people in Europe to understand the House. It will also be very difficult for many people in this country to understand us. [*Amendment passed: 294:136*] – [c. 1009][3]

---

[3] Amendments to Armed Forces Acts to abolish death penalty, *Official Report, House of Commons, 21 October 1998, vol. 317, col.1353*

SECTION 2: INTERPRETATION OF CONVENTION RIGHTS

2. - (1) A court or tribunal determining a question which has arisen in connection with a Convention right must take into account any-

(a) judgment, decision, declaration or advisory opinion of the European Court of Human Rights,

(b) opinion of the Commission given in a report adopted under Article 31 of the Convention,

(c) decision of the Commission in connection with Article 26 or 27(2) of the Convention, or

(d) decision of the Committee of Ministers taken under Article 46 of the Convention,

whenever made or given, so far as, in the opinion of the court or tribunal, it is relevant to the proceedings in which that question has arisen.

(2) Evidence of any judgment, decision, declaration or opinion of which account may have to be taken under this section is to be given in proceedings before any court or tribunal in such manner as may be provided by rules.

(3) In this section "rules" means rules of court or, in the case of proceedings before a tribunal, rules made for the purposes of this section-

(a) by the Lord Chancellor or the Secretary of State, in relation to any proceedings outside Scotland;

(b) by the Secretary of State, in relation to proceedings in Scotland; or

(c) by a Northern Ireland department, in relation to proceedings before a tribunal in Northern Ireland-

(i) which deals with transferred matters; and

(ii) for which no rules made under paragraph (a) are in force.

Effect of section 2

House of Lords, Second Reading
Official Report, House of Lords, 3 November 1997, vol. 582, col. 1230

The Lord Chancellor (Lord Irvine of Lairg): . . . Clause 2 requires courts in the United Kingdom to take account of the decisions of the Convention institutions in Strasbourg in their consideration of Convention points which come before them. It is entirely appropriate that our courts should draw on the wealth of existing jurisprudence on the Convention.

House of Commons, Second Reading
Official Report, House of Commons, 16 February 1998, vol. 307, col. 780

The Secretary of State for the Home Department (Mr. Jack Straw): . . . Clause 2 ensures that, in giving effect to those rights, our domestic courts and tribunals have regard to Strasbourg jurisprudence.

Section 2(1)

Authority of European Convention jurisprudence - meaning of "must take into account"

House of Lords, Committee Stage
Official Report, House of Lords, 18 November 1997, vol. 583, col. 511

Lord Kingsland: . . . The amendment seeks to replace the expression "must take into account any" with the words "shall be bound by".

I can see the superficial attraction of the Government's text. Our courts have hundreds of years of experience in balancing individual rights against public obligations. I am in no doubt that their decisions, if they are examined by the judges in the European [c. 512] Court of Human Rights, carry great weight with them and will in time enrich the jurisprudence of that Court. However, there is another side to which your Lordships' House should give greater weight.

The problem is that if our judges only take account of the jurisprudence of the European Court of Human Rights, we cast them adrift from their international moorings. The Bill, crewed by the judges, will have no accurate charts by which to sail because the judges are obliged only to take into account the provisions of the Convention. That

means that the Bill is effectively a domestic Bill of rights and not a proper incorporation of international rights. It means that the judges, at the end of the day, although they must take account of the Bill, are not obliged to act on it and can go in whatever direction they wish. I have great confidence in Her Majesty's judges, but I believe that they need greater guidance than they receive from the expression "take into account".
[. . .] [c. 514]

The Lord Chancellor (Lord Irvine of Lairg): Clause 2(1) requires a court or tribunal determining a question in connection with a Convention right to take account of relevant judgments, decisions, declarations and opinions made or given by the European Commission and the European Court of Human Rights and the Committee of Ministers of the Council of Europe. [The amendment] would provide that such judgments, etc., were binding if made or given by the European Court of Human Rights, while leaving their status under the Bill unaffected; that is to say, they would have to be taken into account but would not be binding if made or given by the European Commission of Human Rights or the Committee of Ministers.

We believe that Clause 2 gets it right in requiring domestic courts to take into account judgments of the European Court, but not making them binding. To make the courts bound by Strasbourg decisions could, for example, result in the Bill being confusing if not internally inconsistent when the courts are faced with incompatible legislation. In addition, the word "binding" is the language of precedent but the Convention is the ultimate source of the relevant law. It is also unclear to me how "binding" would fit within the doctrine of margin of appreciation under the Convention. I think that "binding" certainly goes further . . . than the Convention itself requires.

We must remember that Clause 2 requires the courts to take account of all the judgments of the European Court of Human Rights, regardless of whether they have been given in a case involving the United Kingdom. That was the point made by the noble Lord, Lord Lester: the United Kingdom is not bound in international law to follow that Court's judgments in cases to which the United Kingdom had not been a party, and it would be strange to require courts in the United Kingdom to be bound by such cases. It would also be quite inappropriate to do so since such cases deal with laws and practices which are not those of the United Kingdom. They are a source of jurisprudence indeed, but not binding precedents which we necessarily should follow or even necessarily desire to follow.

The Bill would of course permit United Kingdom courts to depart from existing Strasbourg decisions and upon occasion it might well be appropriate to do so, and it is possible they might give a successful lead to Strasbourg. For example, it would permit the United Kingdom courts to depart from Strasbourg decisions where there has been no precise ruling on the matter and a commission opinion which does so has not taken into account subsequent Strasbourg court case law. [c. 515]

These cases aside, it is not considered necessary to set out to provide that United Kingdom courts and tribunals are bound by Strasbourg jurisprudence, since where it is relevant we would of course expect our courts to apply Convention jurisprudence and its principles to the cases before them. More fundamentally, this amendment, to my mind, suggests putting the courts in some kind of straitjacket where flexibility is what is required. That is what Clause 2 achieves, and, in my submission, our courts must be free to try to give a lead to Europe as well as to be led. The correct principle is to require our courts to take into account relevant European jurisprudence. That is what Clause 2 and indeed also Clause 8(4) in the special context of damages require our courts to do.

'Undesirable' to make decisions of the European Convention bodies binding

House of Lords, Report Stage

Official Report, House of Lords, 19 January 1998, vol. 584, col. 1268

[**Lord Browne-Wilkinson:** . . . As a serving judge, I shall be concerned if this amendment is agreed to.
[. . .]

I see no reason that we should fetter ourselves in that way in dealing with a jurisprudence that is by definition a shifting one. I am particularly concerned because, although until now the jurisprudence of Strasbourg has been powerful, with the expansion of the European Union there are now a number of judges from jurisdictions which in the past at least have not been famous for their defence of human rights. To find that we were bound by a decision of such a court would be unfortunate.

In practice there will be every encouragement to follow and produce a uniform jurisprudence. But to say that the courts of this country have to produce a result which in their view is unfair, in the sense of being bound by it, would produce an inertia in the development of [c. 1270] human rights law which would be undesirable. For those reasons I prefer that we were required to have regard to the jurisprudence of Strasbourg, but not to be technically bound to follow it whether, in our view, it is right, wrong or indifferent.
[. . .] [c. 1272]

The Lord Chancellor (Lord Irvine of Lairg): As other noble Lords have said, the word "binding" is the language of strict precedent but the Convention has no rule of precedent. The amendment would therefore go further than the Convention required and, for reasons that I shall give in a moment, in an undesirable direction.

[. . .] We take the view that the expression "take in account" is clear enough. Should a United Kingdom court ever have a case before it which is a precise mirror of one that has been previously considered by the European Court of Human Rights, which I doubt, it may be appropriate for it to apply the European Court's findings directly to that case; but in real life cases are rarely as neat and tidy as that. The courts will often be faced with cases that involve factors perhaps specific to the United Kingdom which distinguish them from cases considered by the European Court. I agree with the noble and learned Lord, [c. 1271] Lord Browne-Wilkinson, that it is important that our courts have the scope to apply that discretion so as to aid in the development of human rights law.

There may also be occasions when it would be right for the United Kingdom courts to depart from Strasbourg decisions. We must remember that the interpretation of the Convention rights develops over the years. Circumstances may therefore arise in which a judgment given by the European Court of Human Rights decades ago contains pronouncements which it would not be appropriate to apply to the letter in the circumstances of today in a particular set of circumstances affecting this country. The Bill as currently drafted would allow our courts to use their common sense in applying the European court's judgment to such a case. We feel that to accept this amendment removes from the judges the flexibility and discretion that they require in developing human rights law.
[. . .]

[*Amendment withdrawn c. 1272*]

Effect on judges

House of Commons, Second Reading
Official Report, House of Commons, 16 February 1998, vol. 307, col. 857
The Under-Secretary of State for the Home Department (Mr. Mike O'Brien): . . . I am concerned about the shadow Home Secretary's comments on politicising judges; I do not accept that that will happen. Lord Bingham's words have already been quoted in this debate. He said:

> "Judges already from time to time find themselves deciding cases which have political, sometimes even party-political implications. The judges strive to decide those cases on a firm basis of legal principle; and that is what they will continue to do when the Convention is incorporated if the Bill becomes law."—[*Official Report, House of Lords*, 3 November 1997; Vol. 582, c. 1246.]

It appears that the shadow Home Secretary trusts Strasbourg judges—but not our own judges—to change the law. In his book "What Next in the Law?", Lord Denning said that we have to trust someone, so why not trust the judges. Does the right hon. Gentleman really say that he has no trust in our judges, and that [**c. 858**] they cannot distinguish law from their own "socio-political theories"? He seemed to suggest that our judges would deliver "socio-political theories".

[. . .] Judges will have to apply the law. As clause 2(1) makes clear, they will have to take into account judgments of the European Court of Human Rights and decisions and opinions of other bodies. They will not, of course, be bound by those decisions when our primary legislation says otherwise. They must accept primary legislation if it differs from those decisions, although judges may make a declaration of incompatibility. Our own courts—the House of Lords, the Court of Appeal and the High Court—will soon develop their own jurisprudence, and the lower courts will be bound by that.

[. . .] The Convention will not overrule our primary legislation, and the Bill will preserve parliamentary sovereignty.

Purpose of section 2(1) 'to point our courts towards an interpretation of Convention rights consistent with Strasbourg interpretation' – "must take into account" means 'what words in English say' not 'uniform jurisprudence' – weight to be attached to Strasbourg jurisprudence

House of Commons, Committee Stage
Official Report, House of Commons, 3 June 1998, vol. 313, col. 390

Mr. James Clappison (Hertsmere): . . . We are seeking to explore the margin of appreciation. I hope that he paid close attention when I made it clear that we commended the generally cautious, conservative approach of the European Court, and he will know that that has been widely recognised by commentators. We do not seek to rebel against that, but we need to explore how the Bill will require the margin of appreciation that may be taken into account in decisions by the European Court on other [c. 391] countries to be dealt with in our courts when they consider the decisions and judgments of the European Court. That is an entirely legitimate concern, and we were right to explore it in the other place and here.
[. . .]

First, we need to explore what our courts are intended to understand by the phrase, "must take into account". It was said in another place that those words would permit UK courts to depart from existing Strasbourg decisions and that, on occasion, it might be appropriate to do so and the courts might give a successful lead to Strasbourg. Those words were spoken by another Minister in the other place. We are happy with that. Indeed, it may be recalled that, in our earlier debates, my right hon. and learned Friend the shadow Attorney-General made it clear that, whatever other reservations we might have, one of the benefits of incorporation is that British judges would have an opportunity to have an input into the fashioning of Convention law. That is all well and good, but the Government have not yet been sufficiently clear on what they intend by the phrase, "must take into account".

If those words are not binding—we take it that they are not—the Government must spell out more clearly the nature and extent of the circumstances in which United Kingdom courts may choose not to follow Strasbourg decisions. The Government apparently contemplate that UK courts would be permitted to depart from Strasbourg decisions when there had been no precise ruling on the matter in question. Such an example was given by the [c. 392] Lord Chancellor in the debate on this clause in the other place. What about cases in which there has been a precise ruling by Strasbourg? Do the words, "must take into account" mean that UK courts must follow to the letter rulings in cases in which the Court or the Commission has made a judgment, decision, declaration or opinion in the relevant circumstances? Do our courts have to follow them at all?

Will the Minister say whether UK courts may depart from such decisions when there has been a precise ruling by Strasbourg? The matter was left unclear when it was debated in another place. . . . It is all very well to say that our courts can feel free to go their own way when there is no precise ruling from Strasbourg, but what about cases when there is?

The Parliamentary Secretary, Lord Chancellor's Department (Mr. Geoffrey Hoon): The hon. Gentleman knows the answer to his question. The answer is clear: it is for the independent judgment of a court to resolve the issue before it. Nothing that can be said here will affect that independence. I am surprised to hear him pursue that argument because, by doing so, he seeks to fetter that independence. If a court arrives at an apparently incorrect decision, there is the prospect of an appeal, which, ultimately, could end up in the court in Strasbourg.

[. . .]

Mr. Clappison: The Government have already gone so far as to say that our courts need not feel bound when there is no precise ruling from Strasbourg—they went that far in another place, in a more considered response than the Minister has just given—but what about cases when there is a precise ruling? What do the words, "must take into account" import in those circumstances?

[. . .][c. 393]

Clause 2 requires United Kingdom courts in certain circumstances to take into account decisions of the Commission and the Committee of Ministers. I want to explore two points. First, is it the Government's intention to require the courts to give the same weight to decisions of those bodies as to those of the European Court? Again, I make it clear that I mean no disrespect to the Commission, which I appreciate is of a high calibre and carries out valuable work. However, we need to consider whether it is right in effect to give the commission parity of esteem with the European Court, as the Bill apparently does. Clause 2 puts the Commission on the same footing as the Court. Is that the signal that the Government mean to send out?

My second point concerns the potential problem when the European Court arrives at a different view from the Commission. Under article 31, which is mentioned in clause 2(1)(b), the Commission will, in a matter where it has been unable to bring the parties to a friendly settlement, draw up a report and give its opinion as to whether there has been a breach. That, of course, is standard procedure. I apprehend that subsection (1)(b) requires a United Kingdom court to take into account such an opinion even though the European Court has yet to give a view. No doubt the Minister will correct me if I am wrong.

On that basis, what will happen if the United Kingdom court takes the Commission's opinion into account and the European Court, also having taken into account that opinion, comes to a different conclusion, which is not altogether unknown? That would appear to be a possibility. I assume that the Government have thought that through. Will the Minister tell us what will happen in those circumstances?
[. . .] [c. 402]

Mr. Hoon: . . . [. . .] Clause 2(1) provides that a court or tribunal that is determining a question in connection with a Convention right must take account of the relevant jurisprudence of the European Commission, the European Court of Human Rights and the Committee of Ministers whenever it was made or given. The purpose of the provision is to point our courts towards an interpretation of Convention rights that is consistent with the interpretation in Strasbourg. In other words, we are bringing home the jurisprudence of the Convention rights as well as the rights themselves.
[. . .]

The word "must" in this context clearly means that the courts must take into account the jurisprudence. That is what the words in English say. They do not mean that there has to be uniform jurisprudence. They mean that the courts must take the jurisprudence into account in reaching a decision.

Let me suggest what the effect of the discretionary word "may" will be. It will mean that our courts might produce, on the same set of facts, different results because some may take the jurisprudence into account and some may not. That can hardly be sensible when we are trying to promote consistency in the decision making of our courts. If we allow

courts not to take into account the jurisprudence, we shall end up, on similar facts, with different results. That can hardly be satisfactory.
[. . .]
[. . .] [c. 404]

Mr. Hogg: Will the hon. Gentleman be good enough to tell the Committee the extent to which the Commission and the Committee of Ministers hear argument before expressing an opinion or making a decision? I simply do not know. Therefore, I do not know to what extent the decision results from the process of argument and debate.

Mr. Hoon: It is impossible to give a precise answer to that question because, clearly, it depends on the circumstances of the particular case. An application to the Commission, which first hears the application, may be so manifestly ill founded that it can be dealt with immediately, without a formal hearing. On the other hand, for those cases where clearly there is a substantial issue, there is a full hearing at present before the Commission. Indeed, if the hon. Gentleman were to walk into its courtroom, he would find that it looks very much like a court and like the European Court of Human Rights. As he may know, that is one of the reasons why, after the reform of the process of the European Court of Human Rights, there will be a unified and single court from 1 November this year. Therefore, depending on the circumstances, there will be thorough argument before the Commission. Indeed, its decision may look very much like a decision of the Court.

It is important to recognise that many cases are settled on the basis of an opinion of the Commission and do not necessarily proceed to the Court, but that opinion may nevertheless be extremely relevant to the interpretation of the Convention by the domestic courts. Perhaps more important still, the Commission is responsible currently for decisions on the basic admissibility of complaints, including whether they are manifestly ill founded, as I have mentioned. That is an important part of the body of Strasbourg decisions and one that, on any view, it is right for our courts to take into account.

SECTION 3: INTERPRETATION OF LEGISLATION

3. - (1) So far as it is possible to do so, primary legislation and subordinate legislation must be read and given effect in a way which is compatible with the Convention rights.

(2) This section-

(a) applies to primary legislation and subordinate legislation whenever enacted;
(b) does not affect the validity, continuing operation or enforcement of any incompatible primary legislation; and
(c) does not affect the validity, continuing operation or enforcement of any incompatible subordinate legislation if (disregarding any possibility of revocation) primary legislation prevents removal of the incompatibility.

Effect of s. 3

House Of Lords, Second Reading
Official Report, House of Lords, 3 November 1997, vol. 582, col. 1230
The Lord Chancellor (Lord Irvine of Lairg): ... Clause 3 provides that legislation, whenever enacted, must as far as possible be read and given effect in a way which is compatible with the Convention rights. This will ensure that, if it is possible to interpret a statute in two ways—one compatible with the Convention and one not—the courts will always choose the interpretation which is compatible. In practice, this will prove a strong form of incorporation.

As I have said, however, the Bill does not allow the courts to set aside or ignore Acts of Parliament. Clause 3 preserves the effect of primary legislation which is [c. 1231] incompatible with the Convention. It does the same for secondary legislation where it is inevitably incompatible because of the terms of the parent statute.

House of Commons, Second Reading
Official Report, House of Commons, 16 February 1998, vol. 307, col. 780
The Secretary of State for the Home Department (Mr. Jack Straw): ... Clause 3 provides that legislation, whenever enacted, must as far as

possible be read and given effect in such a way as to be compatible with Convention rights. We expect that, in almost all cases, the courts will be able to interpret legislation compatibly with the Convention. However, we need to provide for the rare cases where that cannot be done. Consistent with maintaining parliamentary sovereignty, clause 3 therefore provides that if a provision of primary legislation cannot be interpreted compatibly with the Convention rights, that legislation will continue to have force and effect.

House of Lords, Committee Stage
Official Report, House of Lords, 27 November 1997, vol. 583, col. 783
The Lord Chancellor (Lord Irvine of Lairg): . . . Clause 3 requires the courts to interpret legislation compatibly with the Convention rights and to the fullest extent possible in all cases coming before them.

New principles of statutory interpretation introduced – comparison with New Zealand provision (Lord Cooke of Thorndon)

House of Lords, Second Reading
Official Report, House of Lords, 3 November 1997, vol. 582, col. 1272
Lord Cooke of Thorndon: . . . Secondly, let us consider the language of Clause 3(1):

> "So far as it is possible to do so, primary legislation and subordinate legislation must be read and given effect in a way which is compatible with the Convention rights".

The clause will require a very different approach to interpretation from that to which United Kingdom courts are accustomed. Traditionally, the search has been for the true meaning; now it will be for a possible meaning that would prevent the making of a declaration of incompatibility. [. . .][**c. 1273**]

The shift of the criterion to a search for possible compatible meanings will confront the courts with delicate responsibilities. Even for lawyers, a must is a must. For surely the difference between mandatory and directory provisions can have no place in interpreting the Human Rights Act, which will itself be primary legislation. Consider, say, an Act making a certain kind of disclosure a criminal offence, enacting one specific defence, but not specifically excluding a defence under Article

10 (freedom to impart information). Without expressing any opinion as to the outcome, one can see that there will be a new kind of problem. In effect, the courts are being asked to solve these problems by applying a rebuttable presumption in favour of the Convention rights.

Clause 3(1) is, if anything, slightly stronger than the corresponding New Zealand section. If it is scrupulously complied with, in a major field the common law approach to statutory interpretation will never be the same again; moreover, this will prove a powerful Bill indeed.

House of Lords, Committee Stage
Official Report, House of Lords, 18 November 1997, vol. 583, col. 533

Lord Cooke of Thorndon: One appreciates that, as the noble Lord, Lord Kingsland, has perhaps suggested, Clause 3(1) of the Bill definitely goes further than the existing common law rules of statutory interpretation, because it enjoins a search for possible meanings as distinct from the true meaning—which has been the traditional approach in the matter of statutory interpretation in the courts.

The difference is not as huge as might be thought at first sight. Even under the New Zealand corresponding provision, the courts have said that the kind of interpretation now enjoined is not a strained interpretation; it is one that is fairly possible. I suspect that the very strength of the clause, as it is now worded, may have been of material assistance to the noble and learned Lord the Lord Chancellor in forming the view which he expressed at Second Reading that declarations of incompatibility would be rare.

The corresponding New Zealand provision is in different language and in some respects the United Kingdom proposed provision may be slightly wider. I shall read the two provisions. It seems to me that in substance in the important matters there is no difference. The New Zealand provision is Section 6 of the New Zealand Bill of Rights Act 1990. It provides:

> "Wherever an enactment can be given a meaning that is consistent with the rights and freedoms contained in this Bill of Rights, that meaning shall be preferred to any other meaning".

The United Kingdom Bill provides that:

> "So far as it is possible to do so, primary legislation and subordinate legislation must be read and given effect in a way which is compatible with the Convention rights".

The words,

"must be read and given effect",

may arguably be slightly wider than the New Zealand words, although I doubt that. What is much more important is that both provisions contain strong mandatory words. In the New Zealand provision those words are "can" and "shall"; in the United Kingdom provision, as proposed, the words are "possible" and "must". It is manifest that any dilution—I avoid the word "wrecking"—any watering down of the strength [c. 534] of the United Kingdom provision, as contained in the Bill, will strike at its very heart. I suggest that Clause 3(1) is a key provision in the proposed legislation, possibly even the most important provision.

In this country the New Zealand Bill of Rights is sometimes stigmatised as weak. That is not necessarily so when its interpretation is in judicial hands; but it would be a sad state of affairs if, when the New Zealand provision is criticised in that way and it is widely urged that the United Kingdom Bill is not strong enough, the United Kingdom Parliament were to enact a measure more timid than, or a weaker version of, the New Zealand Bill. That would be an extraordinary result of the long consideration and the long gestation which the United Kingdom Bill has undergone. I respectfully urge the Committee and the Government not to be persuaded to do anything to weaken Clause 3(1).

Section 3 creates interpretative obligation

House of Lords, Committee Stage

Official Report, House of Lords, 18 November 1997, vol. 583, col. 508

The Lord Chancellor (Lord Irvine of Lairg): . . . It achieves the purpose of the Long Title by requiring primary and secondary legislation to be read and given effect so far as possible in a way that is compatible with Convention rights. It places a requirement on public authorities to act in a way that is compatible with Convention rights and provides for the grant of judicial remedies where they do not do so.

The Convention rights will not, however, in themselves become part of our substantive domestic law. The provisions in Clause 3 operate on an interpretative basis and require legislation to be construed in accordance with the Convention rights so far as it is possible to do so. That interpretative provision interacts with the obligations put upon public authorities in accordance with the generous definition of "public authority" in the Bill. As we will explain in [c. 509] more detail when we come to the relevant clauses, this provides an effective way of giving effect to the Convention rights and avoids constitutional and other difficulties which would arise if we made those rights part of domestic law. For example, Clause 3—which I acknowledge the noble and learned Lord desires to amend—makes provision for the continuing force and effect of legislation that is held to be incompatible with Convention rights.

[. . .] The scheme of the Bill—one may wish to challenge it—is to make provision so as to respect the sovereignty of Parliament for the continuing force and effect of legislation held by the courts by way of a declaration of incompatibility to be incompatible with the Convention rights. If those Convention rights were themselves to constitute provisions of domestic United Kingdom law there would be obvious scope for confusion when the courts were obliged to give effect to legislation that predated the coming into force of the Human Rights Bill. That might give rise to the doctrine of implied repeal. That is a doctrine that can have no application because of the express terms of Clause 3.

The courts need to know where they stand on how the Convention rights on the one hand and legislation on the other should be given effect to when, as will often happen, the two cover the same ground. The scheme of the Bill provides clear information to the courts.

"Possible" preferable to 'reasonable'

House of Lords, Committee Stage

Official Report, House of Lords, 18 November 1997, vol. 583, col. 535

The Lord Chancellor (Lord Irvine of Lairg): . . . We want the courts to strive to find an interpretation of legislation which is consistent with Convention rights so far as the language of the legislation allows and only in the last resort to conclude that the legislation is simply incompatible with them. . . . Our position is that the courts should apply the law and not make it and that they should not be dragged into the area of opinion or into judgment of a political character perhaps to a greater or lesser extent.

The word "possible" is the plainest means that we can devise for simply asking the courts to find the construction consistent with the intentions of Parliament and the wording of legislation which is nearest to the Convention rights. On the other hand, "reasonable" is an evaluative criterion and the proponents of the amendment do not offer us any guidance as to what the criteria might be.

[. . .][W]e want the courts to construe statutes so that they bear a meaning that is consistent with the Convention whenever that is possible according to the language of the statutes but not when it is impossible to achieve that. More generally, we proceed on the basis that Parliament, at least post-ratification of the Convention, must be deemed to have intended its statutes to be compatible with the Convention to which the United Kingdom is bound, and that courts should hold that that deemed general intention has not been carried successfully into effect only where it is impossible to construe a statute as having that effect. This seems to me to be a sensible principle and is consistent both with Parliament's presumed intention post-ratification and with ministerial [c. 536] statements of compatibility, when they come to be made, under Clause 19 of the Bill. . . . [T]o maximise rather than minimise declarations of incompatibility . . . would tend to bring the statute book into unnecessary disrepute.

Act gives judges the strongest jurisdiction possible to interpret Acts of Parliament compatibly with the Convention

House of Lords, Committee Stage

Official Report, House of Lords, 24 November 1997, vol. 583, col. 795

The Lord Chancellor (Lord Irvine of Lairg): The point about the Bill is that it has a coherent intellectual structure. It rests upon giving the strongest jurisdiction possible to the judges to interpret Acts of Parliament so as to make them, whenever possible, compatible with the Convention. But then the Bill reflects the decision that when a court is unable to do that and make a declaration of incompatibility the Bill does not embrace the doctrine of implied repeal—which it could have done—and allow the courts to strike down Acts of Parliament; it goes down the route of a declaration of incompatibility which then leaves Parliament free, a sovereign Parliament which must decide whether to pass a remedial order or indeed a full [c. 796] amending Bill. That is part of the central scheme of the Bill . . .

"So far as it is possible to do so" in s. 3(1), 'moves us on' from previous rule of interpretation of 'Convention legislation'

House of Commons, Committee Stage

Official Report, House of Commons, 3 June 1998, vol. 313, col. 419

Mr. Stinchcombe: . . . Hon. Members may know that there has been some academic discussion about the opening words of the clause. Sir William Wade, who is a member of the chambers of which I was a member before I came to the House, and the hon. Michael Beloff, who is head of those chambers, have publicly disagreed in academic articles and speeches about the meaning of the words. It is now a perfectly appropriate time, given Pepper *v.* Hart, for my right hon. Friend the Home Secretary to resolve the matter once and for all. We must make it clear that the words in clause 3(1) mean what they say and what we said that they meant in paragraph 2.7 of the White Paper—the words go beyond the present rule and, wherever any interpretation of legislation can be made so as to uphold Convention rights, that is what the courts must be invited to do.

[. . .] [c. 423]

Mr. Straw: . . . My hon. Friend the Member for Wellingborough (Mr. Stinchcombe) asked which of the academics I backed. I back those who have read the plain words in this clause and take the view that it moves us on from the way in which the courts currently interpret Convention legislation. Hon. Members should feel reassured by the fact that our courts have had quite a lot of experience in interpreting the Convention. Where there is ambiguity, they come down on the side of the Convention.

[. . .]

The courts have experience. We are moving forward and we intend to ensure, as the wording makes clear, that, in so far as it is possible, primary and subordinate legislation is read and given effect in a way that is compatible with Convention rights.

Courts to find compatible interpretation 'so far as plain words of the legislation allow' – not intention that courts should strain the meaning of statutory wording – Act's relationship with British system of government

House of Commons, Committee Stage
Official Report, House of Commons, 3 June 1998, vol. 313, col. 418

Mr. Douglas Hogg (Sleaford and North Hykeham): . . . It is clear and right that a court should be slow to depart from the decisions of a Parliament in concluding that a Parliament has derogated from Convention rights—that has long been accepted in the jurisprudence of the European Court of Human Rights. I think it right that that should be specified in the Bill, as the Bill will guide the United Kingdom courts in their approach to the Convention. The statute should expressly state that the courts should have due regard to the expressions of parliamentary will, in the hope that the courts will be slow to hold that Parliament has departed and derogated from Convention rights. I believe that there is an advantage in specifying in the Bill the concept of a margin of appreciation.

Mr. Paul Stinchcombe (Wellingborough): The points made by the right hon. and learned Member for Sleaford and North Hykeham (Mr. Hogg) were seductively made, but they were wrong in principle and dangerous in effect. Clause 3(1) and clause 6(1) are the provisions that truly give the Bill teeth—if rights are to be brought home, they will be precisely because of those provisions. Clause 3(1) states:

> "So far as it is possible to do so, primary legislation and subordinate legislation must be read and given effect in a way which is compatible with Convention rights."

Paragraphs 2.7 and 2.8 of the White Paper "Rights Brought Home" make it clear that those words are intended to go beyond pre-existing law:

> "This goes beyond the present rule which enables the courts to take the Convention into account in resolving any ambiguity in a legislative provision. The courts will be required to interpret legislation so as to uphold the Convention rights unless legislation itself is so clearly incompatible with the Convention that it is impossible so to do."

It is precisely because of the opening words of the clause and their effect that Convention law will be moved forward in this country in a way that I believe is desirable.

Mr. Grieve: I understand the hon. Gentleman's point but, like my right hon. and learned Friend the Member for [c. **419**] Sleaford and North Hykeham (Mr. Hogg), I want to know whether the construction of those words will force courts into making artificial interpretations. Would it not be better for the courts to tell Parliament that primary or subordinate legislation was incompatible with the Convention than—as might happen under the current wording—to do painful gymnastic exercises to make existing legislation fit Convention principles when it cannot?

[. . .]

Mr. Straw: This has been a short, but interesting, debate on one of the most fundamental issues about the method that we have chosen to incorporate the European Convention on Human Rights in British law. As hon. Members from both sides of the Chamber will understand, there was considerable debate inside the Labour party and between the Labour party and the Liberal Democrats before the election, and much consideration by the Government after the election, about the form that incorporation should take.

As the White Paper makes clear, we considered how other common law countries had incorporated Bills of Rights. We examined how Canada and New Zealand—both outside the continent of Europe—had dealt with similar issues and whether a Bill of Rights could appropriately be entrenched as a basic and fundamental law with a higher status than the law passed by their Parliaments. We decided to reject Canada's approach, which was, in effect, to establish a fundamental law that, in certain circumstances, took precedence over laws [c. 420] passed by its Parliament. We also considered the New Zealand model. We came up with our own approach—it is a British answer to a British problem—fundamental to which is the sovereignty and supremacy of Parliament.

I have never believed—my colleagues share this view—that it would be sensible in this country to have a supreme court that could override the will of Parliament. Indeed, such a system would be extremely dangerous without a written or codified constitution or—as applies in the United States and almost all other constitutions—the mechanisms to override the fundamental law as laid down by a supreme court.

It would mean that judges in a British supreme court would be accorded more power than is, in practice, accorded to US Supreme Court judges, whose decisions can, in the final analysis, be overridden by the popular will through an amendment to the constitution—without such a facility to override judges who are unelected or who were elected many years before, the democratic processes cannot operate effectively.

For that reason, we decided that, while of course the courts would have clear powers to apply the European Convention—without that, we would not be bringing rights home—ultimately Parliament's will would prevail. We have applied that in a number of ways which I shall place on record before answering the specific points that have been raised by hon. Members on both sides of the Chamber.

Clause 19 requires a Minister introducing a new measure to

> "make a statement to the effect that in his view the provisions of the legislation are or are not compatible with the Convention rights"

or that he is unable to make such a statement.

Nothing could be more compatible with the sovereignty of Parliament than the fact that the Bill incorporating the Convention on Human Rights refers to the possibility—that may happen week by week—that Ministers have to apply it to future legislation. That is not to say that they have to force future Bills into the apparent straitjacket of the Convention; they simply have to make a statement to the House on whether a measure is compatible with the European Convention, and therefore with the Bill.

Obviously, it will be incumbent on Ministers—certainly under the present Administration—to do their best to ensure that Bills are compatible with the Convention. Indeed, that practice was followed for many years by the previous Administration. They also subscribed to decent human rights, and for the practical reason that, if Bills were introduced that were knowingly incompatible with the Convention, the Government could easily end up in trouble, if not with United Kingdom courts, with the European Court of Human Rights, which in practice has a facility to override Parliament so long as Parliament decides to accede to the Convention. That is the first way in which we respect the sovereignty of the House.

The second is through clause 3, which is very clear. . . . [c. 421] Clause 3(1) states:

> "So far as it is possible to do so, primary legislation and subordinate legislation must be read and given effect in a way that is compatible with the Convention rights."

Subsection (2)(b) makes it absolutely clear that

"This section . . . does not affect the validity, continuing operation or enforcement of any incompatible primary legislation".

The issue of incompatibility of legislation can be addressed only by the higher courts. I should explain to the hon. Member for Maidenhead (Mrs. May) that no group of senior judges looking at the clause will come to any other view but that the intention of Parliament is that there may be legislation that is incompatible with the Convention—either in future or previously—and, that even if it is found to be incompatible, it will remain in force unless and until the House, by accelerated or normal procedure, decides otherwise.

Mr. Hogg: The Home Secretary has been making the point that, in this context, the Government are keen not to undermine parliamentary sovereignty. Does he understand that Opposition Members who have studied the argument would have much greater confidence in that approach had he not adopted the remedial order procedure set out in the Bill, which provides for affirmative resolutions for changing primary legislation? [. . .]

Mr. Straw: . . . Even on the most dismal interpretation of clause 10, the will of the House still prevails. It may be a truncated procedure, but it certainly does not give the courts the power to say what the law of the land should be. [. . .]

As I have said, we want the courts to strive to find an interpretation of legislation that is consistent with Convention rights, so far as the plain words of the [c. 422] legislation allow, and only in the last resort to conclude that the legislation is simply incompatible with them. The Opposition want the courts to arrive somewhat earlier at the conclusion that the legislation is simply incompatible with the Convention. I cannot see what could be gained by that, bearing in mind our responsibilities under the Convention, apart from the prospect of more cases ending up in Strasbourg because fewer people would be satisfied with the interpretation of the United Kingdom courts.

Mr. Hogg: There are at least two disadvantages to the Home Secretary's argument. First, the courts may be required to give a strained meaning to language, and that in principle is not a good thing. Secondly, if they give a strained meaning to language in the context of this legislation, it could serve as a precedent that reads across and guides courts in their interpretation of language that is wholly outwith the statute under discussion.

Mr. Straw: The right hon. and learned Gentleman is right on his second point. [. . .] Of course interpretation by one of the higher courts of a particular word will read across into many other circumstances, often anticipated. That is why, as the right hon. and learned Gentleman knows better than I do, parliamentary counsel is so keen on one word rather than another.

I am not convinced, however, by the right hon. and learned Gentleman's first point that the courts will contort the meaning of words until they lose their meaning altogether. In many cases, particularly in respect of statutory interpretation, the whole task of the court is not to make up the law, but to say what it means where that is not clear or where its application in particular circumstances is not clear. The courts are well versed in the interpretation of the law and of Parliament's intention.

Let me say in reply to a point made by the hon. Member for Maidenhead that there was a time when all the courts could do to divine the intention of Parliament was to apply themselves to the words on the face of any Act. Now, following Pepper *v.* Hart, they are able to look behind that and, not least, to look at the words used by Ministers. I do not think the courts will need to apply themselves to the words that I am about to use, but, for the avoidance of doubt, I will say that it is not our intention that the courts, in applying what is now clause 3, should contort the meaning of words to produce implausible or incredible meanings. I am talking about plain words in what is actually a clear Bill with plain language—with the intention of Parliament set out in *Hansard*, should the courts wish to refer to it.

Mr. Grieve: Perhaps the clause should say, "possible and reasonable", but the right hon. Gentleman might then say that the courts are always supposed to be reasonable, so it is not necessary to include that word.

Mr. Straw: Ever since the Wednesbury decision, the courts have chided others for being unreasonable, so it is difficult to imagine them not being reasonable. If we had used just the word "reasonable", we would have created a subjective test. "Possible" is different. It means, [c. 423] "What is the possible interpretation? Let us look at this set of words and the possible interpretations." [. . .]

My bet is that the courts will say that they will adopt a reasonable approach. As the hon. Member for Beaconsfield (Mr. Grieve) said, they would be the last to admit to adopting an unreasonable approach. I am comfortable with the words in the Bill and I do not believe that the courts will contort them in the way that hon. Members implied.

I come back to the point about parliamentary sovereignty. If the higher courts come up with an interpretation that makes the intention of Parliament risible and means that legislation is applied in a way that is unreasonable and has ridiculous results, it is open to the House to change the decision. [. . .] It is open to the House—it is its ultimate right—to change a decision.

My hon. Friend the Member for Wellingborough (Mr. Stinchcombe) asked which of the academics I backed. I back those who have read the plain words in this clause and take the view that it moves us on from the way in which the courts currently interpret Convention legislation. Hon. Members should feel reassured by the fact that our courts have had quite a lot of experience in interpreting the Convention. Where there is ambiguity, they come down on the side of the Convention. [. . .] [c. 424]

Doctrine of implied repeal

Doctrine of implied repeal not relevant to interpretive scheme of the Act – no need for reliance on the doctrine

House of Lords, Committee Stage

Official Report, House of Lords, 18 November 1997, vol. 583, col. 520

The Lord Chancellor (Lord Irvine of Lairg): . . . The central point is that the Bill provides for an interpretative approach. As Clause 3(1) states:

> "So far as it is possible to do so, primary legislation and subordinate legislation must be read and given effect in a way which is compatible with the Convention rights".

The noble Lord, Lord Lester, has consistently said that when in future statements of compatibility are made by Ministers, that will encourage the judiciary in its interpretative endeavours.

Having decided to adopt that interpretative approach it is of course helpful to the courts (and other public authorities) for the Bill to signal what the position is intended to be where a compatible construction is impossible. That information is supplied by subsection (1) itself and also, in conjunction with subsection (2)(a), by paragraphs (b) and (c). Those two paragraphs make it clear that the requirement to interpret legislation in accordance with the Convention rights does not mean that incompatible primary legislation, or inevitably incompatible subordinate legislation, since deriving from parent legislation which itself is incompatible, is to be [c. 522] invalidated or otherwise made inoperable because of that incompatibility. They ensure that the courts cannot disapply, refuse to give effect to, or ignore Acts of Parliament on the grounds of their incompatibility with the Convention rights. That is what we intend. We submit that this scheme is consistent with the sovereignty of Parliament as traditionally understood.

Under the method adopted by the Bill to give effect to the Convention rights, it is just not relevant to cite the doctrine of implied repeal. The Convention rights will not, as I have already said when responding to a previous amendment in the name of the noble and learned Lord, become part of our domestic law, and will therefore not supersede existing legislation or be superseded by future legislation. In both cases the Convention rights will be used to interpret and give effect to that legislation.

. . . It avoids the pitfalls . . . by ensuring that the courts are not brought into conflict with Parliament when a discrepancy is identified. It is also in harmony with the UK's existing constitutional arrangements. [. . .]

I do not accept that the Bill adopts a scheme which is cumbrous and circuitous. On the contrary, I believe that the scheme is right. It rests happily with our traditions. It is intellectually coherent and, with respect to the parliamentary draftsman, it is also elegant. The scheme of this Bill is that if statutes are held incompatible on Convention grounds, then it is for Parliament to remedy that. We do not wish to incorporate the Convention rights, and then, in reliance on the doctrine of implied repeal, allow the courts to strike down Acts of Parliament.

The intended scheme of this Bill rests more comfortably with our tradition of parliamentary sovereignty. I believe also that this is a scheme of incorporation which is welcome to the higher judiciary. The doctrine of implied repeal is not without its own difficulties, but I have no quarrel with the noble and learned Lord's short statement of that doctrine. We are, by Clause 3, inviting Parliament to accept a wholly different scheme of incorporation. It is one which rejects the route of the doctrine of implied repeal, which, together with express incorporation of the Convention rights, the noble and learned Lord would prefer us to follow, but it is one which we do not intend to follow. [. . .][c. 523]

Lord Lester of Herne Hill: I wonder whether he could help in this way: does it follow from what he said that where there is existing legislation, before the Human Rights Bill becomes law that has to be interpreted so far as possible to comply with Convention rights in accordance with Clause 3(1), that the courts' obligation will be to strive, wherever possible, to read the existing legislation in accordance with the Convention, using whatever interpretative tools they think fit, and, if they fail, to grant a declaration of incompatibility, if that is their conclusion? That is how I understand the position. One does not need the doctrine of implied repeal, which would involve saying that the existing statute is, as it were, void, has been overtaken by a subsequent Act, but instead, by a process of judicial interpretation, the existing legislation is to be read in accordance with the Convention rights wherever possible, which is what Clause 3(1) says. If that is the position, I am entirely content.

The Lord Chancellor: In my view that is what the Bill means. The interpretative provision of Clause 3 applies to legislation in being prior to the passage of this Act and legislation that comes into being after the passage of this Act. I see no need for any reliance on the doctrine of implied repeal.

Not Government's intention to repeal any pre-existing legislation that is incompatible with the Convention

House of Lords, Report Stage
Official Report, House of Lords, 19 January 1998, vol. 584, col. 1291

Lord Lester of Herne Hill: . . . [T]he command in the Bill—where possible to construe existing and future legislation to conform with Convention rights—is so strong that it leaves entirely open the possibility that the courts will, in effect, use the doctrine of implied repeal or something like it in order to achieve the correct result, which is no mismatch between our statute book and the Convention.

I was encouraged in that view, in particular, by a remarkable lecture recently given by the noble and learned Lord the Lord Chancellor, the Tom Sargant Memorial Lecture, under the auspices of Justice. With your permission I would like to refer to one or two of the matters in that lecture which seem to me to show exactly the approach that the courts will be adopting.

The Lord Chancellor pointed out that the Act, when it comes into force, will require new judicial techniques of interpretation. He said:

> "The Act will require the courts to read and give effect to the legislation in a way compatible with the Convention rights 'so far as it is possible to do so'. This ... goes far beyond the present rule. It will not be necessary to find an ambiguity. On the contrary the courts will be required to interpret legislation so as to uphold the Convention rights unless the legislation itself is so clearly incompatible with the Convention that it is impossible to do so".

The Lord Chancellor continued:

> "Moreover, it should be clear from the parliamentary history, and in particular the ministerial statement of compatibility which will be required by the Act, that Parliament did not intend to cut across a [c. 1292] Convention right. Ministerial statements of compatibility will inevitably be a strong spur to the courts to find means of construing statutes compatibly with the Convention".

I break off to observe that that, of course, is dealing with post Human Rights Act legislation not pre-Act. Then the Lord Chancellor said this:

> "Whilst this particular approach is innovative, there are some precedents which will assist the courts. In cases involving European Community law, decisions of our courts already show that interpretative techniques may be used to make the domestic legislation comply with the Community law, even where this requires straining the meaning of words or reading in words which are not there".

He gave as an example the well known Litster case decided in 1990. He also referred to the jurisprudence in New Zealand. He then said this:

> "The court will interpret as consistent with the Convention not only those provisions which are ambiguous in the sense that the language used is capable of two different meanings but also those provisions where there is no ambiguity in that sense, unless a clear limitation is expressed. In the latter category of case it will be 'possible' (to use the statutory language) to read the legislation in a conforming sense because there will be no clear indication that a limitation on the protected rights was intended so as to make it 'impossible' to read it as conforming".

I apologise for reading all of that but it is very important because it shows, from the highest authority among the makers of the Bill in this House, that there will be a new approach to statutory interpretation. A declaration of incompatibility will be a systemic failure. I believe that that will very rarely happen, and that our courts will act in a similar way to the Judicial Committee of the Privy Council when construing ordinary legislation in the context of Commonwealth constitutional guarantees of human rights; that is, by reading in and reading down: reading in safeguards to save the statute in accordance with human rights; and reading down—reading narrowly restrictions upon human rights; adopting a generous approach, in the words of the noble and learned Lord, Lord Wilberforce, to give human rights their full scope and avoiding what the noble and learned Lord, described as the austerity of tabulated legalism.

Against that background it seems to me that to go to the doctrine of implied repeal, which has often been criticised by academic commentators, for reasons that I do not need to go into, is now unnecessary. The new principles described by the Lord Chancellor—although of course it is not a matter for him in the end but for the courts themselves to decide how to interpret the provisions of this Bill—seem to me to take care of the problem which the noble and learned Lord has quite properly raised in his amendment. [. . .]

Lord Ackner: . . . It seems to me that the Government's preoccupation with preserving parliamentary sovereignty has caused it to over-complicate the situation. As has been made perfectly clear, we are concerned in this amendment with pre-existing [c. 1293] legislation and not with future legislation. To preserve the sovereignty of Parliament the slightly complex procedure of the declaration of incompatibility followed, one anticipates, with the reaction by Parliament to put the matter right, is quite unnecessary in relation to pre-existing legislation. The mistake made in the White Paper, to which the noble Lord has just drawn attention, is the clue to the unnecessary application of the declaration of incompatibility approach to pre-existing legislation.

It is perfectly clear that the doctrine of implied repeal is an existing part of English law. I cannot find anything in the Bill to prevent the courts, where appropriate, from using the doctrine of implied repeal. All this necessity to adopt an entirely new approach to interpretation in relation to pre-existing legislation is made quite unnecessary if one

follows that doctrine. It involves no problem with regard to infringing parliamentary sovereignty. I think that the strain which is to be imposed upon the judiciary to go through the forensic gymnastics which have been referred to can be so easily relieved in regard to pre-existing legislation, and that is the merit of this amendment.
[...]

Lord Donaldson of Lymington: [...] I do not see that the doctrine of implied repeal solves any problems at all. I do not think it is even intended to solve this problem. As I understand it, it arises where you have two statutes: statute A which sets out certain rights, liabilities or procedures, and statute B, a later statute, which sets out certain rights, liabilities or procedures. You look at the two and find that there is an inconsistency between the earlier statute and the later one. The court, in accordance with this doctrine, says, "Parliament must have intended to repeal the first statute or some part of it, so we can forget about the implied repeal part". That does not work with this Bill because here we have, in theory, an earlier statute giving rise to rights, liabilities or procedures, and then we find an incompatibility. But we do not have an alternative set of rights, liabilities or procedures to judge one against the other to see whether there is an implied repeal. All we know is that the earlier statute is inconsistent. We have nothing else to substitute. [c. 1294] I strongly suspect that in most cases there will be more than one way of remedying the incompatibility. You really would be involving the courts in a legislative function of no mean order if it were pointed out to them that there were, say, three ways of remedying the inconsistency and leaving it to them to choose which.
[...]

The Lord Chancellor (Lord Irvine of Lairg): [...] The Bill sets out a scheme for giving effect to the Convention rights which maximises the protection to individuals while retaining the fundamental principle of parliamentary sovereignty. Clause 3 is the central part of this scheme. Clause 3(1) requires legislation to be read and given effect to so far as it is possible to do so in a way that is compatible with the Convention rights. Clause 3(2) provides that where it is not possible to give a compatible construction to primary legislation or to subordinate legislation whose incompatibility flows from the terms of the parent Act, that does not affect its validity, continuing operation or enforcement.

This ensures that the courts are not empowered to strike down Acts of Parliament which they find to be incompatible with the Convention rights. Instead, Clause 4 of the Bill, together with Clauses 10 to 12, introduces a new mechanism through which the courts can signal to the Government that a provision of legislation is, in their view, incompatible. It is then for Government and Parliament to consider what action should be taken. I believe that this will prove to be an effective procedure and it is also one which accords with our traditions of parliamentary sovereignty. That is why the Bill adopts it.

I agree with the observations of the noble and learned Lord, Lord Donaldson of Lymington. The position under the Bill is that, where pre-existing legislation cannot be construed by the courts compatibly with the Convention, the intention of the Government is that the courts may make a declaration of incompatibility and then Parliament may make a remedial order.

Adopting and not taking up the time of your Lordships repeating the observations of the noble and learned Lord, Lord Donaldson of Lymington, I would add that it is not the intention of the Bill to repeal any pre-existing legislation that is incompatible with the Convention. The noble Lord, Lord Lester of Herne Hill, was kind enough to refer to my recent Tom Sargant Memorial Lecture. I shall not add to whatever authority these extra-judicial observations may have—I doubt much—by repeating in the House anything that I said then.

SECTION 4: DECLARATION OF INCOMPATIBILITY

4. - (1) Subsection (2) applies in any proceedings in which a court determines whether a provision of primary legislation is compatible with a Convention right.

(2) If the court is satisfied that the provision is incompatible with a Convention right, it may make a declaration of that incompatibility.

(3) Subsection (4) applies in any proceedings in which a court determines whether a provision of subordinate legislation, made in the exercise of a power conferred by primary legislation, is compatible with a Convention right.

(4) If the court is satisfied-

(a) that the provision is incompatible with a Convention right, and
(b) that (disregarding any possibility of revocation) the primary legislation concerned prevents removal of the incompatibility, it may make a declaration of that incompatibility

(5) In this section "court" means-

(a) the House of Lords;
(b) the Judicial Committee of the Privy Council;
(c) the Courts-Martial Appeal Court;
(d) in Scotland, the High Court of Justiciary sitting otherwise than as a trial court or the Court of Session;
(e) in England and Wales or Northern Ireland, the High Court or the Court of Appeal.

(6) A declaration under this section ("a declaration of incompatibility")-

(a) does not affect the validity, continuing operation or enforcement of the provision in respect of which it is given; and
(b) is not binding on the parties to the proceedings in which it is made.

Effect of section 4

House Of Lords, Second Reading

Official Report, House of Lords, 3 November 1997, vol. 582, col. 1231

The Lord Chancellor (Lord Irvine of Lairg): . . . Clause 4 provides for the rare cases where the courts may have to make declarations of incompatibility. Such declarations are serious. That is why Clause 5 gives the Crown the right to have notice of any case where a court is considering making a declaration of incompatibility and the right to be joined as a party to the proceedings, so that it can make representations on the point.

A declaration of incompatibility will not itself change the law. The statute will continue to apply despite its incompatibility. But the declaration is very likely to prompt the Government and Parliament to respond.

House of Commons, Second Reading

Official Report, House of Commons, 16 February 1998, vol. 307, col. 780

The Secretary of State for the Home Department (Mr. Jack Straw): . . . A declaration of incompatibility will not affect the continuing validity of the legislation in question. That would be contrary to the principle of the Bill. However, it will be a clear signal to Government and Parliament that, in the court's view, a provision of legislation does not conform to the standards of the Convention. To return to a matter that I discussed earlier, it is likely that the Government and Parliament would wish to respond to such a situation and would do so rapidly. We have discussed how that would operate and no doubt there will be further detailed discussions in Committee on the Floor of the House.

Declarations are discretionary – effect on subordinate legislation – relationship with other sections – responsibility of courts to explain the need for declaration and extent of incompatibility

House of Lords, Committee Stage

Official Report, House of Lords, 18 November 1997, vol. 583, col. 544

The Lord Chancellor (Lord Irvine of Lairg): . . . The position simply is that at present subordinate legislation may be struck down by the courts on the same grounds as in the case of other forms of administrative action. That is most commonly on vires grounds, but also on procedural grounds where a mandatory provision for making the subordinate legislation has not been complied with or, less commonly, on the ground that a discretion has been exercised unreasonably or irrationally.

Clause 6(1) of the Bill, by making it unlawful for a public authority to act in a manner inconsistent with the Convention rights, will make it unlawful for a Minister to exercise a power to make subordinate legislation so as to make provision which is incompatible with the Convention. However, subordinate legislation which is incompatible with the Convention rights will thus become susceptible to challenge on vires grounds in the ordinary way. These provisions deal essentially with a situation where subordinate legislation is incompatible with the Convention because that incompatibility has been dictated by the terms of parent legislation which is in itself incompatible.

. . . The power to make a declaration of incompatibility should be, and is, reserved for those cases where it is needed because the courts have no power to do anything else. The subordinate legislation is necessarily incompatible because the parent legislation causes it to be so. The rational outcome, therefore, is that both the parent and the subordinate legislation are subject to a declaration of incompatibility.
[. . .][c. 546]

Clause 4(2) and (4) give a court, if satisfied that a provision of primary or subordinate legislation is incompatible with the Convention rights, a discretion to make a declaration of incompatibility. [. . .]
The reason Clause 4 only confers a discretion is in part that in our domestic law a declaration is generally a discretionary remedy. A Clause 4 declaration has no operative or coercive effect and in particular does not prevent either party relying on, or the courts enforcing, the law in question unless and until changed by Parliament.

The courts may, therefore, not wish to make a declaration of incompatibility in all cases. It is possible that the facts of particular cases may suggest that legislation as it is applied in that case is incompatible with the Convention, but there may be reasons peculiar to the particular case why the legislation should not be declared incompatible on the occasion when the court would be free to do that.

. . . I suggest that I certainly would expect courts generally to make declarations of incompatibility when they find an Act to be incompatible with the Convention. However, we do not wish to deny them a discretion not to do so because of the particular circumstances of any case.

If the noble Lord asks me for examples of that, I suggest that there might be an alternative statutory appeal route which the court might think it preferable to follow, or there might be any other procedure which the court in its discretion thought the applicant should exhaust before seeking a declaration which would then put Parliament under pressure to follow a remedial route.

I cannot envisage many more particular circumstances, but it appears to me to be sensible to leave the courts a discretion, while I well recognise that in the great majority of cases courts would want to make declarations of incompatibility, where that was appropriate.

House of Commons, Committee Stage
Official Report, House of Commons, 3 June 1998, vol.313, col. 457

Mr. Grieve: . . . I appreciate the point, which I am sure the Minister will make, that one would normally expect a court, when pronouncing on a question of incompatibility, to set out the nature and the extent of that incompatibility as it arises from the nature of the case that is before the court. In principle, that is what one would expect, but, in my experience, courts occasionally do not do that. It is an indispensable prerequisite to Parliament being able to make an objective and correct judgment on incompatibility and on how it wishes to proceed for that decision to be made here.
[. . .] [c. 458]

The Parliamentary Secretary, Lord Chancellor's Department (Mr. Geoffrey Hoon): I agree with Opposition Members to this extent. Clause 4 is central to the careful compromise that the Government propose in the Bill—a compromise between parliamentary sovereignty and the need to give proper effect to the European Convention.

[. . .] It is important to remind the Committee of what the court will do when it makes a declaration of incompatibility by virtue of clause 4. By virtue of clause 3, the court will have done everything possible to find an interpretation of the relevant legislation that is compatible with the Convention rights. If one of the courts that is specified in clause 4 is satisfied that it is simply not possible to find a compatible interpretation, it will be able to say so formally by means of a declaration of incompatibility. That is most likely to have followed the procedure that is set out in clause 5 giving the Crown the right to intervene.

[. . .] There will be a vigorous contest before a court, and both sides of the argument will be extensively debated and discussed before that court reaches a decision. As I have said in an intervention, it will be obvious that the matter has been explored in considerable detail and, clearly, one of the higher courts that are set out in clauses 4 and 5 will be required to explain in some detail the reasons for issuing the declaration.

A declaration of incompatibility will be a statement that, in the court's view, there is a problem with a piece of legislation in terms of its compatibility with the [c. 459] Convention, and it is not open to the court itself to rectify or to make good the legislation. That may happen because a Government may have deliberately provided in a Bill that it is not to be open to the court to strike down primary legislation. That course of action could have been considered by the Government when making our proposals. . . . [T]hat approach is adopted in some countries when dealing with such measures. Nevertheless, the Government decided that, in the interests of maintaining parliamentary sovereignty, that would not be the course we would commend to Parliament.

By enabling the courts to make a declaration of incompatibility, the situation can be brought to the notice of Parliament and the deficiency subsequently rectified by Parliament, whether by primary legislation or by approving a remedial order. That allows Parliament precisely the opportunity for which Opposition Members have been arguing. I am sorry that they have not accepted that during my comments.

. . . As the Bill stands, I would expect a court, when making a declaration, to explain what the difficulty was and why it had been impossible to overcome it by constructive interpretation of clause 3. How the declaration arose would be apparent from the judgment as a whole.

A legislative provision will either be compatible or incompatible. The idea that it is possible for a court to certify the extent of the incompatibility is patent nonsense—forgive me for putting it so brutally. It is not possible to certify the extent of an incompatibility. There is either a breach of the Convention or there is not. That part of the amendments is patently absurd. There will not be degrees of incompatibility, or any difference between one kind of incompatibility and another.
[. . .] [c. 460]

The purpose of a declaration is to draw attention to a legislative incompatibility with the Convention and to act as a trigger for a remedial order under clauses 10 to 12. A declaration of incompatibility has no effect on the case before the court. Clause 4(6) expressly provides that a declaration does not affect the validity, continuing operation or enforcement of the relevant legislative provision. This is because we think that any decision to change primary legislation should be reserved for the consideration of Parliament. Again, the Government are upholding the sovereignty of Parliament and are not in any way breaching that principle.

'A Convention right' in section 4(1) and (2)

Effect of use of 'a Convention right' in section 4(1) and (2) on balancing of rights – effect of Article 17

House of Lords, Report Stage

Official Report, House of Lords, 19 January 1998, vol. 584, col. 1295

Lord Simon of Glaisdale: Even where a claimant relies on an article of the Convention which has no built-in reference to other rights, as Article 8 undoubtedly does, there is the overriding effect of Article 17. Clause 1(1) of the Bill [c. 1297] refers to it. I do not believe that it has been mentioned frequently in your Lordships' House, but Article 17 states:

> "Nothing in this Convention may be interpreted as implying for any state, group or person any right to engage in any activity or perform any act aimed at the destruction of any of the rights and freedoms set forth herein or"—

then these important words—

> "at their limitation to a greater extent than is provided for in the Convention".

That is a classic description of the balancing act which the Government believe is the appropriate task for the courts to perform. Therefore, we suggest that the balancing which I have described quite briefly is much more sophisticated and subtle and is designed specifically to be that, rather than the simple case of two litigants, each asserting conflicting Convention rights.

The balancing is to be carried out in the context of the particular article on which the claimant bases his claim. So in the Article 8 example, the court will be adjudicating on the question whether that article has been infringed. Plainly, there will be different balancing to be done by the courts in different claims.

We believe, on sound historic experience, that the courts in this jurisdiction are peculiarly well equipped to carry out these balancing exercises as the whole development of the common law tradition in this country has been substantially based on the sort of subtle balancing that the courts will be required to carry out. That leads to the question as to the best formulation. Should the Bill refer to "one or more of the Convention rights," or "the Convention rights" or "a Convention right?" We have genuinely and conscientiously given this a good deal of thought and we believe that the phrase "a Convention right" is the proper one to use. It is shorter than "one or more of the Convention rights" and is preferable in drafting terms and a more natural formulation.

[. . .][c. 1301]

It is self[-]evident—I say it, and I almost said, "for the last time", but no one is that fortunate—that this point will involve a balancing exercise. Article 8.1 and 8.2 will not just have to be balanced internally, they will have to be balanced, as the noble and learned Lord the Lord Chancellor has told our friends and colleagues in the media, with Article 10. They will have to be balanced—to take up an implied point put by the noble Viscount, Lord Colville of Culross—with the question of a right to a fair trial. There may be many circumstances with which he and I are well familiar in practice over the years where a fair criminal trial for one person may well involve an infringement of someone else's private confidences or family life. That is a commonplace that we all know.

There is nothing difficult about the balancing in principle. It will be an anxious task for the courts to carry out. We believe that we have the formulation right.

SECTION 5: RIGHT OF THE CROWN TO INTERVENE

5. - (1) Where a court is considering whether to make a declaration of incompatibility, the Crown is entitled to notice in accordance with rules of court.

(2) In any case to which subsection (1) applies-
   (a) a Minister of the Crown (or a person nominated by him),
   (b) a member of the Scottish Executive,
   (c) a Northern Ireland Minister,
   (d) a Northern Ireland department, is entitled, on giving notice in accordance with rules of court, to be joined as a party to the proceedings.

(3) Notice under subsection (2) may be given at any time during the proceedings.

(4) A person who has been made a party to criminal proceedings (other than in Scotland) as the result of a notice under subsection (2) may, with leave, appeal to the House of Lords against any declaration of incompatibility made in the proceedings.

(5) In subsection (4)-

"criminal proceedings" includes all proceedings before the Courts-Martial Appeal Court; and

"leave" means leave granted by the court making the declaration of incompatibility or by the House of Lords.

Effect of section 5

House of Lords, Second Reading
Official Report, House of Lords, 3 November 1997, vol. 582, col. 1231
The Lord Chancellor (Lord Irvine of Lairg): . . . Clause 5 gives the Crown the right to have notice of any case where a court is considering making a declaration of incompatibility and the right to be joined as a party to the proceedings, so that it can make representations on the point.

House of Commons, Committee Stage
Official Report, House of Commons, 17 June 1998, vol. 314, col. 391

The Parliamentary Under-Secretary of State for the Home Department (Mr. Mike O'Brien): The purpose of clause 5 is to give the Crown the right to intervene in proceedings in which the court is considering whether to make a declaration of incompatibility. The need for the Crown to be given that right flows from the importance of such a declaration. It is right that the Government—who answer for the United Kingdom in proceedings at Strasbourg and will have responsibility for considering whether to propose to Parliament the amendment of legislation in respect of which the declaration is made—should have the opportunity to make any relevant arguments to the court before it decides whether to make a declaration. The need for the Government to be able to make such arguments is the reason why clause 5(1) entitles the Crown to be given notice of such a case, and why paragraph (a) of clause 5(2) entitles a Minister to be joined as a party to the proceedings.

Subsection 5(2)

"Person nominated" to enable more appropriate person than Minister to be nominated, eg. Director General of Fair Trading

House of Lords, Committee Stage
Official Report, House of Lords, 18 November 1997, vol. 583, col. 555

Lord Henley: . . . The subsection suggests that it may be a Minister of the Crown or a person nominated by a Minister of the Crown. The question I wish to put to the noble and learned Lord is simply why one needs to have the phrase, "a person nominated". What is wrong with a Minister of the Crown? Surely the phrase "by a Minister of the Crown" includes any person to whom he might delegate such matters. I look forward with interest to hearing the response of the noble and learned Lord the Lord Chancellor.

The Lord Chancellor (Lord Irvine of Lairg): . . . Clause 5(2) entitles a Minister of the Crown or a person nominated by a Minister of the Crown to be joined as a party to the proceedings where a court is considering making a declaration of incompatibility. The effect of this amendment would be to restrict this entitlement to a Minister of the

Crown. It appears to us that it will, or may in some cases, be more appropriate for a person nominated by a Minister of the Crown rather than a Minister to be joined as a party to the proceedings.

That is true, for example, in relation to private Acts or to measures of the Church Assembly or to measures of the General Synod or to regulators of public utilities or to the Director General of Fair Trading, to name but a few. In these cases the court may be considering making a declaration of incompatibility and the appropriate person to intervene may well not be the relevant Government Minister, but the relevant Government Minister may recognise that there is another more appropriate person to represent the court in this particular legislative area, and then will so nominate. So [c. 556] the object of the provision is to enable the responsible Minister to nominate a more appropriate person to assist the court in relation to particular legislation.

Scottish Ministers will also be entitled to be joined – Ministers of Crown entitled to be joined as of right – issues in nominating a person will be: what is the public interest in having such a person giving information to the Court? – not creating a mechanism for parties to be joined– not expected such action will be taken on a large number of occasions

House of Commons, Committee Stage

Official Report, House of Commons, 17 June 1998, vol. 314, col. 391

The Parliamentary Under-Secretary of State for the Home Department (Mr. Mike O'Brien):
[. . .]
As we explained in Committee, a declaration does not affect the validity, continuing operation or enforcement of the relevant legislative provision. It is only if Government and Parliament decide to amend the legislation that anyone would be affected. So interested parties should take up their cases with them rather than with the courts.

[. . .]Why do the Opposition think that the entitlement to be joined should be confined to public authorities? Legislation can affect non-public bodies, and courts can make declarations of incompatibility in cases that do not involve a public authority.

[. . .] Clause 5 provides that, where the court is considering whether to make a declaration of incompatibility, a Minister of the Crown or a person nominated by him is entitled to be joined as a party to the

proceedings. It is envisaged that that will remain the position in all cases, but in Scottish cases which relate to devolved matters, Scottish Ministers should also be entitled to be joined as a party.
[. . .] [c. 393]

In making a nomination, the Government would have to consider the criteria as to what was the public interest in the Government's deciding to nominate a particular organisation to be present during the proceedings. Is there an interest in the court's being better informed, in that that organisation could perhaps put forward information to the court that may allow it to make a better decision?

[. . .] The issue for the Minister is fairly narrow: what is the public interest in having a person nominated by the Minister as a party to the proceedings giving information to the court? That person is there not so much to challenge one side of the argument or the other, as to ensure that the court makes the right decision, with all the necessary information and arguments before it.

The person nominated will speak, in a sense, in his or her own capacity. Such people will be joined by the Minister who regards it as being in the public interest, and in the interests of a proper examination of the issues, that that person be joined. The Minister will decide who the person should be. The criterion is simply who the best person is to raise the arguments about whether legislation is compatible. A nominated person will be joined in his own capacity and would be acting on his own behalf—not on behalf of the Government. If the measures of the Synod were being considered, it is expected that the Synod itself would be nominated by the Minister if it were decided that that was in the public interest. The judgment would be made on those criteria.
[. . .] [c. 397]

It is anticipated that, in considering whether to nominate a particular individual or organisation, the Minister will take into account whether it is in the interests of the Government, Parliament and the nation that the issues should be aired before the court. The issue is not to join the party as a partisan in the case. We want to make sure that all the arguments which need to be put are put before the court, and information which may be relevant should be made available to the court.

It is not expected that the Government or the Minister would take such action on a large number of occasions. Having the power there . . .

is important. It is quite proper for such people to be nominated by the Minister.
[...]

Our view is that it should be a matter for the Government, the Minister and those nominated by him to inform the court's arguments and decisions. It should not be the right of persons who would not otherwise be able to be joined to the proceedings—merely because a declaration of incompatibility has been considered—to make themselves a party. If they have another locus to join in the proceedings, they can pursue that in the normal manner. We do not propose to create new mechanisms for parties to be joined.

In terms of primary legislation, ... we envisage that an individual or organisation would approach the Government, as it is a decision for the Government whether to act on the [c. 398] declaration of incompatibility. In a sense, nobody is affected until the Government have made that legislative change.

Quite rightly, the hon. Member for South Cambridgeshire asked about secondary legislation. Our view is that, if we were to create the circumstances in which anyone who might be affected by a decision could somehow parachute in and create a new situation in the court, it would lead to chaos. If they have the right to be a party to the proceedings, they should, in the normal course of a civil case, become a party to the proceedings. That would not be the effect in a criminal matter. We must be careful not to create new opportunities for persons to become involved in criminal matters.

The best way for persons interested in the outcome of a secondary legislation matter to proceed is that the Government will have to consider how they deal with any decision in relation to secondary legislation by a court. At that point, it is right that any person or organisation interested in any change that the Government may or may not be considering should deal with the Government and Ministers.

The opportunities are there. It may be that those involved have the ability to become a party to a civil proceeding. They almost certainly would not, and should not, have the ability to become a party to a criminal proceeding. In the normal course of events, if they are able to become a party to a proceeding, it is a matter for them to do so. Those who would not have the ability to become a party to a proceeding must deal with the Government afterwards.

Costs

No assurance that extra costs caused by intervention will be met by the Crown – Costs left to the Judge's discretion – Likely to be cases where the Crown is required to meet its own costs, in some cases even those of other parties

House of Lords, Committee Stage

Official Report, House of Lords, 18 November 1997, vol. 583, col. 557

Lord Henley: . . . [I]n Clause 5 we seek an assurance from the Government that in those cases where a Minister of the Crown wishes to intervene, should there be extra costs as a result of that, the other parties in the case will not be subject to the extra costs caused by that intervention and that those costs will be met by the Crown. That is a relatively simple point. I hope that the noble and learned Lord the Lord Chancellor understands it and can give me an assurance that that will be the case.

[. . .]

The Parliamentary Under-Secretary of State, Home Office (Lord Williams of Mostyn): This is of course an important question, but we believe it is best dealt with in a different way. I shall take a moment or two to explain why. As the Committee will be aware, the courts, in particular the higher courts to which this clause is relevant, already have considerable discretion to make [c. 558] orders for costs affecting both parties and non-parties to litigation. Although there are few Members of the Committee present, quite a number of those have had fairly frequent experience of reaching a conclusion about orders for costs.

In relation to civil cases in the High Court and the Court of Appeal, Section 51(3) of the Supreme Court Act 1981 states that,

> "the Court shall have full power to determine by whom and to what extent the costs are to be paid."

Various well known provisions on the award of costs in criminal cases are contained in the Prosecution of Offences Act 1985.

I suggest, with great respect, that there are good reasons why the allocation of costs should be left to the judges' discretion. The important point, among others, is that the court in question has heard the case fully; it knows all the relevant facts and it has had the benefit of submission from counsel for all parties. There are many factors which judges would properly want to take into account when assessing how costs should be allocated. This is not intended to be an exhaustive list, but these would include whether the case put forward by the party seeking the declaration had any substantive merit. Some cases are more meritorious than others and some which get to court have little merit at all except the opportunity of outdoor relief for members of the Bar. Perhaps it ought to be indoor relief for members of the Bar! We all know of litigants who insist on taking up court time when it is not reasonable or legitimate to do so. This is a matter for the judge's decision, having heard— I stress—all the facts of the case and considered all the interlocking legislative provisions.

Another question could be: was there any wider public interest in the case? That ought to be a matter affecting the judge when he decides on the costs order. He would probably want legitimately in this area to consider the financial position of the applicant. That is not, of course, a strong aspect of judicial discretion in costs orders in the generality of cases, but it might—if a particular judge thought it appropriate—be relevant in this class of case. What is the outcome of the case? Is a declaration of incompatibility or a declarator ultimately awarded? How many other members of the public might be affected? What is the ambit of the legislative component which is the subject of a declaration of incompatibility? All those are subtle questions that judges ought to balance rather than being disqualified from carrying out that balance simply by the brutality of this present amendment. It is only right and proper that I should try to protect the judiciary from brutality from any quarter, even probing brutality.

We do not think it would be reasonable or sensible to put a specific provision in the Bill that in every case the Crown should bear the cost of a Minister applying for or being joined as a party. I do not regard this response as in any sense a party political point. It seems to us much better to leave questions of discretion with the judge in question. Judges do this every day of the week and by and large, if I may say so, they do it extremely well. They are well accustomed to deciding those issues, not least, for instance, in the general analogy of which one might think: in cases of judicial review. [c. 559] My noble and learned friend the Lord Chancellor has already plainly indicated—this was reaffirmed on Second Reading—that he regards those cases as particular, because he spoke of—he repeated it earlier today in Committee—a dedicated fund that there may well be for litigation within this general area.

Bearing in mind that this will be peculiar litigation, and the clear indication which my noble and learned friend has given, I should have thought that this was an occasion when one should come to the conclusion: trust the judges. They know the full facts.
[. . .]

We do not believe that it is reasonable or sensible to insert a specific provision in the Bill that in every case the Crown should bear the costs of the Minister. There are likely to be cases—one recognises this—where the Crown would be required to meet its own costs. For instance, a tribunal might feel that the point behind the declaration of incompatibility was so plain that the Minister in question had behaved irrationally or unreasonably in contesting the matter. It might be thought that the interest of the Crown was so marginal that the relevant Minister might perhaps never have applied to be joined, on the powers given him in the Bill.

There is a wide spectrum of possibilities which reinforces our stance. In some cases of course the Crown may be required to meet its own costs, as I said a moment or two ago. It may even be that there would be circumstances where the Crown would have to meet the costs of other parties. There might be some cases where neither would be appropriate. We do not see any grounds for moving away from the general well-known position that the allocation of costs in individual cases is a matter for the courts to determine in the light of individual and particular circumstances. I have taken a moment or two, because, although it is late, and although it does not go to the heart of the Bill, it is an important aspect. I hope that the noble Lord will think that I have done his amendment justice in replying as fully as I can.
[c. 560] [. . .]

Fundamentally, all litigation is about questions of access to justice. Therefore this particular area of litigation, though extremely important, is not different in principle to any litigant wanting his or her rights upheld in the courts.

It would be quite improper for me to give any indication of Crown policy generally which would attempt to bind my colleagues for the future. After all, any government is the steward of public funds and ought not legitimately to say, "This is going to be our policy in these matters".

However, I reiterate—and I should have thought it would be a source of comfort—what the noble and learned Lord the Lord Chancellor said in his Cardiff speech and has reiterated today, and what was said by me on his authority in winding up at Second Reading; namely, of course we regard these cases as important. One signpost of that is his fund, about which he is consulting, which would be devoted entirely to this class of case. Beyond that I do not believe that any Minister ought properly and prudently to go.

Again I reiterate the remarks of my noble and learned friend the Lord Chancellor. The judges who will try this class of case will be High Court judges, well accustomed, well attuned, particularly over the past 10 years—far more attuned than many political figures—to these important questions. They will be alert and astute to the points put forward by the noble Lord, Lord Lester of Herne Hill. I believe it is better to trust the judges on these matters. They know the facts of the case and the importance of the issues. I believe that they will know [c. 561] where their duty, judicially, lies in coming to a proper, fair balance in everyone's interest in relation to applications for costs.

SECTION 6: ACTS OF PUBLIC AUTHORITIES

6. - (1) It is unlawful for a public authority to act in a way which is incompatible with a Convention right.

(2) Subsection (1) does not apply to an act if-

(a) as the result of one or more provisions of primary legislation, the authority could not have acted differently; or
(b) in the case of one or more provisions of, or made under, primary legislation which cannot be read or given effect in a way which is compatible with the Convention rights, the authority was acting so as to give effect to or enforce those provisions.

(3) In this section "public authority" includes-

(a) a court or tribunal, and
(b) any person certain of whose functions are functions of a public nature, but does not include either House of Parliament or a person exercising functions in connection with proceedings in Parliament.

(4) In subsection (3) "Parliament" does not include the House of Lords in its judicial capacity.

(5) In relation to a particular act, a person is not a public authority by virtue only of subsection (3)(b) if the nature of the act is private.

(6) "An act" includes a failure to act but does not include a failure to-
(a) introduce in, or lay before, Parliament a proposal for legislation; or
(b) make any primary legislation or remedial order.

Effect of section 6

House of Lords, Second Reading
Official Report, House of Lords, 3 November 1997, vol. 582, col. 1231
The Lord Chancellor (Lord Irvine of Lairg): . . . Clause 6 makes it unlawful for a public authority to act in a way which is incompatible with the Convention.

House of Commons, Second Reading
Official Report, House of Commons, 16 February 1998, vol. 307, col.. 780

The Secretary of State for the Home Department (Mr. Jack Straw): . . . Clause 6 makes it unlawful for public authorities to act in a way that is incompatible with a Convention right, unless they are required to do so to give effect to primary legislation.

Act only to apply to public authorities – public authorities widely defined – designed to apply to bodies private in some respects but not others

House of Lords, Second Reading
Official Report, House of Lords, 3 November 1997, vol. 582,col. 1231

The Lord Chancellor (Lord Irvine of Lairg): . . . We decided, first of all, that a provision of this kind should apply only to public authorities, [c. 1232] however defined, and not to private individuals.
[. . .]

We also decided that we should apply the Bill to a wide rather than a narrow range of public authorities, so as to provide as much protection as possible to those who claim that their rights have been infringed.

Clause 6 is designed to apply not only to obvious public authorities such as government departments and the police, but also to bodies which are public in certain respects but not others. Organisations of this kind will be liable under Clause 6 of the Bill for any of their acts, unless the act is of a private nature. Finally, Clause 6 does not impose a liability on organisations which have no public functions at all.

Government accountable under Convention for actions of public authorities – Account taken of privatisation of public functions and extension of judicial review

House of Commons, Second Reading
Official Report, House of Commons, 16 February 1998, vol. 307, col. 775

The Secretary of State for the Home Department (Mr. Jack Straw): . . . Before I turn to the detail of the Bill, I should like to comment on two issues that have gained particular prominence: the positions of the media and the Churches. Both have concerns that centre on the provisions of Clause 6, relating to public authorities, so I must briefly explain the principles underlying that clause.

Under the Convention, the Government are answerable in Strasbourg for any acts or omissions of the state about which an individual has a complaint under the Convention. The Government have a direct responsibility for core bodies, such as central Government and the police, but they also have a responsibility for other public authorities, in so far as the actions of such authorities impinge on private individuals.

The Bill had to have a definition of a public authority that went at least as wide and took account of the fact that, over the past 20 years, an increasingly large number of private bodies, such as companies or charities, have come to exercise public functions that were previously exercised by public authorities. Under UK domestic common law, such bodies have increasingly been held to account under the processes of judicial review.

As was generally acknowledged in debates in another place, it was not practicable to list all the bodies to which the Bill's provisions should apply. Nor would it have been wise to do so. What was needed instead was a statement of principle to which the courts could give effect. Clause 6 therefore adopts a non-exhaustive definition of a public authority. Obvious public authorities, such as central Government and the police, are caught in respect of everything they do. Public—but not private—acts of bodies that have a mix of public and private functions are also covered.

Rights to be available against a realistic and modern definition of 'the state' - much guidance from judicial review jurisprudence – two categories created

House of Commons, Committee Stage
Official Report, House of Commons, 17 June 1998, vol. 314, col. 406

The Secretary of State for the Home Department (Mr. Jack Straw): . . . When we were drawing up the Bill, we noted that the Convention had its origins in a desire to protect the individual against the abuse of power by the state, rather than to protect one individual against the actions of another. The history of the establishment of the Council of Europe and the great desire at the end of the war that states in Europe should never again be able to oppress their citizens as Nazi Germany and the axis powers had done, explain why the Convention places on the state responsibilities in respect of its treatment of residents and citizens.

We decided that Convention rights should be available in proceedings involving what might be very broadly described as "the state", but that they would not be directly justiciable in actions between private individuals. Although we were not prepared to go as far as that, we wanted a realistic and modern definition of the state so as to provide correspondingly wide protection against an abuse of human rights. Accordingly, liability under the Bill would go beyond the narrow category of central and local government and the police—the organisations that represent a minimalist view of what constitutes the state. The principle of bringing rights home suggested that liability in domestic proceedings should lie with bodies in respect of whose actions the United Kingdom Government were answerable in Strasbourg. The idea was that if someone could get a remedy in Strasbourg, he or she should be able to get a remedy at home. That point was crucial to the Bill's construction.

[. . .][I]t is worth noting that the Strasbourg court has over the years developed its own concept of the state, and its idea of the bodies for whose actions a Government, as a signatory high contracting party, are answerable goes much wider than the original narrow definition of the state.

[. . .][c. 407]

One of the reasons why we were able to develop our institutions peacefully concerned the development of our legal institutions, with the common law and jurisprudence behind them. Over the years, institutions have evolved that perform functions that are effectively those of the state, in its continental sense, but are not directly under the control of the state. I happen to think that that is a good thing, but it poses some difficulties for the drafting of legislation.

Mr. Grieve: It is a matter, not only of the lack of codification but of the fact that we have deliberately farmed out functions to charitable organisations such as the Royal National Lifeboat Institution that in other European countries would be discharged by the state. That is the nub of the problem. I assume that the RNLI would be a public body.

Mr. Straw: It would be a public body in respect of the public functions that it performs, but not of all its charitable functions.

Our society has placed a high value on the notion of self-regulation.

Essentially, the House has told particular professions or organisations that they should put their house in order and regulate themselves or we will introduce statutory regulation. Many institutions have accepted that incentive.

The best example involves regulation in the City: the Takeover Panel was not established by statute and, as far as I am aware, none of its members are appointed by Ministers, but it plays a crucial role in the regulation of markets and competition policy and has been regarded by our domestic courts as susceptible to judicial review. Although they have not used that language, the courts have effectively said that the Takeover Panel, which may be entirely private in its composition, exercises a public function. That is one of the complexities with which we have had to deal in trying to draft the Bill.

Mr. Rowe: Is the Home Secretary saying that, for the purposes of the Bill, the definition of the state is that which has been evolved by the court in Strasbourg, or that it is what we have traditionally defined as the state? That is quite an important distinction.

Mr. Straw: I take the hon. Gentleman's point, but the distinction is not as great as he thinks. If we are to incorporate the Convention in British law and make sense of it we must, as a basic minimum, ensure that the Bill and its application require that the British courts recognise [c. 408] domestically as public bodies those bodies that would be recognised as such in Strasbourg. Otherwise we will not be bringing rights home and we will simply make a rod for our own back by ruling out adjudication by British courts on questions that can plainly go to Strasbourg.

In that case, we would miss out on what has been recognised by all parties as a benefit, whatever other arguments we may have had in the Chamber, and British judges would not be able to adjudicate on the Convention.

[. . .]

Mr. Edward Garnier (Harborough): . . . In any given case, a court will have to decide whether what a body is doing—be it an omission or a positive act—is public or private. Is the Home Secretary saying that jurisprudence at Strasbourg would allow any given judge to say straight away that an act is clearly public or private, or is he saying that the clause offers the English courts the opportunity to develop a common-law understanding of the difference between public and private acts?

Mr. Straw: . . . As a minimum, we must accept what Strasbourg has developed and is developing, as otherwise we will not be bringing rights home. We wanted to ensure that, when courts were already saying that a body's activities in a particular respect were a public function for the purposes of judicial review, other things being equal, that would be a basis for action under the Bill.

In most cases in which Convention rights are prayed in aid, that will be done by way of an application for judicial review. That will be one of the arguments as to why an administrative decision should be overturned, but others, relating wholly to domestic law, will no doubt be on the application.
[. . .][c. 409]

The most valuable asset that we had to hand was jurisprudence relating to judicial review. It is not easily summarised and could not have been simply written into the Bill, but the concepts are reasonably clear and I think that we can build on them.

I am happy to lift the veil on the considerations of the Cabinet Committee and say that we devoted a great deal of time and energy to this issue, as I hope hon. Members would expect us to. We decided that the best approach would be reference to the concept of a public function. After stating that it is

"unlawful for a public authority to act incompatibly with a Convention right",

Clause 6 accordingly provides that a public authority includes a court or a tribunal, and

"any person certain of whose functions are functions of a public nature."

The effect of that is to create three categories, the first of which contains organisations which might be termed "obvious" public authorities, all of whose functions are public. The clearest examples are Government Departments, local authorities and the police. There is no argument about that.

The second category contains organisations with a mix of public and private functions. One of the things with which we had to wrestle was the fact that many bodies, especially over the past 20 years, have performed public functions which are private, partly as a result of privatisation and partly as a result of contracting out.[. . .]

For example, between 1948 and 1993, a public authority—the British Railways Board—was responsible for every aspect of running the railway. Now, Railtrack plc does that, but it also exercises the public function of approving and monitoring the safety cases of train operating companies. Railtrack acts privately in its functions as a commercial property developer. We were anxious . . . that we should not catch the commercial activities of Railtrack—or, for example, of the water companies—which were nothing whatever to do with its exercise of public functions. [c. 410] Private security firms contract to run prisons: what Group 4, for example, does as a plc contracting with other bodies is nothing whatever to do with the state, but, plainly, where it runs a prison, it may be acting in the shoes of the state. The effect of Clause 6(7) is that those organisations, unlike the "obvious" public authorities, will not be liable in respect of their private acts. The third category is organisations with no public functions—accordingly, they fall outside the scope of Clause 6.

As with the interpretation of any legislation . . . it will be for the courts to determine whether an organisation is a public authority. That will be obvious in some cases, and there will be no need to inquire further; in others, the courts will need to consider whether an organisation has public functions. In doing that, they should, among other things, sensibly look to the jurisprudence which has developed in respect of judicial review.

. . . [T]he courts have said that the Takeover Panel amounts to a public authority for the purposes of judicial review. They have also said, however, that the Jockey Club is not susceptible to judicial review, even though it is established by royal charter and performs functions which would be performed by the state or a state agency in other jurisdictions.

To take a topical example, the courts have said that the Football Association is not such a public body as to be susceptible to judicial review, so they are used to drawing a line, and, up to now, the line which they have drawn has been sensible. The Takeover Panel plainly performs a public function—there can be no argument about that, even though it is a private body—and even though the public enjoy football, it is highly debateable whether the functions of the FA are public functions. The same is true of the Jockey Club and its functions.

The courts have been careful in holding susceptible to judicial review bodies which are not plainly agents of the state.

The courts will consider the nature of a body and the activity in question. They might consider whether the activities of a non-statutory body would be the subject of statutory regulation if that body did not exist, which covers the point about the Takeover Panel; whether the Government had provided underpinning for its activities; and whether it exercised extensive or monopolistic powers.

What I have said is intended to make clear why we have drafted Clause 6 in the way that we have, and what effect it is intended to achieve.

[. . .] [c. 411]

My noble Friend Lord Williams of Mostyn made clear in the House of Lords our considered view that we believe that the PCC would be regarded as a body exercising public functions under Clause 6, but not for the reasons raised by the hon. Gentleman. All bodies that are entirely private are subject to the law of trespass and the law at large. We are not discussing that, but whether they are exercising a public function. Amendment No. 106 states:

> "A public authority is any person or body which—
>
> (a) is established or regulated by statute; or
>
> (b) which has ministerial appointments on its governing body".

Bodies established and regulated by statute would be public authorities only when discharging their statutory functions. If amendment No. 31 is agreed to,

> "the private acts of a public authority shall not be regarded as incompatible with Convention rights".

I do not want to "mix it".

[. . .][c. 412]

Mr. Garnier: . . . The General Medical Council was created by statute, but performs an internal disciplinary function. It disciplines doctors who fall into error, but its functions are not set out in statute. It is not a statutory body in the sense that some nationalised industries are statutory bodies. Nor is it even a body to which the law of contempt applies when it sits as a court. That was decided only this week in the Court of Appeal.

We have here a delicious mixture. The General Medical Council is a body created by statute—as, I believe, is the Law Society—or at least recognised by statute; but it performs internal disciplinary functions of a quasi-court-like nature. As we discovered this week, it is not susceptible to the law of contempt. In carrying out its judicial and disciplinary function, will the GMC fall foul of Clause 6 as it is now drafted, or does the Home Secretary believe that our amendment would assist public understanding of the issue by introducing at least a degree of clarity?

Mr. Straw: . . . The General Medical Council is plainly performing the function that the state expects it to perform—regulating the conduct of doctors.

Mr. Grieve: Surely any body that regulates a profession of any kind must be a public body for the purpose of that regulation.

Mr. Straw: That is true.[. . .] [c. 413]
The most obvious reason why amendment No. 106 will not do—I have given technical reasons, but this is really important—is that it does not include Secretaries of State like myself. The Secretary of State for the Home Department is not a

"person or body which . . . is established and regulated by statute";

nor are Departments generally. Most are not legal entities in their own right. Ministers and Departments exercise a range of statutory powers, but many of the powers that I exercise relate to the royal prerogative, or are common-law powers.

If the amendment were adopted, it would go both too far and not far enough. It would go too far by including the private acts of bodies such as Railtrack and the water companies, which were established by statute, when we want only the public functions to be included. It would not go far enough, by a long way, in that it would not include Government Departments. It would also exclude other bodies that are at present judicially reviewable. The most obvious example is the panel on takeovers and mergers, which was held to be judicially reviewable following the judgment of the Court of Appeal in the ex parte Datafin case in 1987, but which is not regulated by statute. The same applies to the British Board of Film Classification.

That is a very interesting body. As I know all too well, following the interesting discussions in which I have had to engage with the board to

get it to do the job that is expected of it, it is an entirely private organisation. It is not regulated by statute. It has a curious connection with the Video Recordings Acts, but hon. Members on both sides of the House—on behalf of the public—are pressurising it to do a job on behalf of the public, and classify films properly. In any other jurisdiction, a state body would probably do the work. Here, it is done by a self-regulating body that clearly has a public function. I believe—and I think the public would believe—that that body should be seen as exercising public functions.
[. . .]

I wanted to make another point before talking about the press. [. . .][c. 414] We think that tribunals should be public authorities, at least in so far as they are bodies in which legal proceedings may be brought. If they were not, there would be a significant gap in the protection of human rights offered by the Bill. "Tribunals" include industrial tribunals, the employment appeals tribunal, immigration adjudicators and the immigration appeals tribunal. If those bodies are not required to comply with Convention rights, it is hard to think of bodies that should be. If the employment appeals tribunal were deemed not to be a public body, the cases would go straight to the court in Strasbourg.

Attempt is to replicate the Strasbourg definition as 'best we can' – respondents will be liable for costs – privatised utilities must be allowed level playing field with commercial competitors – test must relate to substance and nature of the act

House of Commons, Third Reading
Official Report, House of Commons, 17 June 1998, vol. 314, col. 432

The Secretary of State for the Home Department (Mr. Straw): . . . I should have explained before that we could not directly replicate in the Bill the definition of public authorities used by Strasbourg, because, of course, [c. 433] the respondent to any application in the Strasbourg Court is the United Kingdom, as the state. We have therefore tried to do the best we can in terms of replication by taking into account whether a body is sufficiently public to engage the responsibility of the state. [. . .]

[. . .] [W]ho would pay in domestic actions [?] The organisations concerned will pay, so some aspects will depend on the depth of their pockets. That was one of the reasons why I made that clear a couple of weeks ago when we debated the subject in respect of the Churches. I wanted to avoid vexatious litigation against the Churches, which is why I was persuaded to provide them with additional protection in the Bill. The hon. Member for Bury St. Edmunds (Mr. Ruffley) picked me up on paragraph 2.2 of the White Paper, which mentions privatised utilities. That put the matter in a general way, to make the point that, if we had a list of public authorities, it would quickly go out of date. I am absolutely clear that we must, to use the old cliche, provide a level playing field between BT and other, wholly private, operators. They would have to be treated the same under the Bill.

[...]

Overall, the difference between some Opposition Members and other Members on both sides of the House is whether we seek to define a public authority and a public function by reference to the substance and nature of the act, or to the form and legal personality of the institution. As we are dealing with public functions and with an evolving situation, we believe that the test must relate to the substance and nature of the act, not to the form and legal personality.

If we were to do as the Opposition recommend, we would have a definition too wide in some respects, which would cop Railtrack's purely commercial activities as it should not, and too narrow in others—that is, it would exclude the Home Secretary, and I think that I ought to [c. 434] be covered by the Bill.

Definition of public authority part of central scheme of the Act – policy decision to use principles rather than a list of bodies

House of Lords, Committee Stage
Official Report, House of Lords, 24 November 1997, vol. 583, col. 796
The Lord Chancellor (Lord Irvine of Lairg): ... There are some bodies which are obviously public authorities such as the police, the courts, government departments and prisons. They are obviously public authorities under Clause 6(1). However, under Clause 6(3)(c) the term "public authority" includes,

> "any person certain of whose functions are functions of a public nature".

I ask the noble Baroness, Lady Young, to abstain from asking herself the question: is this a public authority just looking at the body in the round? That is what Clause 6(1) invites us to do. However, Clause

6(3)(c) asks whether the body in question has certain functions—not all—which are functions of a public nature. If it has any functions of a public nature, it qualifies as a public authority. However, it is certain acts by public authorities which this Bill makes unlawful. In Clause 6(5) the Bill provides:

> "In relation to a particular act, a person is not a public authority by virtue only of subsection (3)(c) if the nature of the act is private".

Therefore Railtrack, as a public utility, obviously qualifies as a public authority because some of its functions, for example its functions in relation to safety on the railway, qualify it as a public authority. However, acts carried out in its capacity as a private property developer would no doubt be held by the courts to be of a private nature and therefore not caught by the Bill.

[. . .][W]e took a policy decision to avoid a list. [. . .] The disadvantage of a list is precisely . . . that it would be easy to regard it as exhaustive or to suggest that any non-listed body could be a public authority only if it was sufficiently analogous in its essential characteristics to a body that had qualified in the list. There are obvious public authorities—I have mentioned some—which are covered in relation to the whole of their functions by Clause 6(1). Then there are some bodies some of whose functions are public and some private. If there are some public functions the body qualifies as a public authority but not in respect of acts which are of a private nature. Those statutory principles will have to be applied case by case by the courts when issues arise. We think that it is far better to have a principle rather than a list which would be regarded as exhaustive.

[. . .][c. 797] Lord Simon of Glaisdale, would extend [the application of the Bill]. He would include any person supplying goods or services to the public. The Convention, I suppose, would catch window cleaners, jobbing joiners, the girl who keeps the window cleaner's accounts and the boy who delivers the flyers from the local restaurant. I think that that is far too broad.
[. . .]

What we have sought to do in Clause 6 is to set out a principle: first, that the effects of Clauses 6 to 8 should apply in the first place to bodies which are quite plainly public authorities such as Government departments; and, secondly, to other bodies whose functions include functions of a public nature, and therefore the focus should be on their functions and not on their nature as an authority. In the latter case the provisions of the Bill would not apply to the private acts of the bodies in question.

That is the principled approach that we have chosen. Another approach would have been to draw up lists of the bodies to which the Bill did or did not apply. But we rejected that approach as a matter of principle. In particular, there would be the difficulty of compiling such a list, the arguments about it, and the difficulty at the end of the day of preserving any coherent rationale [c. 798] in such a list. The debate that we have had today strengthens me in the view that it was right as a matter of principle to go for a principle and not a list.

Against that background, there is not a great deal more that I wish to say about the particular cases cited. What is most obvious is that the lists could scarcely end where the Opposition have suggested that they might. I appreciate what the noble Lord, Lord Henley, said: that the amendments are put down primarily to probe. We agree of course that local authorities, the police, and so on, will be subject to the Bill. Any expression such as "public authority" is bound to cover them. But it is equally obvious that the list produced in the amendment does not delineate all the obligations that we have under the European Convention which we seek to make justiciable by means of the Bill in our own courts. As to the bodies which noble Lords opposite would wish specifically to exclude, I think that they would be the first to agree, at any rate in private, that it would be extremely difficult to justify excluding those bodies, however worthy they are, and not others. Some of them I do not doubt carry out some functions which are functions of a public nature. It is possible that others do not. But we see no reason why bodies which carry out functions of a public nature should not be amenable to the Convention rights as interpreted and applied by our own courts as they are already indirectly in Strasbourg unless, as I said, the nature of the act complained of is of a private nature.

[. . .] I cannot see any rationale in a society such as ours for regarding the fact of supplying goods or services as qualifying people to be treated as on a par with public bodies, or other organisations of at least a semi-public nature having regard to certain of their functions which will be of a public nature. It would be the smallest step from there, and perhaps more honest, to give the Convention full horizontal effect, as it is sometimes called—that is, to regard the Convention as applying to private individuals as well as to public authorities. I sense that the noble and learned Lord might not be too averse to that. But we think that

that would be a step too far in a Bill which, I repeat, is designed to allow the Convention rights to be invoked in this country by people who would have already a case in Strasbourg.

Two categories of public authorities created
House of Lords, Committee Stage
Official Report, House of Lords, 24 November 1997, vol. 583, col. 810
The Lord Chancellor (Lord Irvine of Lairg): . . . Interpreting Clause 6(3)(c) as applying to all public authorities, even obvious ones, they already qualify as public authorities under Clause 6(1), with the result that Government departments, for example, would not be bound by the Convention in respect of their private acts. Of course, once a body qualifies as a public authority under Clause 6(1), if any of its acts are incompatible with one or more of the Convention rights, it acts unlawfully. [. . .][c. 811]

Clause 6(1) refers to a "public authority" without defining the term. In many cases it will be obvious to the courts that they are dealing with a public authority. In respect of Government departments, for example, or police officers, or prison officers, or immigration officers, or local authorities, there can be no doubt that the body in question is a public authority. Any clear case of that kind comes in under Clause 6(1); and it is then unlawful for the authority to act in a way which is incompatible with one or more of the Convention rights. In such cases, the prohibition applies in respect of all their acts, public and private. There is no exemption for private acts such as is conferred by Clause 6(5) in relation to Clause 6(3)(c).

Clause 6(3)(c) provides further assistance on the meaning of public authority. It provides that "public authority" includes,

> "any person certain of whose functions are functions of a public nature".

That provision is there to include bodies which are not manifestly public authorities, but some of whose functions only are of a public nature. It is relevant to cases where the courts are not sure whether they are looking at a public authority in the full-blooded Clause 6(1) sense with regard to those bodies which fall into the grey area between public and private. The Bill reflects the decision to include as "public authorities" bodies which have some public functions and some private functions.

Perhaps I may give an example that I have cited previously. Railtrack would fall into that category because it exercises public functions in its role as a safety regulator, but it is acting privately in its role as a property developer. A private security company would be exercising public functions in relation to the management of a contracted-out prison but would be acting privately when, for example, guarding commercial premises. Doctors in general practice would be public authorities in relation to their National Health Service functions, but not in relation to their private patients.

The effect of Clause 6(5) read with Clause 6(3)(c) is that all the acts of bodies with mixed functions are subject to the prohibition in Clause 6(1) unless— I emphasise this—in relation to a particular act, the nature of which is private.

Clause 6 accordingly distinguishes between obvious public authorities, all of whose acts are subject to Clause 6, and bodies with mixed functions which are caught in relation to their public acts but not their private acts. [. . .][c. 812] In relation to employment matters, for example, I do not see a distinction between a private security company which has a contracted-out prison in its portfolio and one which does not. There is no reason to make the first company liable under Clause 6 in respect of its private acts and the second one not liable simply because the first company is also responsible for the management of a prison. As far as acts of a private nature are concerned, the two private security companies are indistinguishable; nor do I see a distinction in this area between Railtrack and other property developers or between doctors with NHS patients and those without.

Right in principle for organisations exercising public functions and courts to be covered – duty of courts to act compatibly in developing the common law

House of Lords, Committee Stage

Official Report, House of Lords, 27 November 1997, vol. 583, col. 783

The Lord Chancellor: . . . We believe that it is right as a matter of principle that organisations which are, on a reasonable view and as decided by the courts, exercising a public function should be so treated under the Bill and should have the duty, alongside other organisations having public functions, to act compatibly with the Convention rights in respect of those functions. That means (among other things) that, in doing what they do, they should pay due regard to Article 8 (on privacy) as well as to Article 10 (on freedom of expression, which includes also the freedom of the press).

We also believe that it is right as a matter of principle for the courts to have the duty of acting compatibly with the Convention not only in cases involving other public authorities but also in developing the common law in deciding cases between individuals. Why should they not? In preparing this Bill, we have taken the view that it is the other course, that of excluding Convention considerations altogether from cases between individuals, which would have to be justified. We do not think that that would be justifiable; nor, indeed, do we think it would be practicable. As the noble and learned Lord, Lord Wilderforce, recognised, the courts already bring Convention considerations to bear and I have no doubt that they will continue to do so in developing the common law and that they have the support of the noble and learned Lord in making that use of the Convention. Clause 3 requires the courts to interpret legislation compatibly with the Convention rights and to the fullest extent possible in all cases coming before them.

Section 6(1)

Effect of section 6(1) on Minister's power to make subordinate legislation

House of Lords, Committee Stage

Official Report, House of Lords, 18 November 1997, vol. 583, col. 544

The Lord Chancellor (Lord Irvine of Lairg): . . . Clause 6(1) of the Bill, by making it unlawful for a public authority to act in a manner inconsistent with the Convention rights, will make it unlawful for a Minister to exercise a power to make subordinate legislation so as to make provision which is incompatible with the Convention.

Meaning of 'a Convention right'
See under section 4

Distinction between judicial review and unlawful act under the Act

House of Lords, Committee Stage

Official Report, House of Lords, 24 November 1997, vol. 583, col 807

The Lord Chancellor (Lord Irvine of Lairg): . . . It is of the first importance to distinguish clearly between judicial review and unlawful action under the Convention. They are two different things. So far as I am aware, the Bill does not affect the ordinary law of judicial review. What it does do, however, is make it unlawful for a public authority to act in a way which is incompatible with one or more of the Convention rights. That is set out in Clause 6(1).

Definition of persons for Clause 6(3)

Persons includes natural and legal persons

House of Lords, Committee Stage

Official Report, House of Lords, 24 November 1997, vol. 583, col. y

Lord Mackay of Drumadoon: . . . While I fully accept what has been said about the problems associated with having an exhaustive list, it nevertheless may be valuable to set it clear on the face of the Bill that in Clause 6(3)(c) the person or persons to whom reference is made can be either natural or legal persons. When one looks at the Convention rights set out in Schedule 1 to the Bill, one sees that in Article 1 of the First Protocol, on page 17 of the Bill, there is reference to "every natural or legal person", making it clear that both categories are protected when it comes to the peaceful enjoyment of their possessions. That contrasts with the provisions of the Convention itself which, when dealing with, for example, the right to liberty and security in Article 5, restricts itself to the use of the word "person". I therefore hope that the Government will be persuaded of the merit of looking at this matter when they reconsider the terms of Clause 6.

The Parliamentary Under-Secretary of State, Home Office (Lord Williams of Mostyn): I am most grateful for that explanation. We have looked at the matter in the context of the schedule and the terms of the Convention article to which the noble and learned Lord, Lord Mackay of Drumadoon, referred. We believe that the present draft of [**c. 803**] the Bill achieves what the noble and learned Lord wishes to achieve since Clause 6(3)(c) refers to "any person". Unlike the situation when one looks at the drafting of Article 1, the term is well known as a term of art in our law. It is defined in the Interpretation Act 1978 and is relied upon throughout the statute book as including any person or body of persons corporate or unincorporate. I suggest that that is clearly wide enough to cover the natural or legal person to which the amendment refers.

A 'matter for the courts' if body that spends public money, fulfills statutory function or has Govermnent appointees on governing body constitutes public authority

House of Commons, Second Reading

Official Report, House of Commons, 16 February 1998, vol. x, col. 860

Sir Brian Mawhinney: . . . Does a body that spends taxpayers' money, or fulfils a statutory function, or has Government appointees on its governing body constitute a public authority for the purposes of the Bill?

The Parliamentary Under-Secretary of State for the Home Department (Mr. Mike O'Brien): That will be a matter for the courts, but it would appear to be likely to be so.

Definition of public authority 'could not be wider'

House of Lords, Committee Stage

Official Report, House of Lords, 18 November 1997, vol. 583, col. 475

The Lord Chancellor (Lord Irvine of Lairg): . . . The very ample definition of public authority in Clause 6 makes it plain that there is no intention to protect persons acting in an official capacity. On the contrary, our definition of public authority in that clause could not be wider.

Interaction of ss. 6(3) and 6(5)

House of Lords, Committee Stage

Official Report, House of Lords, 24 November 1997, vol. 583, col. 758

The Parliamentary Under-Secretary of State, Home Office (Lord Williams of Mostyn): . . . We suggest that "public authority" is plainly defined in Clause 6. When the Bill is enacted, one will be dealing with two types of public authority—those which everyone would recognise as being plainly public authorities in the exercise of their functions, and those public authorities which are public authorities because, in part of their functions, they carry out what would be regarded as public functions. Examples vary, but I believe that the courts will have in mind changing social economic and cultural conditions when they come to consider particular decisions on particular aspects of a public authority. [...]

I believe that my noble and learned friend the Lord Chancellor gave an illustration on an earlier occasion. For example, Railtrack has statutory public powers and functions as the safety regulatory authority; but, equally, it may well carry out private transactions, such as the disposal of, the acquisition of, or the development of property.

If one follows the scheme through, we suggest that it is perfectly capable of being understood. The amendment would exempt from the prohibition in [c. 759] Clause 6(1) a public authority falling within Clause 6(3) in respect of its private acts. However, I venture to suggest to the Committee that that is already achieved, we say satisfactorily, by subsection (5). The other public authorities specified in Clause 6(3) are courts and tribunals which, we think, are in a very similar position to obvious public authorities, such as Government departments, in that all their acts are to be treated as being of such a public nature as to engage the Convention. I hope that I have given a helpful explanation . . .
[*Amendment withdrawn – c. 759*]

Public authorities covered

BBC would be covered, Channel 4 might well be, other private television stations might not be

House of Lords, Second Reading

Official Report, House of Lords, 3 November 1997, vol. 582, col. 1309

The Parliamentary Under-Secretary of State, Home Office (Lord Williams of Mostyn):
The noble and learned Lord, Lord Simon of Glaisdale, asked what would or would not be a public body. He rightly conjectured that we would anticipate the BBC being a public authority and that Channel 4 might well be a public authority, but that other commercial organisations, such as private television stations, might well not be public authorities. I stress that that is a matter for the courts to decide as the jurisprudence develops. Some authorities plainly exercise wholly public functions; others do not. There is no difficulty here.

Status of BBC

House of Commons, Second Reading

Official Report, 16 February 1998, vol. 307, col. 778

Mr. David Ruffley (Bury St. Edmunds): In the context of Articles 8 and 10, would the BBC and independent television companies be public authorities for the purposes of Clause 6?

The Secretary of State for the Home Department (Mr. Jack Straw): That is ultimately a matter for the courts, but our judgment is that the BBC will be regarded as a public authority under Clause 6; independent television companies will not, but the Independent Television Commission will be.

Status of Press Complaints Commission

House of Commons, Second Reading

Official Report, House of Commons, 16 February 1998, vol. 307, col. 778

Mr. Kaufman (Manchester, Gorton): Will my right hon. Friend assure the House that the arrangements are the only ones arrived at, and that there is no question of the Press Complaints Commission being excluded from the definition of a public authority under Clause 6?

We have before us, in the annexe that lays out the Convention, a series of rights and freedoms that will be available under this legislation to all citizens of the United Kingdom. My assumption, when the Bill was introduced, was that all those rights and freedoms would be given equal weight. My right hon. Friend now appears to be telling the House—only a satisfactorily drafted amendment could possibly allay any misgivings on the matter—that the Article 10 right will have greater weight than the Article 8 right. Many Labour Members would be seriously disturbed by such a change.

The Secretary of State for the Home Department (Mr. Jack Straw): The answer to my right hon. Friend's first point is that we do not propose to table amendments that [c. 779] would exempt any particular body, including the Press Complaints Commission, from the operations of Clause 6. There are a number of reasons for that; we can go into detail in Committee. We do not believe that exemptions are the appropriate means of dealing with Clause 6, about which I shall speak in a moment.

On my right hon. Friend's second point, I ask him to look carefully at the document that I shall deposit in the Library, which sets out the development of jurisprudence by the European Court in Strasbourg on matters relating to Articles 10 and 8. It is always the case that some legal concepts have greater force than others; it happens to be the case that the European Court has given much greater weight to Article 10 rights of freedom of expression than to Article 8 rights to privacy. We want to reflect that in our domestic law.

Editor's note: The debate concerning the relationship between Articles 8 & 10 and the impact of the Human Rights Bill is dealt with extensively in Part 3 on pages 217–230, below

Newspapers not covered
House of Lords, Second Reading
Official Report, House of Lords, 3 November 1997, vol. 582, col. 1310
Lord Donaldson of Lymington: . . . [C]an he tell me whether a newspaper which has never been publicly funded and which has never been a public body comes within the definition? I never understood that the definition required anybody to be an authority; I thought that one had to be either a company or an individual.

The Parliamentary Under-Secretary of State, Home Office (Lord Williams of Mostyn): My Lords, subject to the cautious proviso that this is a matter for the courts to determine in due time, it is our belief that a newspaper is not a public authority. A court is a public authority which is obliged to act lawfully. I have developed that point in the context of the question about the press and privacy.
[*See below under Article 8 & 10*]

House of Commons, Committee Stage
Official Report, House of Commons, 2 July 1998, vol. 314, col. 561
The Parliamentary Under-Secretary of State for the Home Department (Mr. Mike O'Brien): An important point that has, to some extent, been overlooked is that newspapers will not be public authorities and could not be proceeded against directly under the Bill, but an Article 8 point could be raised in proceedings for harassment or a libel action, for example.

Position of the Churches

Principles of Bill are that religious organisations exercising public functions should be covered, eg. School underpinned by a religious foundation

Editor's note: For a detailed examination of the position of Churches see section 13 on pages 177–189 below

House of Lords, Committee Stage
Official Report, House of Lords, 24 November 1997, vol. 583, col. 800

The Lord Chancellor (Lord Irvine of Lairg): . . . If a court were to uphold that a religious organisation, denomination or church, in celebrating marriage, was exercising a public function, what on earth would be wrong with that? If a court were to hold that a hospice, because it provided a medical service, was exercising a public function, what on earth would be wrong with that? Is it not also perfectly true that schools, although underpinned by a religious foundation or a trust deed, may well be carrying out public functions? If we take, for example, a charity whose charitable aims include the advancement of a religion, the answer must depend upon the nature of the functions of the charity. For example, charities that operate, let us say, in the area of homelessness, no doubt do exercise public functions. The NSPCC, for example, exercises statutory functions which are of a public nature, although it is a charity. We believe that the principles of the Bill are right and that the courts will come to answers in which the public will have confidence.

Position of the Armed Forces

Armed forces fall squarely within the category of an obvious public authority

House of Lords, Third Reading
Official Report, House of Lords, 5 February 1998, vol 585, col. 766

The Lord Chancellor: . . . The noble Lord, Lord Goodhart, is also correct in saying that the Armed Forces are already subject to the Convention and to the Strasbourg court. In the Findlay case . . . the relevant statutory provisions governing courts martial, in particular as they concern the role of commanding officers in courts martial, were found to breach the Convention. Accordingly, our predecessors had to bring forward [c. 767] primary legislation to deal with that. So there is nothing in particular that is new here. The only point is that under the Bill these matters can be dealt with through our domestic courts and will not have to await Strasbourg.

The key point, in the Government's view, is that the Armed Forces fall squarely within the category of an obvious public authority. If they are not that, it is difficult to say who is. What I mean is that it is scarcely conceivable that there could be a Bill of this kind which did not cover the Armed Forces. Secondly, the Government are plainly answerable in Strasbourg for the actions of the Armed Forces which engage the responsibility of the state. Thirdly, if the intention is to bring rights home so as to allow our own courts to adjudicate on Convention issues, this seems to be a clear case. Therefore, we cannot see any justification for excluding the Armed Forces from the scope and reach of the Bill.

Position of 'hybrid bodies'

Jockey Club suggested to be included – cf. position in judicial review

House of Commons, Committee Stage

Official Report, House of Commons, 20 May 1998, vol. 312, col. 1018

The Secretary of State for the Home Department (Mr. Jack Straw):
[. . .] There will be occasions—it is the nature of British society—on which various institutions that are private in terms of their legal personality carry out public functions. That includes the Churches in the narrow circumstances that I have described. I would suggest that it also includes the Jockey Club.

Other countries have public bodies to regulate racing; in this country, we do it in a different way. That is how we have always done it, and I know of no proposals to change the system. The Jockey Club is a curious body; it is entirely private, but exercises public functions in some respects, and to those extents, but to no other, it would be regarded as falling within Clause 6.

Privatised utilities

House of Lords, Second Reading

Official Report, House of Lords, 3 November 1997, vol. 582, col. 1310

The Parliamentary Under-Secretary of State, Home Office (Lord Williams of Mostyn):
Perhaps I may cite Railtrack as a simple example. It is the statutory safety regulator, but equally it carries out private functions of property development or property acquisition. It is perfectly easy for a judiciary, which is as well accustomed as is ours to questions of judicial review, to resolve such problems. It is a mistake to think that we are hobbling authorities because they are now private whereas they used to be public utilities. The point is not the label or description; it is the function. I hope that I have made that plain.

Position of prosecutors

Effect of Articles 5 and 6 on prosecutors

House of Lords, Committee Stage

Official Report, House of Lords, 24 November 1997, vol. 583, col. 807

The Lord Chancellor (Lord Irvine of Lairg): . . . It is of the first importance to distinguish clearly between judicial review and unlawful action under the Convention. They are two different things. So far as I am aware, the Bill does not affect the ordinary law of judicial review. What it does do, however, is make it unlawful for a public authority to act in a way which is incompatible with one or more of the Convention rights. That is set out in Clause 6(1).

In England, certainly today, decisions not to prosecute are reviewable. The test would be whether no reasonable prosecutor could have abstained from prosecuting. I do not see in principle why that should not apply to a decision to prosecute where no reasonable prosecutor would prosecute. I would also agree with the noble [**c. 808**] Lord, Lord Lester, that a decision to prosecute only those who were black but not those who were white would be perverse and judicially reviewable. That, however, is not what is touched by the Bill. I am not aware of—and no noble and learned Lord has drawn my attention to—any provision of the Convention which a decision to prosecute or not to prosecute might be said to infringe. So, as at present advised, I do not see how a prosecutor—
Lord Lester of Herne Hill: . . . The example I had in mind was the right to liberty under Article 5 of the Convention. Perhaps I may give, as an example, internment without trial, which was the subject matter of the Irish state case where I had the honour to represent the United

Kingdom Government. A discriminatory use of internment without trial would plainly breach Article 5 and a decision to arrest and detain with a view to prosecution might breach Article 6 read with Articles 5 and 14. That is the risk that could arise since people would then find themselves facing criminal charges on a discriminatory basis. Some such argument might be mounted in relation to the discretion of the prosecutor. The example I have given of Article 10, where the prosecution related to free speech, was why Lord Diplock considered that the prosecutor needed to have regard to the Convention in that context.

The Lord Chancellor: The noble Lord refers to Article 5. I should have thought that internment or detention was not a matter of prosecutorial decision and therefore would fall outside Article 5. As at present advised, I am not persuaded that a decision to prosecute or not to prosecute is caught by the Convention or by any provision of the Convention. But I shall look at that with greater care.

I can see that certain provisions of Article 6 and in particular those in paragraph (3) which confer certain minimum rights on persons charged with a criminal offence could be infringed by a prosecutor. So I am not saying that it appears to me that prosecutors are free of any duties under the Convention. But for the present I do not see how a decision whether to prosecute would be caught by any particular provision of the Convention. But I shall look at it and write to the noble and learned Lords who have spoken in support of the amendment.

In developing our proposals in Clause 6 we have opted for a wide-ranging definition of public authority. We have created a correspondingly wide liability. That is because we want to provide as much protection as possible for the rights of individuals against the misuse of power by the state within the framework of a Bill which preserves parliamentary sovereignty.

As a matter of principle it is plain that a prosecuting authority is a public authority and that it is right that it should abstain from acting in a way which is incompatible with one or more of the Convention rights, but if it does so act, then it acts unlawfully.

Given the central role played in our criminal justice by independent public prosecutors, it would create a significant gap in the protection provided by the Bill if they were not subject to Clause 6. I do not see why they [c. 809] should be exempted. I do not see why public prosecutors should not be required to act in a way which is compatible with the Convention in just the same way as the courts themselves and investigators such as the police are required to act compatibly.

[. . .]In my view, it would be subversive of the rule of law to provide that independent public prosecutors should be above the Convention when no other public body is so placed. My right honourable and learned friend the Attorney-General and my noble and learned friend the Lord Advocate do not desire to be above the Convention. In my view it would be bizarre if they were above it, while, in the case of the Attorney-General, the body for which he is responsible—namely, the Crown Prosecution Service—must comply with the Convention. For these reasons, I oppose this amendment in its own terms but on the narrow issue of whether a decision to prosecute could arguably be said to infringe any Convention rights, I shall consider it and write to the noble and learned Lords.

House of Lords, Report Stage
Official Report, House of Lords, 19 January 1998, vol. 584, col. 1363

Lord Mackay of Drumadoon: . . . The current procedure in practice is that neither the civil nor the criminal courts in Scotland will entertain proceedings, whether at the instance of an accused man or his alleged victim, seeking to review the decisions as to whether the Lord Advocate should prosecute in a particular case and, if he decides to do so, on what charge such a prosecution should be brought. There is also the position in relation to the procurators fiscal who, as your Lordships know, initiate and conduct summary criminal proceedings in the various sheriff courts throughout Scotland.
[. . .]

However, the courts in Scotland, at least until this moment, will not seek to inquire of a Lord Advocate why he has reached his decisions and will not therefore seek to review the soundness of them.

When the issue was last debated, the noble and learned Lord the Lord Chancellor promised to write to me about the matter. Again I am grateful to the noble Lord, Lord Williams, for having taken the trouble to do so in ample time for me to put down the amendment. In his letter, the noble Lord confirms what had been accepted on all sides during our debates in Committee; namely, that the Lord Advocate is a public authority within the meaning of Clause 6. He also confirmed what I asserted in Committee; namely, that it is possible to envisage circumstances in which a decision as to whether or not to prosecute could arguably be said to infringe a Convention right. He therefore accepted what I think the noble and learned Lord the Lord Chancellor had been reluctant to accept when we last looked at the issue: that these decisions might infringe Convention rights.

The noble Lord went on to suggest that it would seem natural for any judicial challenge to a decision to be brought, as appears to be the position in England, by way of judicial review in the civil courts. In a kindly manner, and with the sense of humour with which we now associate the noble Lord, his letter went on to reassure me by stating that he did not believe this should be a matter of concern. He stated that decisions not to prosecute have already been reviewed in England where the courts have not adopted the strict self-denying ordinance followed by the Scottish courts. [. . .] He went on to say that the case law here—referring to England—has shown the courts to be very careful when exercising their jurisdiction. They have used their [c. 1364] discretion to intervene sparingly and their role has not been to second guess the decision taken by the prosecutor.

I have no difficulty in accepting that were such a jurisdiction to be introduced in Scotland, it would be exercised with caution. Nevertheless, I believe that it would be a serious mistake to proceed along those lines—a view which I have reason to believe is shared by others involved in the criminal justice system in Scotland.

[. . .] [U]ntil the very helpful letter was received by me from the noble Lord, Lord Williams, no public recognition had been made by any Minister that the decisions of a Lord Advocate might be susceptible to review against Convention rights.
[. . .][c. 1366]

The Lord Chancellor: . . . It is the case that decisions not to prosecute have been reviewed in England where the noble and learned Lord suggests that the Scottish courts would be unwilling to review. Certainly, case law in England has shown the courts to be very careful when exercising their discretion in this area. I am sure that the courts in Scotland, when considering whether to review a decision concerning the bringing of a prosecution on Convention grounds would pay due regard to the factors which have influenced the prosecution and would allow the Lord Advocate an appropriately generous discretion.

The noble and learned Lord asks: why the Court of Session rather than the High Court of Justiciary? We will consider any representations that are made; but the immediate response would be that the natural court to consider complaints of denial of Convention rights would be a civil court and not a criminal court. Nor, is it argued, is there any inconsistency with the established rule—established, I believe, since the Act of Union—that on matters of criminal law no appeal lies in Scotland to the House of Lords.

Section 6(6)

Section 6(6) protects Ministers from claims for failures to legislate

House of Lords, Committeee Stage

Official Report, House of Lords, 24 November 1997, vol. 583, col. 814

The Lord Chancellor (Lord Irvine of Lairg): . . . If a person believes that his Convention rights have been violated as a result of action by a public authority which is not governed by legislation the right course is for him to bring legal proceedings against the authority under Clause 7 of the Bill or to rely on his Convention rights in any other legal proceedings to which he and the authority are a party. If the court finds in his favour it will be able to grant whatever remedy is within its jurisdiction and appears just and appropriate. The fact that there is no specific legislation for the court to declare incompatible with the Convention does not affect the ability of the person concerned to obtain a remedy. The absence of legislation entails that there is no legislative warrant for acts in breach of the Convention by the public authority. The Minister, however, as the noble Lord, Lord Lester, rightly points out, is protected by Clause 6(6) from any claim that he is in breach by failing to bring forward legislation. That is part of the scheme of the Bill to underpin parliamentary sovereignty.

Further, the purpose of a declaration of incompatibility is to allow the courts to make a public statement that they cannot interpret legislation in a way which is [c. 815] incompatible with the Convention rights. It is just not possible to do so. This provides a trigger for the power to make a remedial order in Clause 10. Because the Bill protects public authorities which are acting so as to give effect to primary legislation, even if the action is incompatible with the Convention rights, there is nothing that the courts can do to provide a remedy to the

person affected by their actions. That is why the power to make a declaration of incompatibility is needed in these cases. There is no corresponding need to make a declaration of incompatibility in cases where the problem is an absence of legislation, because there is nothing to stop the courts providing a remedy in those cases. There is no legislative bar or block on the courts doing so. On the contrary.
[...]
Clause 6(6) exempts from Clause 6 a failure by a public authority to,

> "introduce in, or lay before, Parliament a proposal for legislation; or . . . make any primary legislation or remedial order".

This amendment would remove that exemption so that a failure by a public authority to do one of those things would be capable of being challenged in the courts on the grounds that it was unlawful because it was incompatible with one or more of the Convention rights.

In effect—and I believe this to be the compelling argument against the amendment—it would make a decision not to enact primary legislation justiciable before the courts. That would be inconsistent with a fundamental precept of our constitutional arrangements; namely, that the courts do not interfere with the proceedings of Parliament. In short, the Bill is designed to preserve parliamentary sovereignty and this amendment would encroach upon that.

[. . .] I should add also that judges do, in their judgments from time to time, draw attention to the need for Parliament to consider legislative change and after the passage of this Bill they will remain as free to do that as they have always been and have felt themselves free to do.

SECTION 7: PROCEEDINGS

7. - (1) A person who claims that a public authority has acted (or proposes to act) in a way which is made unlawful by section 6(1) may-

(a) bring proceedings against the authority under this Act in the appropriate court or tribunal, or
(b) rely on the Convention right or rights concerned in any legal proceedings, but only if he is (or would be) a victim of the unlawful act.

(2) In subsection (1)(a) "appropriate court or tribunal" means such court or tribunal as may be determined in accordance with rules; and proceedings against an authority include a counterclaim or similar proceeding.

(3) If the proceedings are brought on an application for judicial review, the applicant is to be taken to have a sufficient interest in relation to the unlawful act only if he is, or would be, a victim of that act.

(4) If the proceedings are made by way of a petition for judicial review in Scotland, the applicant shall be taken to have title and interest to sue in relation to the unlawful act only if he is, or would be, a victim of that act.

(5) Proceedings under subsection (1)(a) must be brought before the end of-

(a) the period of one year beginning with the date on which the act complained of took place; or
(b) such longer period as the court or tribunal considers equitable having regard to all the circumstances, but that is subject to any rule imposing a stricter time limit in relation to the procedure in question.

(6) In subsection (1)(b) "legal proceedings" includes-
(a) proceedings brought by or at the instigation of a public authority; and
(b) an appeal against the decision of a court or tribunal.

(7) For the purposes of this section, a person is a victim of an unlawful act only if he would be a victim for the purposes of Article 34 of the Convention if proceedings were brought in the European Court of Human Rights in respect of that act.

(8) Nothing in this Act creates a criminal offence.

(9) In this section "rules" means-

(a) in relation to proceedings before a court or tribunal outside Scotland, rules made by the Lord Chancellor or the Secretary of State for the purposes of this section or rules of court,
(b) in relation to proceedings before a court or tribunal in Scotland, rules made by the Secretary of State for those purposes,
(c) in relation to proceedings before a tribunal in Northern Ireland-
  (i) which deals with transferred matters; and
  (ii) for which no rules made under paragraph (a) are in force,

Rules made by a Northern Ireland department for those purposes, and includes provision made by order under section 1 of the Courts and Legal Services Act 1990.

(10) In making rules, regard must be had to section 9.

(11) The Minister who has power to make rules in relation to a particular tribunal may, to the extent he considers it necessary to ensure that the tribunal can provide an appropriate remedy in relation to an act (or proposed act) of a public authority which is (or would be) unlawful as a result of section 6(1), by order add to-

(a) the relief or remedies which the tribunal may grant; or
(b) the grounds on which it may grant any of them.

(12) An order made under subsection (11) may contain such incidental, supplemental, consequential or transitional provision as the Minister making it considers appropriate.

(13) "The Minister" includes the Northern Ireland department concerned.

Effect of section 7

House of Lords, Second Reading

Official Report, House of Lords, 3 November 1997, vol. 582, col. 1232

The Lord Chancellor (Lord Irvine of Lairg): If people believe that their Convention rights have been infringed by a public authority, what can they do about it? Under Clause 7 they will be able to rely on Convention points in any legal proceedings involving a public authority; for example as part of a defence to criminal or civil proceedings, or when acting as plaintiff in civil proceedings, or in seeking judicial review, or on appeal. They will also be able to bring proceedings against public authorities purely on Convention grounds even if no other cause of action is open to them.

House of Commons, Second Reading

Official Report, House of Commons, 16 February 1998, vol. 307, col. 780

The Secretary of State for the Home Department (Mr. Jack Straw): ... Clause 7 enables individuals who believe that they have been a victim of an unlawful act of a public authority to rely on the Convention rights in legal proceedings. They may do so in a number of ways: by bringing proceedings under the Bill in an appropriate court or tribunal; in seeking judicial review; as part of a defence against a criminal or civil action brought against them by a public authority; or in the course of an appeal. Clause 7 ensures that an individual will always have a means by which to raise his or her Convention rights. It is intended that existing court procedures will, wherever possible, be used for that purpose.

Section 7(1)

Government 'decided to follow the Convention practice' in adopting victim test

House of Commons, Second Reading

Official Report, House of Commons, 16 February 1998, vol. 307, col. 856

The Parliamentary Under-Secretary of State for the Home Department (Mr. Mike O'Brien): ... My hon. Friend the Member for Hull, North (Mr. McNamara), who has great knowledge of Northern Ireland, raised the important issue of human rights there. He asked us to consider allowing organisations that are not themselves victims to bring class actions and to anticipate issues. We considered doing that, but decided to follow the Convention practice and enable victims of breaches to raise issues as they occur. On the question of a preamble or a purposive clause, we believe that the Bill as it stands is clear about what it is intended to achieve and that a preamble or purposive clause is unnecessary.

Section 7 part of principle that individuals should have access to rights including in Tribunals – Effect of s.7 on criminal proceedings and private prosecutions

House of Commons, Committee Stage
Official Report, House of Commons, 24 June 1998, vol. 314, col. 1055

The Parliamentary Under-Secretary of State for the Home Department (Mr. Mike O'Brien): . . . I remind the Committee that one of the Bill's key principles is that all courts and tribunals should take account of Convention rights whenever they are relevant to the case before them. Otherwise, people would have no access to their rights unless they went to the European Court of Human Rights or to the Commission. We shall ensure that individuals can rely on their Convention rights and have access to them at the earliest opportunity. We shall also make the Convention rights an integral part of our legal system. [c. 1056]

One of the many drawbacks of the current arrangements is that the Convention rights are cut off from people in the United Kingdom and viewed as something alien to us. In bringing rights home, we want everyone in Britain to view the basic principles set out in the Convention as part of their national heritage. We shall not achieve that by practising an internal system of apartheid, keeping the Convention rights as the exclusive preserve of the courts. That way, people will continue to see those rights as separate from their daily lives, not as something intrinsic to them.

It is in keeping with that principle that tribunals as well as courts are required by Clause 3 to read and give effect to legislation as far as possible in a way that is compatible with the Convention rights. It is also in keeping with that principle that tribunals should be able to take account of the Convention rights when a person alleges that he or she has been the victim of an unlawful act by a public authority.

[. . .] It is our expectation that the great majority of cases in which the Convention arguments are raised will fall within the scope of such proceedings. That is because, in most cases, it is likely that a victim of an act made unlawful by Clause 6(1) will have available to him an existing course of action or other means of legal challenge, such as a judicial review.

Furthermore, in a significant proportion of such cases, a tribunal, not a court, will be the forum in which a case is brought. Social security, employment, housing and immigration are but a few of the many areas where tribunals handle the bulk of cases.
[. . .]

To prevent individuals from raising Convention points in tribunals would cause unnecessary delay, expense and frustration. How would they be expected to raise them on appeal? [. . .] If one has concerns about the ability of tribunals to deal with Convention issues, one should surely wish people to be able to rely on their Convention rights when the matter is appealed up to the appropriate court.

[In relation to c]ases brought under Clause 7(1)(a)—that is, cases brought solely on Convention grounds. As I have said, we expect that such cases will be relatively infrequent, but where they do arise, it is likely that a tribunal will sometimes be the most appropriate forum for hearing the case.

If the case concerns a subject which is usually heard, in the first instance, by a tribunal, there is a good prima facie case for assuming that a tribunal will be the correct place in which to hear the Convention case. [c. 1057]
[. . .]

We do not for one moment underestimate the amount of preparatory work that will have to be undertaken to ensure that both courts and tribunals are able to handle the Convention issues that will come before them. I assure the Committee that the training issue is being taken very seriously, and that we will not bring the Bill into force until we are confident that the legal system is in a position to cope with the changes.
[. . .]

The vast majority of criminal proceedings will be caught directly by Clause 7(5)(a), as they are

"proceedings brought by or at the instigation of a public authority".

The very few private prosecutions that are undertaken will also be caught by Clause 7(5)—as it is an inclusive definition, and such prosecutions would be regarded as legal proceedings. In such cases, the private prosecutor would not be a public authority, although the court, as a public authority, would be required to act not incompatibly with the Convention rights. Therefore, Tesco, for example, would not become a public authority. The court itself will be required to take account of the Convention rights.

If the hon. and learned Gentleman's concern is whether Clause 7 covers criminal proceedings, I can assure him that it does. It will be possible for individuals to rely on their Convention rights in criminal proceedings as in other proceedings.

I should make it clear also that the RSPCA—which the hon. and learned Member mentioned—will be performing a public act when that act has a statutory basis. Although it will be a matter for the court to decide whether it is behaving as a public authority, it may be doing so if it is acting on a basis conferred by statute. Tesco, for example, would not be acting as a public authority, although, as I said, the court must take account of the Convention in reaching any decision.

Section 7(3): Standing for public interest groups

Narrower test of standing will be applied than in judicial review but interest groups may provide assistance to victims – Strasbourg victim test believed to be right – the Act does not prevent third party interventions – no intention to alter the Scots or English rules of standing in judicial review

House of Lords, Committee Stage

Official Report, House of Lords, 24 November 1997, vol. 583, col. 830

The Lord Chancellor (Lord Irvine of Lairg): . . . The basic point, the critical issue, can be shortly and easily stated. It is whether the judicial review standing test domestically should apply to Convention cases as well rather than the Strasbourg victim test, which is perhaps naturally more appropriate when we are bringing Convention rights home. [. . .]

The purpose of the Bill is to give greater effect in our domestic law to the Convention rights. It is in keeping with this approach that persons should be able to rely [**c. 831**] on the Convention rights before our domestic courts in precisely the same circumstances as they can rely upon them before the Strasbourg institutions. The wording of Clause 7 therefore reflects the terms of the Convention, which stipulates that petitions to the European Commission (or to the European Court once the Eleventh Protocol comes into force) will be ruled inadmissible unless the applicant is the victim of the alleged violation.

I acknowledge that a consequence of that approach is that a narrower test will be applied for bringing applications by judicial review on Convention grounds than will continue to apply in applications for judicial review on other grounds. But interest groups will still be able to provide assistance to victims who bring cases under the Bill and to bring cases directly where they themselves are victims of an unlawful act.

I also point out that Clause 7, consistently with the position in Strasbourg, also treats as victims those who are faced with the threat of a public authority proposing to act in a way which would be unlawful under Clause 6(1). So potential victims are included. Interest groups will similarly be able to assist potential victims to bring challenges to action which is threatened before it is actually carried out.

My noble friend, Lord Williams of Mostyn, reminded the House, both at Second Reading and on our first Committee day, that I am committed to implementing measures that will improve access to justice, and that I am giving serious consideration to Sir Peter Middleton's proposal that there should be a separate fund for public interest cases, including those involving Convention rights.

I said in my speech to the Law Society's annual conference at Cardiff on 18th October that I believed it right to make special arrangements for cases that raise issues of wider public interest and that I intended to consult about the details. I am planning to issue a consultation paper early next year, but my officials have already begun informal discussions with various interest groups. That will of course include those bodies such as the Public Law Project, Justice, Liberty and the Child Poverty Action Group which regularly support applicants in the courts.
[. . .] [c. 832]

I focus first on the essential and critical point—that is, whether there should be a victim test in relation to a complaint of an unlawful act on Convention grounds. Essentially we believe the victim/potential victim test to be right. If there is unlawful action or if unlawful action is threatened, then there will be victims or potential victims who will complain and who will in practice be supported by interest groups. If there are no victims, the issue is probably academic and the courts should not be troubled.

We are right to mirror the law as Strasbourg applies it. I understand that to be generally accepted by Members of the Committee who have spoken in favour of the amendment. But they depart from that because of a greater affection for the English judicial review test than for the Strasbourg victim test in relation to Convention cases.
[...]

I turn to the point ... in relation to third party intervention. The European Court of Human Rights rules of procedure allow non-parties such as national and international non-governmental organisations to make written submissions in the form of a brief. There is no reason why any change to primary legislation in this Bill is needed to allow the domestic courts to develop a similar practice in human rights cases, which is the answer to the noble Lord's question on how I would respond to the point that an interest group would have the right to be heard in a judicial review case under the English domestic test but that, if there was not a victim, could the individual interest group be heard on the Convention point? So now, in its proper context, I address an answer to that question.

This is a development—that is to say, allowing third parties to intervene and be heard—which has already begun in the higher courts of this country in public law cases. Provisions as to standing are quite different. They determine who can become parties to the proceedings. The standing rule which the Bill proposes in relation to Convention cases simpliciter is identical to that operated at Strasbourg; and why not? Is that not right in principle? It would not, however, prevent the acceptance by the courts in this country of non-governmental organisational briefs here any more than it does in Strasbourg.

Your Lordships' House, in its judicial capacity, has recently given leave for non-governmental organisations to intervene and file amicus briefs. It has done that in [c. 833] Queen v. Khan for the benefit of Liberty and it has done that in Queen v. Secretary of State for the Home Department ex parte Venables and Thompson for the benefit of Justice. So it appears to me, as at present advised, that the natural position to take is to adopt the victim test as applied by Strasbourg when complaint is made of a denial of Convention rights, recognising that our courts will be ready to permit amicus written briefs from non-governmental organisations; that is to say briefs, but not to treat them as full parties.
[...]

The incorporation of the Bill will put a burden on all lawyers and courts to learn a great deal more about Strasbourg jurisprudence. I do not think that there is any particular burden in learning about the victim test that Strasbourg applies, which appears to me to be entirely intelligible and which requires an actual or potential victim and therefore precludes academic cases. [c. 834]

Clause 7(1)(b), states:

"A person who claims that a public authority has acted (or proposes to act) in a way which is made unlawful by section 6(1) may—
(b) rely on the Convention right or rights concerned in any legal proceedings"—

to my mind that entails a party—

"but only if he is (or would be) a victim of the unlawful act".

It does not touch a third party who has not ex hypothesi been the victim of the infringement of a Convention right. It in no way precludes a third party from making submissions about the implication of Convention rights in written briefs if a written brief is invited or accepted by the court, as I believe will happen.

As regards oral interventions by a third party, I dare say that the courts will be equally hospitable to oral interventions provided that they are brief.

[...]

It is no part of the intention of this Bill to alter the standing rules in relation to judicial review in either England or Scotland. It is no part of the intention of this Bill to impose uniformity on the Scottish courts—that is to say, to be uniform with England and Wales—in relation to the rules of practice of the English courts which I have described in permitting third party interventions by way of a written brief. It is part of the intention of this Bill to import the Strasbourg victim test in relation to complaints based solely on denial of Convention rights. That appears to us to be right in principle.

Act in no way affects judicial review standing rules – Act based on mirroring the Strasbourg approach

House of Lords, Third Reading

Official Report, House of Lords, 5 February 1998, vol 585, col. 810

The Lord Chancellor (Lord Irvine of Lairg): . . . As regards the proposed statutory test, I believe that the concerns expressed about applying the victim test are misplaced. [T]here is nothing in our Bill which would prevent pressure groups—interest groups—from assisting and providing representations for victims who wish to bring cases forward.

There is a flexible Strasbourg jurisprudence on the victim test which I suggest the English courts would have no difficulty applying. Although I hesitate to take up time, and indeed abstain from doing so, I could cite example after example of an expansive approach by the Strasbourg court to the victim test.

As we have said a number of times, the purpose of the Bill is to give further effect in our domestic law to our Convention rights, and it is in keeping with that approach that a person should be able to rely on those rights before our courts in the same circumstances that they can rely upon them before the Strasbourg institutions, and not in different circumstances. Bringing rights home means exactly what it says—to mirror the approach taken by the Strasbourg court in interpreting Convention rights.

I acknowledge that as a consequence, and despite the flexibility of the Strasbourg test, a narrower test will apply for bringing applications on Convention grounds than in applications for judicial review on other grounds. But I venture to think that interest groups will plainly be able to provide assistance to victims who bring cases under the Bill, including, as I mentioned in Committee, the filing of amicus briefs. Interest groups themselves will be able to bring cases directly where they are victims of an unlawful act. I do not believe that different tests for Convention and non-Convention cases will cause any difficulties for the courts or prevent interest groups providing assistance to victims of unlawful acts.

As to the questions raised about giving access to the courts, I mentioned in Committee that I am giving serious consideration to Sir Peter Middleton's proposal that there should be a separate fund for public interest cases, including those involving rights under this Bill. Informed consultation with various interest groups on that matter is already well under way and I hope to publish a consultation document by the end of February.

Therefore, we consider that the wording of Clause 7 is wholly consistent with the proposition that rights should be brought home to this country from Strasbourg on the [c. 811] same terms as they may be enjoyed there.

Relationship of section 7 to Article 34 ECHR – Application of standing rules to public interest groups –Courts can develop their own law taking into account the Strasbourg jurisprudence– examples of European Court of Human Rights caselaw

House of Commons, Committee Stage

Official Report, House of Commons, 24 June 1998, vol. 314, col. 1084

The Parliamentary Under-Secretary of State for the Home Department (Mr. Mike O'Brien): . . . The intention is that a victim under the Bill should be in the same position as a victim in Strasbourg. A local [**c. 1085**] authority cannot be a victim under Clause 7 because it cannot be a victim in Strasbourg under current Strasbourg jurisprudence.

On the definition, the Convention provides that

> "The Commission may receive petitions . . . from any person, non-governmental organisation or group of individuals claiming to be a victim of a violation by one of the High Contracting Parties of the rights set forth in this Convention".

Applying the victim requirement, the basic approach of the Commission and the Court has been to require that the applicant must claim to be directly affected in some way by the matter complained of. In some cases, they have interpreted fairly flexibly the requirement for the applicant to be directly affected, although the jurisprudence on the issue is not always entirely consistent. The victim requirement was, for example, applied restrictively in a series of sado-masochist cases, in which the Commission considered that applications from persons claiming to indulge in certain acts that were prohibited by law did not satisfy the victim test because, at that stage, there had been no interference by the police or prosecuting authorities in what they were doing.

There are other examples of a more expansive approach and it is important to put some before the House—indeed, the hon. Member for Gainsborough has already cited some. Individuals can sometimes complain of a particular practice in the absence of a measure of implementation if they run the risk of being directly affected by it. For example, children attending a school where corporal punishment was practised have been treated by the Commission as having a direct and immediate personal interest in complaining about such a punishment, even though they had not been punished. That was in the case of Campbell and Cosans *v.* UK in 1982.

The Court and Commission have shown a readiness to accept that the category of persons affected by a particular measure—and accordingly the number of potential victims—may be broad. The hon. Member for Gainsborough has referred to the case of Open Door and Dublin Well Woman *v.* Ireland in 1992, in which the Irish Supreme Court had granted an injunction preventing the provision of information regarding abortion facilities outside Ireland. The Commission and Court considered that women of child-bearing age could claim to be victims of the injunction, as they belonged to a class of women that might have been adversely affected by the restriction.

Applications have been allowed not only by the person immediately affected—sometimes referred to as the direct victim—but by indirect victims. Where there has been an alleged violation of the right to life and the direct victim is dead, for example, close relatives of the deceased can be treated as victims on the basis that they were indirectly affected by the alleged violation.

A number of hon. Members have referred to family members. Obviously, they can be victims in appropriate circumstances. For example, a decision to deport someone might allow the family of the person to claim to be a victim of a violation of Article 8—the right to respect for family life.[. . .] I can confirm that we have no intention of restricting guardians ad litem or [c. 1086] others who could normally undertake cases from doing so. Likewise, a case can be brought on behalf of a dead victim by his or her family or relatives. The best known case, of which we have all heard, is the "Death on the Rock" case, brought on behalf of a dead IRA terrorist shot in Gibraltar. That is the sort of area that we are considering. A person may be able to claim that he or she is directly affected as a consequence of a violation of the rights of someone else. Where complaints are brought by persons threatened by deportation, that may arise.

[. . .] The difficulty is that if [interest] groups are to have that right [to assist the court], how many of them will claim that they want to participate in a court proceeding? Under the provisions of the Human Rights Convention, many groups may feel that they have an interest in a particular issue and wish to assist the court. We are talking not only of Liberty, as there are a large number of different groups. For example, the Right to Life could produce a series of litigation cases, which might involve many interest groups that might want to assist the court. Interest groups, such as professional associations and NGOs, can bring an application in Strasbourg only if they can demonstrate that they themselves are victims of a breach—that is, that they are in some way affected by the measure complained of. It is not enough that the actual victim, whether a member of the organisation or not, consents to them acting on his behalf.

In B *v.* the UK, both Mrs. B and the Society for the Protection of the Unborn Child brought an application complaining of the way in which the law affected electoral expenses. The Commission ruled the application by SPUC inadmissible because it was not directly affected by the law—only Mrs. B had been prosecuted. On the other hand, in Council of Civil Service Unions *v.* the UK, the Commission accepted that the CCSU was itself a victim of the GCHQ ban and could therefore bring an application, although it was rejected on different grounds. An NGO may represent its members in certain contexts and, in that case, it needs to identify them and produce the evidence of authority. In such circumstances, the NGO does not, however, thereby become a party itself.

Our courts will develop their own jurisprudence on the issue, taking account of Strasbourg cases and the Strasbourg jurisprudence. As a Government, our aim is to grant access to victims. It is not to create opportunities to allow interest groups from SPUC to Liberty—in which I must declare an interest because I am a member—to venture into frolics of their own in the courts. The aim is to confer access to rights, not to license interest groups to clog up the courts with test cases, which will delay victims' access to the courts. There is nothing undemocratic about conferring rights on victims, rather than interest groups that are non-victims. Interest groups can always support victims, and that is enough.

Section 7(5): Limitation periods for section 7 actions

Introduction of Section 7(5) by Committee Stage amendment - New 1 year limitation periods introduced for s. 7(1)(a) actions only – limitation periods for actions relying on s. 7(1)(b) not affected

House of Commons, Committee Stage
Official Report, House of Commons, 24 June 1998, vol. 314, col. 1094

The Parliamentary Under-Secretary of State for the Home Department (Mr. Mike O'Brien): The amendments[4] relate to the time within which proceedings against public authorities under the Bill are to be brought. To some extent, this is a matter of judgment and the judgment of various parties in the House appears to differ. At present, the Bill makes no provision about limitation periods in which proceedings under Clause 7(1)(a)—that is, proceedings brought on Convention grounds alone and not under any pre-existing cause of action—have to be brought. We think, as do those who are moving the other amendments on the subject, that such proceedings should be no different from other civil proceedings in having a limitation period. [. . .] I should, for the avoidance of any doubt, make the point that our amendment relates only to proceedings under clause 7(1)(a). If a plaintiff proceeded under clause 7(1)(b)—that is to say, he brought proceedings under an existing cause of action and relied on his Convention rights as an additional argument in support of his case—the limitation period would be the one that applies in the normal way to the existing cause of action.

The Government amendment provides that proceedings under Clause 7(1)(a) must be brought within one year, beginning with the date on which the act complained of took place, or within such longer period as the court or tribunal considers equitable, having regard to all the circumstances. However, that time limit is subject to any stricter time limit in relation to the procedure in question. The most obvious such case is judicial review. Assuming that the new rules of court that will be needed for the Bill provide that a procedure analogous to judicial review may [c. 1095] be used for cases under Clause 7(1)(a), it is reasonable that the time limit for that procedure—which is three months—should continue to apply. It would not be right for applicants who choose to bring their claims by way of judicial review to benefit from the longer 12-month period proposed for claims under the Bill.

---

[4] The text of the amendment reads: in Clause 7 insert—

'(5) Proceedings under subsection (1)(a) must be brought before the end of—
(a) the period of one year beginning with the date on which the act complained of took place; or
(b) such longer period as the court or tribunal considers equitable having regard to all the circumstances,

but that is subject to any rule imposing a stricter time limit in relation to the procedure in question.'.—

As the right hon. Member for Caithness, Sutherland and Easter Ross (Mr. Maclennan) suggested, there is at present a range of limitation periods in our law. For judicial review proceedings, an application for leave must be made promptly and in any event within three months; for cases of personal injury caused by negligence, it is three years; and for most other actions in tort, it is six years. There is no off-the-shelf answer to the question of how long the limitation period for claims under Clause 7(1)(a) should be. What we have tried to do in our amendment is to strike a balance between the legitimate needs of the plaintiff and the legitimate needs of the defendant, which is what all limitation periods should do.

Scope of time limits – Relationship of section 7 actions to other actions -
House of Commons, Committee Stage
Official Report, House of Commons, 24 June 1998, vol. 314, col. 1095
The Parliamentary Under-Secretary of State for the Home Department (Mr. Mike O'Brien): . . . I am aware that some people consider that the 12-month time limit is too short, although there are no amendments before the Committee which would provide for a much longer basic period. It has been suggested that the ordinary limitations for civil proceedings should apply, as they do, for example, in New Zealand. If I might take the New Zealand example first, the legislation in that country has no precise equivalent to Clause 7(1)(a). As the Committee will be aware, Clause 7(1)(a) creates a cause of action, and the Bill would be open to criticism if it did not clearly state what limitation period was to apply to proceedings under that paragraph.

As I have said, we believe that the right balance is provided by a 12-month period, with a power to extend it for the benefit of the complainant. Suggestions for a two or three-year period fail to take account of the existing three-month period for judicial review, to which many claims under Clause 7(1)(a) will be similar.

We recognise, however, that there may be circumstances where a rigid one-year cut off could lead to injustice. Our amendment does not therefore seek to provide a rigid limit, but enables a court to extend the period where it is appropriate to do so. There will be cases in which an individual has a good reason for delay. In judicial review cases, for example, the courts have extended time where the applicant has been seeking redress by other proper means, such as by pursuing internal grievance procedures, or where he has had to apply for legal aid. I have no doubt that the courts will continue to exercise their discretion so as to prevent prejudice to one party or the other where an application is made to extend time.

The Government amendment provides that the limitation period is to be one year

"or such longer period as the court or tribunal considers equitable having regard to all the circumstances".

We have said no more than that because I think to expand on those circumstances might be likely to prove unhelpful to the court. We do not wish to narrow the range of circumstances which might influence the court.

[...][c. 1097]

It may be helpful if I draw attention to the limitation provisions in another area. The Sex Discrimination Act 1975 has a number of limitation periods—all less than a year—but . . . a court or tribunal can consider an application out of time

"if, in all the circumstances of the case, it considers that it is just and equitable to do so."

No further guidance is given in the Act, but a body of law has been built up when it is appropriate to exercise the discretion. We have no doubt that the same would happen under the Bill.

Principles behind Section 7 time limits

House of Commons, Committee Stage
Official Report, House of Commons, 24 June 1998, vol. 314, col. 1099

The Parliamentary Under-Secretary of State for the Home Department (Mr. Mike O'Brien): . . . He is trying to ask whether we would be creating novel legal procedures to circumvent judicial review. In considering any application that sought to do that, the courts would take account not only of the wording of the Bill, but, under Pepper *v.* Hart, what I said as the Minister presenting the Bill.

It is not our intention to create a vast array of novel features that would allow litigants to pursue cases in courts in a way that the courts and Parliament had not intended. However, someone with a genuine human rights grievance will be entitled to pursue it under Clause 7(1)(a), whether or not he is within the time limit for judicial review. We accept that that should be so. The amendment seeks to insert a one-year time limit for Clause 7(1)(a) so that the courts have time to make a judgment. We have not sought to constrain that time too much because paragraph (b) of our amendment allows the courts to decide when they wish to go beyond the 12-month period, should it be equitable to do so.

We are conscious that it is important that the person is allowed to pursue any action under Clause 7(1)(a). We do not want to create an artificial time limit of three months, as the Opposition seek to do, without giving the level of flexibility that is needed. The amendment would tie the procedure too tightly to the judicial review procedure. The courts will develop their own jurisprudence on this issue, over time. I agree with the hon. Member for Beaconsfield that we want to keep matters simple and straightforward, but the courts will take note of what Parliament has said and will be able to consider the points that I have made as Minister at the Dispatch Box. They will understand that we are seeking not to create novel areas of litigation, but to continue to pursue matters in the proper and most appropriate way.

Section 7(8)

Whether prosecutions should be brought where a public authority has acted unlawfully

House of Commons, Committee Stage
Official Report, House of Commons, 24 June 1998, vol. 314, col. 1106

The Parliamentary Under-Secretary of State for the Home Department (Mr. Mike O'Brien): Amendment No. 54 would delete Clause [7(8)], which states:

> "Nothing in this Act creates a criminal offence."

We considered whether the Bill should enable criminal proceedings to be brought when a public authority has acted unlawfully, and we concluded that it should not. The Bill contains ample provisions for challenging the acts of a public authority, and the courts have wide-ranging scope to grant an appropriate remedy to the [c. 1107] individual affected by an unlawful act. We see no reason to impose a criminal sanction specifically for a breach of the Convention.

That is the normal approach. For example, both the Sex Discrimination Act 1975 and the Race Relations Act 1976 specifically preclude criminal proceedings for breaches of the prohibition on discriminatory treatment under those Acts. I should perhaps add, for the avoidance of doubt, that some incompatible acts may amount to criminal offences in their own right, and the Bill, including Clause [7(8)], does not affect that. For example, ill-treatment that is contrary to Article 3 of the Convention on the Prohibition of Torture may amount to an offence under the Offences Against the Person Act 1861. In such circumstances, criminal proceedings could be brought, but they would be for an alleged breach of the 1861 Act, not for an alleged failure to comply with Article 3.

Section 7(11)

Introduction of sub-section – extension of jurisdiction of special adjudicators in asylum cases – general nature of provision

House of Lords, Report Stage

Official Report, House of Lords, 19 January 1998, vol. 584, col. 1361

Lord Williams of Mostyn: A person appearing in difficult circumstances before the special adjudicator would not be able to rely on the Convention rights. He would not be left without any remedy under the Human Rights Bill, because he would be able to rely on those rights in separate proceedings under Clause 7(1)(a) of the Bill. The better course, however, would be for him to be able to rely on Convention points at the time when the case was before the special adjudicator. [. . .]The effect of [sub-section 7(11)] is to enable a Minister to confer jurisdiction on a tribunal to determine Convention issues or to grant a remedy where a public authority has acted incompatibly with the Convention rights. The jurisdiction is to be conferred by order. It will be in addition to the existing statutory provisions relating to tribunal jurisdiction. . . . [I]t will enable the Secretary of State to confer jurisdiction on the adjudicator to consider claims relating to Convention rights, notwithstanding the restriction in the 1993 [Asylum and Immigration Appeals] Act, and to provide a remedy if a public authority acts in a way which is incompatible with those rights.

The intention would be to use the order-making power to extend the jurisdiction of the special adjudicators who hear asylum appeals so as to allow a person appealing on one of the grounds set out in Section 8 of the 1993 Act to appeal also on the ground that his removal from the United Kingdom would be unlawful under Clause 6(1) of the Human Rights Bill. An appellant who succeeded on that ground would not be granted asylum but would be irremovable from the United Kingdom and eligible for exceptional leave to remain. Therefore, the effect of such an order would be to make the ECHR jurisdiction in asylum appeals consistent with that in non-asylum appeals under Section 19 of the Immigration Act 1971.

The order conferring jurisdiction is to be subject to affirmative resolution under the scheme that we propose. We sought to make general provision of this kind rather than to operate directly on the Act of 1993. That is because we do not think it appropriate for a Bill of general application, such as this one, to remedy problems in a particular piece of legislation. Moreover, we are not certain that the problem identified by the noble Earl is necessarily confined to tribunal hearings in immigration appeals cases. We are not aware at present of similar problems arising from statutory restrictions on the jurisdiction of other tribunals, but if such problems do emerge we would look to a general provision which I hope the noble Earl can welcome because, although consonant with his approach, it goes beyond the ambit of his particular concern. We are looking for a general provision in order to deal with such problems.

Editor's note: The relevant provision was made by s.65 of the Immigration and Asylum Act 1999

Power to add to remedial powers and grounds for granting of them

House of Commons, Committee Stage

Official Report, House of Commons, 24 June 1998, vol. 314, col. 1109

The Parliamentary Under-Secretary of State for the Home Department (Mr. Mike O'Brien): . . . The power conferred by clause [7(11)][5] has been included to cater for situations where the grounds on which proceedings may be brought before a tribunal are extremely narrowly defined either by statute or by restrictive judicial interpretation

---

[5] Now section 7(11).

of statutory provisions. In those rare cases, a tribunal would, unless its powers were suitably amplified, be precluded from determining issues relating to the Convention rights. The issue that prompted the inclusion of Clause [7(11)] is the constraints placed on special adjudicators hearing appeals under the Asylum and Immigration Appeals Act 1993.

It was pointed out in another place that the terms of the 1993 Act are such that they would prevent a special adjudicator hearing an asylum case from determining whether an appellant's removal from the United Kingdom would breach his Convention rights when such appeals were dealt with.

Even without subsection (13), an individual would not be left without a remedy under the Human Rights Bill, as he would be able to rely on the Convention rights in a subsequent application for judicial review. The better course is for him to rely on Convention rights at the time the case is before the special adjudicator. Clause [7(11)] would allow that result to be achieved. In addition, as it has been cast in general terms, it could also be used to benefit other tribunals in the same position as the special adjudicator.

There is, however, a risk that the current wording will be misinterpreted. In particular, there is a possibility that some might read it as implying that no tribunal will be able to take account of the Convention rights unless and until a Minister makes an order under clause [7(11)]. The argument might run that, since no tribunals have in their parent statute express authority to determine Convention questions or to grant remedies in respect of Convention [c. 1110] violations, tribunals may conclude that they are not to have regard to the Convention rights without being given express authority to do so.

That is not our intention. The great majority of tribunals would not be debarred from having regard to the Convention rights. It is an important principle of the Bill that they should do so. The amendment simply seeks to achieve the purpose of Clause [7(11)] in a way which does not lead to any misunderstanding on that score. It makes it clear that the power to make an order applies only where it is necessary to ensure that the tribunal in question can provide an appropriate remedy in respect of an unlawful act. I should add that, by virtue of Clause 20(4), any order would need to be approved in draft by both Houses of Parliament.

One other change to Clause [7(11)] to which I wish to draw the attention of the Committee is the removal of the reference to a tribunal's "jurisdiction". On reflection, we consider that the meaning of the term in this context is unclear. That adjustment leads to a consequential change in the wording of Clause 8(1) on remedies. Amendment No. 129 accordingly substitutes a reference to "powers" in place of "jurisdiction".

SECTION 8: JUDICIAL REMEDIES

8. - (1) In relation to any act (or proposed act) of a public authority which the court finds is (or would be) unlawful, it may grant such relief or remedy, or make such order, within its powers as it considers just and appropriate.

(2) But damages may be awarded only by a court which has power to award damages, or to order the payment of compensation, in civil proceedings.

(3) No award of damages is to be made unless, taking account of all the circumstances of the case, including-

(a) any other relief or remedy granted, or order made, in relation to the act in question (by that or any other court), and
(b) the consequences of any decision (of that or any other court) in respect of that act,

the court is satisfied that the award is necessary to afford just satisfaction to the person in whose favour it is made.

(4) In determining-

(a) whether to award damages, or
(b) the amount of an award,

the court must take into account the principles applied by the European Court of Human Rights in relation to the award of compensation under Article 41 of the Convention.

(5) A public authority against which damages are awarded is to be treated-

(a) in Scotland, for the purposes of section 3 of the Law Reform (Miscellaneous Provisions) (Scotland) Act 1940 as if the award were made in an action of damages in which the authority has been found liable in respect of loss or damage to the person to whom the award is made;
(b) for the purposes of the Civil Liability (Contribution) Act 1978 as liable in respect of damage suffered by the person to whom the award is made.

(6) In this section-
"court" includes a tribunal;
"damages" means damages for an unlawful act of a public authority; and
"unlawful" means unlawful under section 6(1).

See also section below on Article 13 of the Convention.

Effect of Section 8

House Of Lords, Second Reading
Official Report, House of Lords, 3 November 1997, vol. 582, col. 1232
The Lord Chancellor (Lord Irvine of Lairg): . . . If a court or tribunal finds that a public authority has acted in a way which is incompatible with the Convention, what can it do about it? Under Clause 8 it may provide whatever remedy is available to it and which seems just and appropriate. That might include awarding damages against the public authority.

House of Commons, Second Reading
Official Report, House of Commons, 16 February 1998, vol. 307, col. 780
The Secretary of State for the Home Department (Mr. Jack Straw): . . . Clause 8 deals with remedies. . . . If a court or tribunal finds that a public authority has acted unlawfully, it may grant whatever remedy is available to it that it considers just and appropriate.

Section 8(1)

No definition of public authority in section 8 because bill is aimed solely at public authorities as defined in section 6

House of Lords, Committee Stage
Official Report, House of Lords, 18 November 1997, vol. 583, col. 477
The Lord Chancellor (Lord Irvine of Lairg): "Acts of public authorities" in respect of which our courts may grant remedies if they deny Convention rights and therefore act unlawfully are amply defined in Clause 6 of the Bill. The Bill is aimed at public authorities and unlawful acts by public authorities acting contrary to Convention rights. That is not in the back of my mind; it is in the front of my mind.

Clause 8(1) refers to remedies in respect of acts of public authorities because that is what the Bill is about.

Relationship with Article 13

'inconceivable' that section 8(1) would not provide an effective remedy for the purpose of Article 13 of the Convention

House of Lords, Committee Stage

Official Report, House of Lords, 18 November 1997, vol. 583, col. 479

Lord Kingsland: The vast majority of the rights that are guaranteed by the European Convention are already guaranteed by our own common law rules or by statute. Those common law rules or statutory rules are backed in our courts by an array of enforceable remedies. Let us suppose that a judge is presented with a situation whereby the substance of the common law or statute rule complies with the Convention but the remedy available does not comply with the remedy that a citizen would gain under Article 13 if that citizen went to the court. What happens next? Under Clause 8(1) a court can grant any order within its jurisdiction. Is the noble and learned Lord saying that since Article 13 is automatically incorporated, although not on the face of the Bill, that judge is entitled to give effect to a remedy which is sanctioned by Article 13? Alternatively, is he saying that the judge is not so entitled? If the judge is not so entitled, is the judge then entitled to make a declaration of incompatibility with respect to remedies rather than the substance of the law and to ask for a fast-track solution from Parliament?

The Lord Chancellor (Lord Irvine of Lairg): . . . At present, I cannot conceive of any state of affairs in which an English court, having held an Act to be unlawful because of its infringement of a Convention right, would under Clause 8(1), be disabled from giving an effective remedy. I believe that the English law is rich in remedies and I cannot conceive of a case in which English law under Clause 8(1) would be unable to provide an effective remedy.

However, during the earlier course of the debate I did not say that Article 13 was incorporated. The debate is about the fact that it is not incorporated. In reply to the noble Lord, Lord Lester, I said that in my view the English courts, in the examples which he offered, would be able to have regard to Article 13[6].

---

[6] *Official Report, House of Lords, 18 November 1997, vol. 583, col. 477*

Section 8(1) is 'of the widest amplitude' – no examples of remedies which it would prevent

House of Lords, Report Stage

Official Report, House of Lords, 19 January 1998, vol. 584, col. 1266

The Lord Chancellor (Lord Irvine of Lairg): My Lords, I have not the least idea what the remedies the courts might develop outside Clause 8 could be if Article 13 was included. The noble and learned Lord has really made my point for me. Clause 8(1) is of the widest amplitude. No one is [c. 1267] contending that it will not do the job. When we have challenged the proponents of the amendment on a number of occasions in Committee to say how Clause 8 might not do the job, they have been unable to offer a single example. Therefore, the argument is all one way. What we have done is sufficient.

Proposal to amend section 8 to be in accordance with Article 13 – likely to be productive only of uncertainty – nothing further is needed

House of Lords, Report Stage

Official Report, House of Lords, 29 January 1998, vol. 585, col. 383

Lord Lester of Herne Hill:
A ... problem was, and is, that, on the face of it, Clause 1(1)(a) gives the impression that Parliament is innumerate and illiterate in terms of the law of the Convention by inviting us to count from two to 12 and 12 to 14, omitting Article 13 altogether, even though we know that Article 13 creates a substantive right which has to be complied with by all the public authorities of the United Kingdom, including the courts. The problem is then aggravated by the fact that although Clause 8— with which this amendment is concerned—gives ample powers to the court to grant just and appropriate remedies there is still no link with Article 13 of the Convention. Various attempts have been made to create that link. Notwithstanding the assurances that the noble and learned Lord the Lord Chancellor has given in previous debates which are, as it were, Pepper *v.* Hart assurances, it is essential that our courts should be able to continue to do what they have already been doing in developing the common law and in interpreting statutory discretion.

As I explained earlier, in libel cases the Court of Appeal has at least twice referred to Article 13, and the Appellate Committee of your

Lordships' House has done the same in ex parte Khan. It would be most unfortunate if the deliberate exclusion of Article 13 in Clause 1(1)(a) were to be construed as intended to cut down the power of our courts to have regard to Article 13 as well as to the other substantive provisions of the Convention.

[. . .]

The Lord Chancellor (Lord Irvine of Lairg): My Lords, . . . Clause 8(1) provides that,

> "In relation to any act (or proposed act) of a public authority which the court finds is (or would be) unlawful, it may grant such relief or remedy, or make such order, within its jurisdiction as it considers just and appropriate".

In my respectful view, that gives the courts the amplest discretion.
[. . .][c. 385]

The key point is this. Given the wealth of remedies available to a court under Clause 8(1), nothing further is needed, in the Government's judgment. We are confident that Clause 8 will allow the courts to do full justice in the cases that come before them. I repeat that it is noteworthy that on the several occasions that we have now debated this general issue, no one has been able to point to any particular deficiency within Clause 8(1).

Article 13 might give rise to damages being granted 'in more circumstances than we had envisaged'

House of Common, Committee Stage

Official Report, House of Commons, 20 May 1998, vol. 312, col. 979

Mr. Garnier: Will the right hon. Gentleman give one or two examples of the remedies he envisages that would go beyond those set out in Clause 8?

The Secretary of State for the Home Department (Mr. Jack Straw): In considering Article 13, the courts could decide to grant damages in more circumstances than we had envisaged. We had to consider that matter carefully, because of the effect on the public purse. We are dealing with breaches of rights by public bodies, some of which are financed by Government—whose purse is, apparently, endless and seamless—whereas others do not have access to the full resources of

Her Majesty's Government and the Bank of England printing works in my home town of Loughton in Essex. We had to think carefully about the scope of the remedies that we should provide.

Amendment of 'jurisdiction' to 'powers' in Section 8(1) so that Civil Liability (Contribution) Act 1978 will apply to damages awarded under Section 8

House of Commons, Committee Stage

Official Report, House of Commons, 24 June 1998, vol. 314, col. 1113

The Parliamentary Under-Secretary of State for the Home Department (Mr. Mike O'Brien): . . . The Civil Liability (Contribution) Act 1978 provides a right to contribution when more than one person is liable for the same damage. We see no reason why that standard provision should not apply when damages are awarded against a public authority under clause 8 of the Bill. The amendment makes it clear that the terms of the 1978 Act and the relevant provisions in Scotland—Section 3 of the Law Reform (Miscellaneous Provisions) (Scotland) Act 1940—apply to the award of such damages. I heard what the hon. and learned Gentleman said and will, therefore, take that matter no further.

Taking into account the conduct of the injured party in assessing damages

House of Commons, Committee Stage

Official Report, House of Commons, 24 June 1998, vol. 314, col. 1114

The Parliamentary Under-Secretary of State for the Home Department (Mr. Mike O'Brien): . . . It may help if I say something about the principles applied by the European Court of Human Rights in relation to the award of compensation. Article [41] provides that in the event of a finding of a violation,

> "the decision of the Court shall, if necessary, afford just satisfaction to the injured party".

There is no entitlement to an award, and the court's discretion is guided by the particular circumstances of each and every case. On many occasions, the court has held that no award should be made because the finding of a violation itself constituted just satisfaction. It appears from the court's judgments that matters such as the applicant's conduct and the limited nature of the breach are relevant factors. An interesting case in that regard, and one that most of us would remember, is the 1995 judgment in the case of McCann and others *v.* UK, in which the court had regard to the fact that the three terrorist suspects who were killed had intended to plant a bomb in Gibraltar in dismissing the applicants' claim for damages.

In our view, therefore, the requirement to take into account the principles applied in Strasbourg already allows the court to have regard to the conduct of the applicant, and it is unnecessary to amend the Bill to insert a specific reference to it. Also, it would be undesirable to do so, because the purpose of the Bill is to reflect Strasbourg thinking on the award of compensation, and the insertion of an additional condition of this kind could imply only that we wanted to gloss the court's thinking in some way. That is not our purpose. Our purpose is to use the way in which those decisions are reached to guide our courts.

Damages in judicial review proceedings

Unclear whether damages could be awarded on an application for judicial review for breach of Convention where there is no misfeasance in public office – criminal court unable to award damages for breach of the Convention

House of Lords, Committee Stage
Official Report, House of Lords, 24 November 1997, vol. 583, col. 854

Lord Lester of Herne Hill: . . . As those Members of the Committee who are judges or practical lawyers will know, one cannot obtain compensation under traditional English legal principles for maladministration unless there is misfeasance in public office, unless there is bad faith. However under the European Convention on Human Rights, the position is somewhat different.

It is clear that where a public authority acts in breach of legitimate expectations in a public law context and causes direct damage, there is a right under the Convention to compensation. What I am not clear about as regards the structure of Clause 8 as it stands is what happens in, for example, judicial review proceedings, where what is at stake is a public law tort (a government tort) giving rise to direct loss, as distinct from the normal private law tort. That distinction does not normally arise under our legal system as it stands, except, as I say, where there is misfeasance in public office.

If I am right about the position under the European Convention—it arises in a Irish case called Pine Valley Developments, where the European court held that there needed to be compensation for breach of legitimate expectations in the planning context—it seems to me that one needs to be clear whether, by means of a Pepper *v.* Hart statement, or under the wording of Clause 8, the Bill permits the remedy of compensation for what I call public law wrongdoing as distinct from normal private law tort in the context in which the Convention would require it.

The Lord Chancellor (Lord Irvine of Lairg): Clause 8 provides the courts and tribunals with wide powers to grant such relief or remedy which they consider just and appropriate where they find that a public authority has acted unlawfully by virtue of Clause 6(1) of the Bill. Under Clause 8(2),

> "damages may be awarded only by a court which has power to award damages, or to order the payment of compensation in civil proceedings".

Under Clause 8(3):

> "No award of damages is to be made unless"—

and I miss out the intervening words—

> "the court is satisfied that the award is necessary to afford just satisfaction to the person in whose favour it is made".

That is a comprehensive and comprehensible code. However, it is necessary to put down certain limits on what remedies a court or tribunal can provide. Subsection (2), which I have just read, provides one such restriction. It states that,

> "damages may be awarded only by a court which has power to award damages . . . in civil proceedings".

Quite clearly, this means that a criminal court will not be able to award damages for a Convention breach, even if it currently has the power to make a compensation order unless it also has the power to award damages in civil proceedings. [c. 855] So as to make the intention plain, it is not the Bill's aim that, for example, the Crown court should be able to make an award of damages where it finds, during the course of a trial, that a violation of a person's Convention rights has occurred. We believe that it is appropriate for an individual who considers that his rights have been infringed in such a case to pursue any matter of damages through the civil courts where this type of issue is normally dealt with; in other words, to pursue the matter in the courts that are accustomed to determining whether it is necessary and appropriate to award damages and what the proper amount should be. For that reason, we regard the inclusion of subsection (2) as an entirely proper part of the scheme.

We say that the Crown court, in cases of crime, should not award damages. The remedy that the defendant wants in a criminal court is not to be convicted. We see very considerable practical difficulties about giving a new power to award damages to a criminal court in Convention cases. It would seem to me to open up the need for representation in the Crown court to any person whom it might appear in the course of criminal proceedings might be at risk of damages. We believe that that would be potentially disruptive of a criminal trial. Similarly, a magistrates' court is a criminal court and, under the amendment, it could award damages. We believe that it is appropriate that the civil courts, which traditionally make awards of damages, should, alone, be enabled to make awards of damages in these Convention cases.

[. . .][c. 856]

I am tempted simply to rely upon the answer that in the circumstances to which the noble Lord alludes an award of damages will be made if— I quote from Clause 8(3)—

> "the court is satisfied that the award is necessary to afford just satisfaction to the person in whose favour it is made".

Effect of section 8 on fair trial guarantees

Wrong to interfere with a criminal court's discretion to give remedies where Convention points are concerned

House of Commons, Committee Stage

Official Report, House of Commons, 24 June 1998, vol. 314, col.1107

The Parliamentary Under-Secretary of State for the Home

Department (Mr. Mike O'Brien): Amendment No. 59[7] would insert a new subsection in Clause 8 to the effect that a person should not be acquitted in a criminal trial by reason only of a finding that an act of a public authority was unlawful unless the court had made a declaration of incompatibility in relation to those proceedings. I shall first address what I take to be the intention behind the amendment—to restrict the ability of the courts, especially the lower courts, to acquit a person solely on the basis that he has been the victim of an unlawful act by a public authority.

The amendment seems to imply that a person would be "getting away with it" if an acquittal were founded on that ground alone. It suggests that, unlike the many existing domestic freedoms already enjoyed by people in the United Kingdom, Convention rights are not to be regarded as inherent rights. I disagree with that: they are supposed to part of our own law. We are giving access to Convention rights as part of our own law on the same basis as laws that are dealt with by Strasbourg and subject to the appropriate derogations and reservations.

The way in which the courts will approach a case in criminal proceedings in which Convention points are raised is clear. As a public authority, a court will be required not to act in a way that is incompatible with the Convention. It will be unlawful for a court to give a judgment that is incompatible with a Convention right, unless it is required to do so to give effect to a provision of primary legislation or a provision made under it. The fact that, in a particular trial, a public authority is found to have acted unlawfully will not automatically lead to an acquittal. The nature of the act and its impact on the trial as a whole will have to be considered. If the effect of the act is such that, for example, a fair trial is impossible, an acquittal would be the appropriate outcome. That will not always follow; it will depend on the circumstances of the case. That is no different in principle from decisions that the courts already take—for example, when deciding whether to stay proceedings on the ground of abuse of process.

It would be quite wrong to attempt to interfere with the courts' discretion in these matters, as the amendment tries to do. In fact, the

---

[7] The amendment stated:
"In the case of criminal proceedings, no person shall be acquitted by reason only of a finding that an act of a public authority is unlawful, unless the court has made a declaration of incompatibility under section 4 in relation to those proceedings."

amendment seems to be misconceived, as it links unlawfulness with the making of a declaration of incompatibility. It implies that in a criminal trial there [c. 1108] will be both an unlawful act by a public authority and an incompatible provision of legislation that attracts a declaration from the court. If the public authority is acting to give effect to that legislation, then, by virtue of Clause 6(2), its act would be protected, and hence not unlawful. To put it the other way, if a public authority has acted unlawfully, it cannot have been acting so as to give effect to an incompatible provision of primary legislation or a provision made under it. No declaration of incompatibility would therefore arise.

There are some other difficulties, which may or may not have been intended by those who tabled the amendment. Magistrates courts and the Crown court do not have the power to make declarations of incompatibility. The amendment would, therefore, risk triggering a flood of appeals from those courts, as no defendant could be acquitted by them on the sole ground of an unlawful act by a public authority. That would clog up the court system for no good purpose, and would be contrary to our intention that all courts and tribunals should take account of Convention rights.

The hon. and learned Member for Harborough (Mr. Garnier) referred to terrorists. An act covered by the derogation in schedule 2[8] is not an unlawful act for the purposes of the Bill, so it cannot form the basis of a finding that a public authority has acted unlawfully. The hon. and learned Gentleman asked me whether someone would [be able to use] the Convention to found an acquittal. It would be used in the same way as the rules in the Police and Criminal Evidence Act 1984 and as any of the other provisions of natural justice.

We are giving each person in the United Kingdom the ability to access the rights that they already have at Strasbourg. It all comes back to that point. The hon. and learned Gentleman seems to be suggesting that someone could be acquitted because that person was able to claim a Convention right. That person would have the right to go to Strasbourg if we did not provide him with access to a decision in a domestic court. He would still have that right, but he would have to go to Strasbourg to access it.

The Bill is about access. We are enabling our courts to make decisions much more effectively and to take into account our jurispru-

---

[8] Covering the Prevention of Terrorism Acts

dence. We are also ensuring that the Strasbourg court, when reaching decisions, is able to take into account the way in which we have developed our jurisprudence.

The Bill is beneficial in that it establishes rights and ensures that procedures are properly followed. I understand why the hon. and learned Gentleman has tabled the amendment, but I suspect that, if proper methods of investigation are used, it is unlikely that new problems will be created. A claim in a British court that a particular method of collecting information was inappropriate could be raised in a Strasbourg court; the only difference is where one accesses one's rights. Some seem to think that our people should be able to access their rights only in Strasbourg. We think it best that such matters should be dealt with by our own courts in Britain.

SECTION 9: JUDICIAL ACTS

9. - (1) Proceedings under section 7(1)(a) in respect of a judicial act may be brought only-

(a) by exercising a right of appeal;

(b) on an application (in Scotland a petition) for judicial review; or

(c) in such other forum as may be prescribed by rules.

(2) That does not affect any rule of law which prevents a court from being the subject of judicial review.

(3) In proceedings under this Act in respect of a judicial act done in good faith, damages may not be awarded otherwise than to compensate a person to the extent required by Article 5(5) of the Convention.

(4) An award of damages permitted by subsection (3) is to be made against the Crown; but no award may be made unless the appropriate person, if not a party to the proceedings, is joined.

(5) In this section-

"appropriate person" means the Minister responsible for the court concerned, or a person or government department nominated by him;

"court" includes a tribunal;

"judge" includes a member of a tribunal, a justice of the peace and a clerk or other officer entitled to exercise the jurisdiction of a court;

"judicial act" means a judicial act of a court and includes an act done on the instructions, or on behalf, of a judge; and

"rules" has the same meaning as in section 7(9).

Effect of section 9

House Of Lords, Second Reading

Official Report, House of Lords, 3 November 1997, vol. 582, col. 1232

The Lord Chancellor (Lord Irvine of Lairg): . . . Clause 9 is concerned with what happens when a court or tribunal acts in a way which is incompatible with the Convention. Here we have preserved the existing principle of judicial immunity and have provided that proceedings against a court or tribunal on Convention grounds may be brought only by an appeal or application for judicial review.

House of Commons, Second Reading
Official Report, House of Commons, 16 February 1998, vol. 307, col. 780

The Secretary of State for the Home Department (Mr. Jack Straw): . . . Clause 9 serves two main functions. It preserves the general principle of judicial immunity when a court or tribunal is found, or alleged, to have acted in a way that is made unlawful by Clause 6, and it provides for the possibility of damages being awarded against the Crown in respect of a judicial act, to the extent necessary to comply with Article 5(5) of the Convention

Section 9(1) and Article 5(5) of the European Convention on Human Rights

House of Lords, Report Stage
Official Report, House of Lords, 29 January 1998, vol. 585, col. 389

The Lord Chancellor (Lord Irvine of Lairg): . . . I indicated at Committee stage that the Government were alive to the need to make appropriate provision for the Article 5(5) requirement and that we were considering how best to give effect to this obligation in relation to judicial acts of courts and tribunals. The effect of Clauses 6, 7 and 8 of the Bill is that there is an enforceable right to compensation in relation to public authorities generally. But special provisions are needed in relation to judicial acts of courts and tribunals.

Where a complaint is made that Article 5 has been breached as a result of a judicial act or omission it will be necessary first to establish whether the judicial act complained of was unlawful, then to rule on whether the aggrieved person is entitled to compensation under Article 5(5) and then to determine the amount of compensation. In determining those questions the court will take into account the Strasbourg jurisprudence on unlawful detention and on the award of damages, as required by Clauses 2 and 8 of the Bill.

Subsections (1) and (2) of the clause require that proceedings under Section 7(1)(a) in respect of a judicial act may be brought in three ways: by exercising a right of appeal; on an application for judicial review (or in Scotland a petition for judicial review) or in such other forum as may be prescribed by rules.

A finding that an inferior court has acted unlawfully will most commonly be reached in England and Wales by way of appeal to the Court of Appeal or the Divisional Court, or by an application by way of judicial review to the High Court. The higher court will then be able to reach a decision of unlawfulness and make an award of damages. Clause 8(2) will enable the courts, which already have power to award damages, to do so in proceedings under this Bill. However, in criminal proceedings in Scotland, if the High Court on appeal finds that some act of an inferior court has contravened the complainant's rights under Article 5(5) it would have no power to award damages. It would therefore be necessary for the amount of damages to be determined by the civil courts. The clause therefore enables proceedings to be brought in such other forum as may be prescribed by rules. The Court of Appeal in England, as a single entity, has the power to award damages. [c. 390]

Rules will provide as to whether the Criminal or Civil Division should hear compensation claims. Again, Clauses 9(1) and 7(2) provide the necessary powers to make rules.

Subsection (2) underlines that no new right to judicial review is being created. For example, a challenge to a decision of the Crown Court in a matter relating to a trial on indictment will be made on appeal since there cannot be judicial review in respect of trials on indictment.

Subsection (3) has two purposes. It restates the current position under common law and statutory rules that the Crown is not liable in respect of judicial acts and that judges and magistrates acting within their jurisdiction, or outside their jurisdiction if doing so in good faith, are immune from proceedings for damages. But it also makes provision that damages may be awarded to compensate a person to the extent required by Article 5(5) of the Convention in respect of a judicial act of a court.

The noble Lord, Lord Meston, has written me a most helpful letter in which he has indicated that he himself had thought of making clear in Clause 9 that existing personal immunity of judges and magistrates was preserved, but he had decided that it was probably unnecessary to do so. It is helpful to know that he had in mind the second purpose of the government amendment—that is, preserving judicial immunity—

as well as the first of providing an enforceable right to compensation under Article 5(5).

[...]

Subsection (4) provides that an award of damages permitted by subsection (3) should be made against the Crown rather than against the judge personally. It also ensures that whichever Minister is responsible for the court or tribunal concerned is joined to the proceedings if not already a party. This is similar in effect to the provision of Clause 5 which provides that where a court is considering whether to make a declaration of incompatibility, the Crown is entitled to notice and, on an application to the court, to be joined as the party to the proceedings. In practice, the Lord Chancellor will be the appropriate person in many cases concerning judges and magistrates, in England and Wales. In Scotland, the relevant Minister will usually be the Secretary of State. But there may be cases where the breach of the Article 5 provisions arises from a wholly proper judicial decision required by inconsistent legislation, primary or secondary legislation. In this case it would be helpful for the Minister responsible for the legislation to be joined. "Appropriate person" therefore allows me, or the Secretary of State for Scotland, to nominate a person or Government department.

The definitions in subsection (6) make it clear that judicial acts include acts undertaken by court officers performing judicial functions or acting on behalf of the judge or on the instructions of the judge. [c. 391]

At present, this clause refers both to a "judicial act", in subsection (1) and to a "judicial act of a court" in subsection (3). This may give rise to confusion and the Government will therefore be moving a minor amendment at Third Reading to clarify this small point.

I said in Committee that the amendment proposed by the noble Lord, Lord Meston, might be the best way of providing compensation for breaches of Article 5 by judicial acts. I warned the Committee then that the complex and delicate issues of judicial immunity and Crown liability for judicial decisions required consideration before an amendment was made to this clause. The Government amendments before the House seek to deal with that situation. They go rather further than the noble Lord's amendment. I hope that he will therefore consider withdrawing his amendment and that the House will agree that the Government amendments achieve what is required.

Background: Government acknowledges and will address gap between section 9 and the requirements of Article 5(5)

House of Lords, Committee Stage

Official Report, House of Lords, 27 November 1997, vol. 583, col. 856

Lord Meston: . . . Clause 9(3) provides a general immunity for acts of courts. However, the relationship between this subsection and Article 5(5) of the Convention—which the Committee will find on page 14 of the Bill—needs to be addressed. Article 5(5) gives an enforceable right to compensation to those who have been victims of arrest or detention in contravention of the provisions of Article 5. In this respect the United Kingdom has been in breach of Article 5(5) for a long time. Clause 9(3) of the Bill seems to preserve that continuing breach. It should be possible to introduce a scheme of compensation for those who are victims of arrest or detention in breach of the Convention without affecting the important personal immunity of judges and magistrates. [. . .]

The Lord Chancellor (Lord Irvine of Lairg): . . . The Government are aware that Clause 9, as currently drafted, makes no explicit provision for the requirement of Article 5(5) that everyone who has been the victim [c. 857] of arrest or detention in contravention of the provisions of Article 5 shall have an enforceable right to compensation.

Clause 8 provides for such an enforceable right to compensation in relation to public authorities generally. Clause 9, as currently drafted, preserves the common law and statutory rules which, broadly speaking, provide that the Crown is not liable in tort in respect of judicial acts and that judges and magistrates acting within their jurisdiction, or outside their jurisdiction if doing so in good faith, are immune from having proceedings brought against them personally.

I can assure the noble Lord, Lord Meston, that the Government are alive to the need to make appropriate provisions for the Article 5(5) requirement and are considering how best to give effect to this obligation in relation to courts and tribunals. [. . .]

SECTION 10: POWER TO TAKE REMEDIAL ACTION

Editor's note—In the original Bill, Section 10 consisted of three separate clauses: 10, 11 and 12. Those aspects found in Clauses 11 and 12 are now located in the second schedule. For the debates concerning that schedule see pages 208–217 below.

10. - (1) This section applies if-

(a) a provision of legislation has been declared under section 4 to be incompatible with a Convention right and, if an appeal lies-

(i) all persons who may appeal have stated in writing that they do not intend to do so;

(ii) the time for bringing an appeal has expired and no appeal has been brought within that time; or

(iii) an appeal brought within that time has been determined or abandoned; or

(b) it appears to a Minister of the Crown or Her Majesty in Council that, having regard to a finding of the European Court of Human Rights made after the coming into force of this section in proceedings against the United Kingdom, a provision of legislation is incompatible with an obligation of the United Kingdom arising from the Convention.

(2) If a Minister of the Crown considers that there are compelling reasons for proceeding under this section, he may by order make such amendments to the legislation as he considers necessary to remove the incompatibility.

(3) If, in the case of subordinate legislation, a Minister of the Crown considers-

(a) that it is necessary to amend the primary legislation under which the subordinate legislation in question was made, in order to enable the incompatibility to be removed, and

(b) that there are compelling reasons for proceeding under this section,

he may by order make such amendments to the primary legislation as he considers necessary.

(4) This section also applies where the provision in question is in subordinate legislation and has been quashed, or declared invalid, by reason of incompatibility with a Convention right and the Minister proposes to proceed under paragraph 2(b) of Schedule 2.

(5) If the legislation is an Order in Council, the power conferred by subsection (2) or (3) is exercisable by Her Majesty in Council.

(6) In this section "legislation" does not include a Measure of the Church Assembly or of the General Synod of the Church of England.

(7) Schedule 2 makes further provision about remedial orders.

Effect of and rationale behind section 10

House of Lords, Second Reading
Official Report, House of Lords, 3 November 1997, vol. 582, col. 1231 . . .
The Lord Chancellor (Lord Irvine of Lairg): . . . We have taken the view that if legislation has been declared incompatible, a prompt parliamentary remedy should be available. Clauses 10 to 12 of the Bill provide how that is to be achieved (*Editor's note - in the Human Rights Act 1998 remedial orders are dealt with in section 10 and Schedule 2*). A Minister of the Crown will be able to make what is to be known as a remedial order. The order will be available in response to a declaration of incompatibility by the higher courts. It will also be available if legislation appears to a Minister to be incompatible because of a finding by the European Court of Human Rights.

We recognise that a power to amend primary legislation by means of a statutory instrument is not a power to be conferred or exercised lightly. Those clauses therefore place a number of procedural and other restrictions on its use. [. . .] So we have built in as much parliamentary scrutiny as possible.

In addition, the power to make a remedial order may be used only to remove an incompatibility or a possible incompatibility between legislation and the Convention. It may therefore be used only to protect human rights, not to infringe them. And the Bill also specifically provides that no person is to be guilty of a criminal offence solely as a result of any retrospective effect of a remedial order.

No reassurance that affirmative resolution procedure will only be activated in cases of real emergency - Purpose of remedial action is to confer rights

House of Commons, Second Reading

Official Report, House of Commons, 16 February 1998, vol. 307, col. 773

Mr. Douglas Hogg (Sleaford and North Hykeham): Does the right hon. Gentleman accept that hon. Members who support the principle of incorporation remain deeply concerned about the provisions of the remedial order procedure, which depend on secondary legislation Orders in Council? Can he reassure us that, in the great generality of cases, primary legislation will be amended only by primary legislation, and that the provisions in Clauses 10 to 12, which deal with the affirmative resolution procedure, will be activated only in instances of real emergency? If he were able to say that, he might gain much more support in the House than would otherwise be forthcoming.

The Secretary of State for the Home Department (Mr. Jack Straw): I understand the concerns expressed by the right hon. and learned Gentleman; they were raised in the other place and were the subject of extensive debate. I cannot give him the undertaking that he seeks. However, I can say, first, that occasions on which the courts declare an Act of this Parliament to be incompatible are rare; there will be very few such cases. Secondly, the purpose of remedial action is to try to resolve the current paralysis, which is to nobody's advantage. It is not to take away anyone's rights; it is to confer rights. Thirdly, hon. Members will have every opportunity to discuss this matter in great detail in Committee.

In our judgment, these fast-track provisions offer far more safeguards than were provided under the European Communities Act 1972 . . . Under the 1972 Act, Parliament cannot vote on any declaration of the European Court of Justice that our law is outwith the ECJ; the law must be changed.

Discretionary nature of power to make remedial orders

House of Lords, Committee Stage

Official Report, House of Lords, 27 November 1997, vol. 583, col. 1139

The Lord Chancellor (Lord Irvine of Lairg): . . . As I have made clear, we expect that the Government and Parliament will in all cases almost certainly be prompted to change the law following a declaration. However, we think that it is preferable, in order to underpin parliamentary sovereignty, to leave this on a discretionary basis. The decision whether to seek a remedial order is a matter for government to decide on a case-by-case basis. It would be wrong for a declaration automatically to lead to a remedial order. It would in effect be tantamount to giving the courts power to strike down Acts of Parliament if there were an obligation in all cases to bring remedial orders forward. [. . .]

Effect of final draft of section 10

House of Commons, Committee Stage

Official Report, House of Commons, 24 June 1998, vol. 314, col. 1120

The Secretary of State for the Home Department (Mr. Jack Straw): Clause 10(1) describes the circumstances in which the power to make a remedial order applies. The first—Clause 10(1)(a)—is where a domestic court has made a declaration of incompatibility and there is no prospect of an appeal, either because those who may appeal have stated that they do not intend to do so, or for other specified reasons. The provisions about appeals were inserted in another place to guard against the possibility of legislation being amended by a remedial order in response to a declaration of incompatibility which was then overturned on appeal. [. . .][T]he only way in which Clause 10(1) can operate in practice will be for the person making the order, if he wishes to proceed urgently before the time for appealing has expired, to take proactive steps by seeking statements from all interested parties to the effect that they do not propose to appeal. I should like to thank the hon. and learned Gentleman for spotting what could have been an ambiguity in the Bill. . . .

The second circumstance in which the power to make a remedial order applies—Clause 10(1)(b)—is where the European Court of Human Rights has found a violation of the Convention in proceedings against the United Kingdom, and it appears to a Minister of the Crown or to Her Majesty in Council that a provision of legislation is incompatible with an obligation of the United Kingdom arising from the Convention.
[. . .]

The point of having the Minister of the Crown is that he or she normally has to exercise those duties. The burden of the hon. and learned Gentleman's remarks is [c. 1121] contained in new Clause 2, which provides for no remedial order to be made following a declaration of incompatibility if a Minister of the Crown considers that the issues raised by the declaration should be considered in Strasbourg.

New Clause 2 seems to be based on two assumptions. The first is that a declaration of incompatibility will have some legal effect unless a ministerial certificate is issued. The second is that the Government must make a remedial order following a declaration of incompatibility. Neither of those assumptions is true. As Clause 4(6) makes clear, a declaration of incompatibility does not affect the continuing validity, operation or enforcement of the provision in respect of which it is given. That is a crucial part of the Bill to preserve the sovereignty of this Parliament.

In most cases, a Minister's view is endorsed by Parliament, and if a Minister decides that it is not appropriate for the Government to take action in respect of the declaration of incompatibility, no action need be taken. In controversial cases, the Minister's decision might have to be endorsed by the House. Indeed, the Opposition could force it to be endorsed, so it would always be subject to that possibility, which is right.

Nor is there any obligation on the Government to remedy any incompatibility by means of a remedial order. We expect that the Government will generally want to do so, just as successive Governments have sought, as we will discuss on the next group of amendments, to put right any declaration by the Strasbourg court by way of legislation or Executive action in the United Kingdom. That is the effect of Clause 10, and it is the logical consequence of our decision that the courts are not to have a power to set aside Acts of Parliament under this Bill.

Therefore, although I understand the point of new Clause 2, it would not achieve anything. Nothing in it could not equally be achieved—and will not equally be achieved—within the framework of the Bill as it stands.

Mr. Maclennan: Obviously this is hypothetical, but in the event of the circumstance that he described arising and a Minister recommending that no action be taken, does the right hon. Gentleman assume that the Government would feel obliged to derogate from the relevant provision of the European Convention?

Mr. Straw: No, I do not. That would arise only if there had been an adverse judgment by the court—I was about to deal with that. Normally in such a circumstance, if the Government had refused to accept a clear declaration of incompatibility—for example, by the Judicial Committee of the other place, the highest court of the land—the victim, who would be the applicant in the action, would take the matter to the Strasbourg court. In practice, in most cases, an appeal to the European court in Strasbourg would naturally follow.

The assumptions implicit in new Clause 2 and some of the other remarks made by the hon. and learned Member for Harborough demonstrate a misreading of the Convention—that it is somehow possible for a Government party to effect an appeal to the Strasbourg court. The Convention is so drawn that the only parties that can make an application to the Strasbourg court are the citizens, or residents, of the country, as the Convention exists to protect the rights of the individual against the state. [c. 1122] A state has never, under the Convention, been able to take action before the Strasbourg court. Given the conceptual, jurisprudential structure of the Convention, that would be entirely otiose—it would entirely reverse the Convention's purpose. Even if the House of Commons was determined that the state should have a right of appeal in the Strasbourg court against the decision of a higher court in this country, that could not be effected under the Convention.

I should also say to Conservative Members, whose interest in the sovereignty of Parliament is at least as strong as ours, that, if we were to seek to do that, we would genuinely be open to the charge that we were undermining the power of Parliament by setting above it a supreme international court with powers over this country's courts. The only way in which to avoid that would be to withdraw from the Convention, which we would not want to do. We believe that the way in which the Convention has been applied over the years, particularly with the margin of appreciation, is sensible, so I suggest that it would not be desirable to go down that road.

Mr. Lansley: The Home Secretary will correct me if I am wrong, but is it not entirely possible, under new Clause 2, not so much that the Government would contemplate resolving issues through the European Convention on Human Rights or the court, as that parties to those proceedings might do so?

Mr. Straw: Of course it is correct to say that parties to the proceedings may voluntarily decide to take a case to the Strasbourg court. Even if there is a declaration of incompatibility, and a remedial order amending primary legislation is put through the House of Commons and the other place, it is still open to the other party to the proceedings to take the matter to the court, although I suggest that they would get short shrift if they sought to do so.

New Clause 2 would effect a right of appeal to the Government. It tries to get around the way in which the Convention has been constructed by requiring the victim to exercise his existing rights to go to Strasbourg so that the case could be considered there before anything happened at home.

I do not think that that is a sensible way in which to proceed. In practice, if the Government and Parliament refused to act on a declaration of incompatibility, the so-called victim—the citizen—would almost certainly take the case to Strasbourg. If the victim did not, but accepted that the Government and Parliament were right to ignore the declaration of incompatibility, I see no reason why anyone would want to pursue the matter to Strasbourg. For those reasons, I hope that the Opposition will see fit not to press new Clause 2 and amendment No. 63.

Mr. Garnier: The right hon. Gentleman is perfectly right to suggest that the new clause is a device. It has to be a device, for the reasons that I had hoped I had explained and that he himself expressed—the state does not have a right to go to Strasbourg; it is for the citizen to do that. What happens in this example, however? A case fought between a citizen and a public authority—be it a Government authority or some other public authority—[c. 1123] eventually reaches the Judicial Committee of the House of Lords, which says that the legislation we are discussing is incompatible with the citizen's Conventional rights. The citizen therefore wins in our domestic courts. However, the political will of Parliament and the advice of the Government are that that is a mistake.

What does the Home Secretary suggest the Government—it does not matter which Government—should do in those circumstances? Under the Bill, the Government are stuck. The purpose of new Clause 2 is to overcome a logjam.

Mr. Straw: Let me try to put the hon. and learned Gentleman's mind at rest. There will be no logjam. If there had been a declaration of incompatibility, and the Government and Parliament had decided not to act on it, I would guess that, in most cases, the applicant would take the case to Strasbourg. That almost certainly follows. However, in the rare examples where that did not happen, the status quo ante would obtain because of Clause 4(6), which makes it clear that

> "A declaration under this section ("a declaration of incompatibility")—
> (a) does not affect the validity, continuing operation or enforcement of the provision in respect of which it is given; and
> (b) is not binding on the parties to the proceedings in which it is made."

If the issue before the Judicial Committee of the House of Lords was, say, whether a statutory instrument was ultra vires, the Committee could use its existing powers to deal with that issue. If, however, the issue was a piece of primary legislation that was incompatible with the Convention, on which the Judicial Committee had made a declaration that the Government and Parliament had decided not to accept, and on which there had been no appeal to Strasbourg, the original piece of primary legislation would stay in force. There would be no logjam, and that is why the new clause is not necessary.

To set up, by whatever device, a system by which the Government of the day—and therefore Parliament—would be able to appeal to the Strasbourg court, would be to elevate that court to a position of supremacy over Parliament, a circumstance that very few Members on either side of the House wish to bring about.

[. . .] [c. 1128]

Derogation arises only from the Convention. In addition, it is not open to member states to derogate judgment by judgment from decisions of the European Court of Human Rights in Strasbourg. It is possible to derogate only in case of war or other emergency that threatens the life of the nation. As hon. Members will see if they turn to the back of the Bill, schedule 2 sets out the one derogation that this country has made in respect of the Convention, which arises from the threat of terrorism and the need for us to operate the Prevention of Terrorism (Temporary Provisions) Act 1984.

[. . .] The powers of any Minister to bring a remedial order before the House or the other place are very circumscribed.

However, as I shall spell out when we discuss the next group of amendments, we have accepted the strong views expressed in the other place and by many hon. Members in this House about the need further to constrain the opportunity for Ministers to bring remedial orders.[...]

[T]he courts already have power to strike down subordinate legislation, and they do so with some regularity. If they feel that a statutory instrument has been introduced in a way that is ultra vires the primary legislation, they can do so. When we discussed the matter in detail in the Cabinet Ministerial Sub-Committee on Incorporation of the European Convention on Human Rights, it seemed to us that, as that power was already there, it would be very odd not to continue to allow courts to strike down subordinate legislation if it was incompatible with the Bill. [c. 1129]

In a sense, that does not affect the sovereignty of Parliament, because it is open to Ministers to try to put the subordinate legislation right by simply introducing further regulations. That happens quite often, as any Minister who has held office in the Department of Social Security can testify.

The issue is whether the courts have power to strike down primary legislation, and we are clear in our minds that they should not.
[...]

A question arises, which is dealt with under Clause 4(3), in respect of a small category of inevitably incompatible subordinate legislation which cannot be quashed by the courts and can only be declared incompatible because of the nature of the primary legislation that brought about that subordinate legislation. In those cases, again to ensure that the sovereignty of Parliament is not inadvertently challenged by striking down subordinate legislation and, in so doing, striking down the primary legislation, we have adopted the other approach and said that, in those cases, all the courts can do is to make a declaration of incompatibility in respect of the subordinate legislation as well.

Mr. Lansley: I accept what the Home Secretary says about primary legislation, but, in this instance, is not the question not as much about the sovereignty of Parliament as about whether it is desirable that there should be a mechanism ... for the Government to suspend, as it were, the courts' quashing of secondary legislation in this respect, based on Convention rights, until the interpretation of Convention rights has proceeded all the way through to the European Court of Human Rights, where the Government consider that to be desirable?

Mr. Straw: I am sorry; I do not accept that. We might equally take the example of social security, but let us take the prison rules as an example.

The prison rules are subordinate legislation, which I change from time to time, under the powers given me under the prison Acts. If they were struck down for incompatibility with the Convention, the important thing would be to introduce new prison rules that were compatible with the legislation, not to leave a hole in the provision.

On the other hand, if the [P]rison Acts were declared incompatible, it would be a much more serious matter, and the important thing would be for the Government and Parliament to make a judgment about whether to take action in respect of that declaration. We have dealt with that.

[. . .] [c. 1137]

Having decided on the concept of declarations of incompatibility, we had to determine what procedures to put in place where such a declaration was made. One option available to Government and Parliament is simply to ignore the declaration of incompatibility, and we have discussed the possibilities that can arise in such a circumstance when no action is taken. However, in most cases when there is a declaration of incompatibility, any Government who are committed to promoting human rights will want to do something about that part of the law that the Judicial Committee in another place has declared outwith the Convention.

It is certainly possible for primary legislation to be introduced and passed very quickly in certain circumstances, and the previous Government had an honourable record of introducing the necessary legislation to give proper effect to the judgments of the European Court of Human Rights. Successive Governments have always acknowledged that it is their duty to bring into law—and into effect—judgments of the European Court of Human Rights.

Opposition Members who have served in previous Parliaments have experience of the pressures on the legislative timetable that sometimes mean that it is not always possible to bring legislation into force timeously. The power to make a remedial order exists for cases—we do not think that there will be very many—when there is a very good reason to amend the law following a declaration of incompatibility or a finding by the Strasbourg court, but no suitable legislative vehicle is available.

Let me give an example . . . A declaration of incompatibility might arise where the legislation in question had touched on the liberty of the subject. In most cases, the Judicial Committee in another place has said that primary legislation here is outwith the Convention [c. 1138] because it has taken the view that the rights of the subject spelled out in the Convention have been unjustifiably interfered with by the primary legislation of this Parliament. Therefore, a remedial order aims to restore, or to give to the subject for the first time, liberties that the subject had previously been denied by Parliament. In those cases, I believe that Parliament would wish to act swiftly, but it could well be that there was no criminal justice Bill before the House through which amendments could be made. In those circumstances, the power to make specific and necessary amendments by means of a remedial order could be useful.

[...]

... I should like to refer to the case of Mr. Chahal, in which the European Court declared that the arbitrary powers of the Home Secretary to deport an individual on the ground that his presence here was not conducive to the public good was not acceptable and that there had to be a judicial element in the decision. Primary legislation has now been passed, but, because of the time that it took, individuals were left in limbo with no proper procedure for making decisions on whether people could be deported. Mr. Chahal was released, but in other circumstances such an individual would have to continue to be detained, perhaps for many months or a year, before primary legislation was passed. That is not acceptable and a remedial order would be right for such a case.

[...]

We are deleting the word "appropriate" in Clause 10 and saying that a remedial order can be brought forward only if there are compelling reasons. We are setting a very high test. Only the changes necessary to remove the incompatibility will be possible. We have also made provision for representations to be made about non-urgent orders. The appropriate Minister will have to bring before Parliament a clear statement of those representations and whether they have been accepted, with a provision for amending the original remedial order if appropriate.

Under amendment No. 64, if Parliament signified that it did not agree with a declaration of incompatibility made by the domestic courts, the case in relation to which the declaration was made would

"stand in abeyance, save for any appeal to the European Court of Human Rights."

As a declaration of incompatibility has no effect on the proceedings in which it is made, the provision would serve no purpose other than to stay the proceedings. The amendment does not refer to only that part of the case in respect of which a declaration of incompatibility is made. Several points could be raised on the matter that went before the other place, some of which required relief, and [c. 1139] for which relief should and would be forthcoming from a domestic court but for the operation of amendment No. 64. I do not believe that the hon. and learned Member for Harborough had that in mind, but the perverse effect of the amendment would be to stay the whole case and therefore to stay the relief that would otherwise be available. For that reason, as for many others, I hope that the hon. and learned Member for Harborough will not press his amendment.

We have worked carefully on the amendments. I accept that they do not deal with all the concerns raised about remedial orders, but I suggest that we have listened with great care to those concerns and have sought to meet them as far as possible.

Effect of later inconsistent judgment of European Court of Human Rights after operation of remedial order arrangements

House of Lords, Report Stage

Official Report, House of Lords, 19 January 1998, vol. 584, col. 1271

Lord Kingsland: If a domestic court makes a decision which is then incorporated into domestic law under the fast-track procedure, and meanwhile the litigant goes to the European Court of Human Rights and gets a decision that is different from that which has been incorporated in domestic law, does it mean that the government of the day will not under any circumstances incorporate the decision of the European Court of Human Rights in domestic law to the extent that it differs from their reaction to the domestic decision? Put another way, if a declaration of inconsistency by a domestic court has been incorporated in our own law does that set the limits of what the Government are prepared to accept from a decision of the European Court of Human Rights, whatever it is?

The Lord Chancellor (Lord Irvine of Lairg): My Lords, I am not sure that I entirely understand the force of the question. As I understand it, the supposition is that the courts of the United Kingdom make a declaration of incompatibility and give their reasons for holding a statute to be incompatible; alternatively, Parliament moves fast and passes a remedial order which is of legislative effect in a certain legislative sense. As I understand the question, I am asked further to suppose that the European Court of Human Rights in Strasbourg pronounces on that point, or something very close to it, in a sense not quite in accord with the reasons given by the court in making [c. 1272] its declaration of incompatibility or the purpose of the remedial order. I can only say that in those circumstances the Government would obviously think again.

Section 10(1)(a)

Background: problem of remedial orders where appeal lies against declaration of incompatability

House of Lords, Committee Stage

Official Report, House of Lords, 27 November 1997, vol. 583, col. 1100

The Parliamentary Under-Secretary of State, Home Office (Lord Williams of Mostyn): . . . [W]hat if the relevant Minister seeks to initiate the fast-track procedure in response to a declarator or declaration of incompatibility, only to find that the declaring court is overturned or varied on appeal? We believe that such a situation would be most unlikely to arise in practice because it is a discretion that the Minister has to introduce the fast-track procedure. I would find it hard to envisage circumstances in which the Government would want to exercise the power conferred by Clause 10 before the appeal process had been concluded.

Nevertheless, I recognise the concern behind the amendment. Perhaps I ought to take the matter away, consider whether a limitation of the kind suggested should be made on the face of the Bill—but I am bound to say that, as at present advised, it may not be—and also consider whether the present drafting might need a little attention.

Requirement of 'compelling reasons' strikes the right balance

House of Commons, Report Stage

Official Report, House of Commons, 21 October 1998, vol. 317, col. 1330

The Parliamentary Under-Secretary of State for the Home

Department (Mr. Mike O'Brien): ... The requirement for compelling reasons in clause 10(2) is itself a response to concern expressed here and in another place about the remedial order provisions. It is there to make it absolutely clear that a remedial order is not a routine response in preference to fresh primary legislation. We would not want to go further ... and limit "compelling reasons" to the ... categories mentioned. There may be other circumstances that constitute compelling reasons sufficient to justify a remedial order: for example, a decision of the higher courts in relation to basic provisions of criminal procedure affecting the way in which, perhaps, all criminal cases must be handled. An example is a provision that might invalidate a crucial part of the codes of practice under the Police and Criminal Evidence Act 1984, or provisions relating to the detention of suspects. Therefore, there are a number of issues where we would want to proceed with care. We also might need to respond very quickly simply to avoid the criminal justice system in such cases either collapsing or not being able to deliver justice and proper convictions.

"Compelling" is a strong word. We see no need to define it by reference to particular categories. In both the outstanding cases that the hon. and learned Member for Harborough has put to me, our view is likely to be that those would not create the compelling reasons that would justify a remedial order. In any event, on those issues—electoral law and chastising children—everyone would expect primary legislation rather than a remedial order. I hope that that gives some reassurance.

I noted that the hon. and learned Member for Harborough said that this is, in a sense, a probing amendment. He has asked me some clear questions about how we would perceive those two cases and I hope that those are clear answers. We do not expect that those will be the sort of issues in which remedial orders would be likely. [c. 1331]

[. . .][A] document must be laid before Parliament containing certain information. It must explain the incompatibility that the remedial order or draft remedial order seeks to remove, and it must state the reasons for proceeding under Clause 10 and for making an order in the terms in which it is made.

Therefore, the document is bound to explain why the Government believe that there are compelling reasons for making a remedial order and what those are. The document must be laid before Parliament and will be available for the debate in each House on the motion for affirmative resolution, which will be necessary before a draft remedial order

can be made, or in order for an urgent remedial order to continue in existence . . .
[. . .]

It would be open to the Government to take no action in response to a declaration of incompatibility—that issue has already been rehearsed during this afternoon's debates—but, where a declaration is made, a Government who are committed to promoting human rights, as we are, will want to do something about the law in question. It is possible for primary legislation to be introduced and passed quickly, but the pressures on the timetable can make it very difficult to find a slot.

The power to make a remedial order is there for cases where there is a very good reason to amend the law following a declaration of incompatibility or a finding by the Strasbourg court, but no suitable legislative vehicle is available. Where a remedial order is made or proposed, we accepted that the procedures for parliamentary scrutiny needed to be strengthened. That is why the requirement to provide a document containing all the relevant information and a statement providing a summary of any representations on an order or draft order was added to schedule 2 in Committee.

We think that we have the balance right here. Clause 10 and schedule 2 enable Parliament to fulfil its responsibilities and ensure that onerous powers are not given to the Government. Our proposals safeguard parliamentary procedures and sovereignty, ensure proper supervision of our laws and ensure that we can begin to get the ability both to enforce human rights law and to create a human rights culture. They also ensure that we can do it in the context of not having to worry that, if something is decided by the Strasbourg court or by our courts that creates an incompatibility, we do not have a mechanism to deal with it in the quick and efficient way that may be necessary.

Section 10(6)

Meaning of Section 10(6)

House of Lords, Report Stage
Official Report, House of Lords, 29 January 1998, vol. 585, col. 396
The Parliamentary Under-Secretary of State, Home Office (Lord Williams of Mostyn): . . . As it was indicated in Committee, Clause 10 would enable a Minister of the Crown to make a remedial order

amending a measure of the General Synod or of its predecessor, the Church Assembly, following a declaration of incompatibility. The Minister of the Crown could do that without any reference to the General Synod.

The Church of England, perfectly properly, pointed out that that would sit uneasily with our present arrangements whereby a Church measure can only be approved or disapproved by Parliament in its entirety—in other words, with no opportunity for amendment. To provide for amendment of a Church measure by a Minister, even in response to the serious situation of a declaration of incompatibility, would obviously have significant implications for the Church. Neither do we feel that it would be appropriate for a Minister of the Crown to be in that situation. It would not tie appropriately with our present relations between Church and state.

We came to the conclusion that if an amendment to Church measures were required to remove a Convention incompatibility, it is better done by the Church itself rather than by the exercise of the order-making power by a Minister of the Crown. I express the Government's confident hope that if there were a court declaration of Convention incompatibility, then the General Synod would speedily consider whether the measure should be amended. We do not believe that the Church of England would be found inactive if its legislation were found to be in breach of human rights.

Application to Court findings pre-dating coming into force of Section 10 – Implicit that remedial order powers will not apply pre-existing court decisions

House of Lords, Committee Stage

Official Report, House of Lords, 27 November 1997, vol. 583, col. 1104

The Parliamentary Under-Secretary of State, Home Office (Lord Williams of Mostyn): . . . [W]e think that it is implicit that the power to make a remedial order does not extend to cases where the Court finding pre-dates the coming into force of Clause 10. Clause 22 makes express provision for the circumstances in which another provision of the Bill—Clause 7(1)(b)—may apply to acts committed before it comes into force, and that implies that, in the absence of express provision to the contrary, the Bill should not have retrospective effect. However, as we said at the outset of our deliberations on this Bill, we are eager to see whether it can be improved consistent with the scheme of the Bill, as the noble and learned Lord the Lord Chancellor said. I am perfectly content to consider before the next stage whether this measure should be made clear on the face of the Bill.

SECTION 11: SAFEGUARD FOR EXISTING HUMAN RIGHTS

Editors' note - in the Bill as originally published what is now section 11 of the Human Rights Act 1998 appeared as Clause 13. In an attempt to minimise confusion, where the debate referred to Clause 13, this text will report it as Clause [11].

11. A person's reliance on a Convention right does not restrict-

(a) any other right or freedom conferred on him by or under any law having effect in any part of the United Kingdom; or
(b) his right to make any claim or bring any proceedings which he could make or bring apart from sections 7 to 9.

Effect of Section 11

House of Commons, Second Reading

Second Reading, House of Commons, 16 February 1998, vol. 307, col. 738

The Secretary of State for the Home Department (Mr. Jack Straw): ... Clause [11] confirms that a person's reliance on a Convention right does not restrict any other right or freedom that he enjoys under United Kingdom law.

House of Lords, Committee Stage

Official Report, House of Lords, 18 November 1997, vol. 583, col. 509

Lord Lester of Herne Hill: ... I remain in the dark about exactly what is intended. Clause [11] provides that a person may rely on a Convention right in proceedings other than a challenge to the act of a public authority.

Clause 1 informs us that the Convention rights mean the rights set out in Articles 2 to 12 and 14 of the Convention, and so on. Under Clause [11], in an appropriate dispute involving, let us say, libel law where someone seeks to rely on Article 10 of the Convention as a guarantee of the right to free speech, in arguing that there was proper scope for the law of defamation, as I read the Bill, the person may rely on

Clause [11], as he can indirectly at present and as was done in the Derbyshire libel case a few years ago.

If I am right on that point, it seems to me that the Convention rights are to that extent part of our domestic law and can be relied upon, as Clause [11] states. Will the noble and learned Lord the Lord Chancellor say [c. 510] whether I am right on that; or is the intention to cut down the existing position where, for example, common law as developed in the courts matches the Convention rights and under this Bill treats the Convention rights as part of our law?

The Lord Chancellor (Lord Irvine of Lairg): I shall consider what the noble Lord said. The position appears to me to be quite straightforward. It may be more complicated; I shall reflect upon it.

As I understand it, Clause [11] means only that a person may rely on the Convention right in the way in which the Bill provides that individuals may rely upon Convention rights, but his Convention rights are, as it were, a floor of rights; and if there are different or superior rights or freedoms conferred on him by or under any law having effect in the United Kingdom, this is a Bill which only gives and does not take away.

House of Lords, Committee Stage

Official Report, House of Lords, 27 November 1997, vol. 583, col. 1157

The Lord Chancellor (Lord Irvine of Lairg): Clause [11](1) provides:

> "A person may rely on a Convention right without prejudice to any other right or freedom conferred on him by or under any law having effect in any part of the United Kingdom".

The purpose of that provision is to ensure that the Bill gives but does not take away. A person may rely on a Convention right, but he may also rely on any other right or freedoms he enjoys under the law.

Clause [11](1) relates back to Clause 7(1)(b) which provides:

> "A person who claims that a public authority has acted ... in a way which is made unlawful by section 6(1) may—
>
> (a) bring proceedings against the authority under this Act in the appropriate court or tribunal, or
>
> (b) rely on the Convention right or rights ... in any legal proceedings".

So a person can rely on the Convention rights concerned in any legal proceedings. Next of course, any court or tribunal must take into account the judgments, decisions, declarations, or advisory opinions of the European Court of Human Rights because Clause 2(1) so provides. It appears to me that it is for the court in question, and for individual judicial decision in any particular case, to decide when the point, based on Convention law, is to be adjudicated upon. It is a matter to decide in its discretion whether the argument that is put before it, based on the Convention, is one upon which it should decide, as, for example, a preliminary issue at the outset.

House of Lords, Report Stage

Official Report, House of Lords, 29 January 1998, vol. 585, col. 410

The Parliamentary Under-Secretary of State, Home Office (Lord Williams of Mostyn): . . . My Lords, this amendment[9] is designed to clarify the purpose of Clause [11] and to remove any possible misunderstanding. Clause [11] as presently drafted, and as it would be in this new clause, is simply to provide a saving for other human rights. It is there to ensure that if a person has existing rights, nothing in this Bill shall detract from them in any way. We believe that this amendment brings that out more clearly than the current formulation. That, briefly, is the purpose of the amendment. [c. 411] There are, of course, two kinds of relationship created in the Bill between Convention and domestic law: the interpretive principle in Clauses 3 to 5, and the right to rely on Convention rights against a public authority in Clauses 6 to 9. We do not wish to have any misunderstanding. We believe that the new formulation makes the position, as was intended, rather plainer. [. . .]

Lord Lester of Herne Hill: My Lords, I greatly welcome the amendment. I do so because it makes clear that which is already implicit in the Bill—namely, that the European Convention contains a floor of minimum rights guaranteed under international law, but does not create a ceiling. Therefore, if Parliament chooses to go further or if the common law goes further in protecting our basic rights and freedoms, which are

---

[9] Introducing the wording:

Safeguard for existing human rights

A person's reliance on a Convention right does not restrict—
(a) any other right or freedom conferred on him by or under any law having effect in any part of the United Kingdom, or
(b) his right to make any claim or bring any proceedings which he could make or bring apart from Sections 7 to 9..

inherent in us as citizens and human beings, the Convention and the Bill are not to restrict that. The fact that that is a minimum and not a maximum is made clear in the Convention itself. It does not mean that there will never be conflict and difficult questions to be resolved as a result of people arguing that, say, the Race Relations Act is an infringement of some basic right in the Convention, or other such points. It is important that one does not concentrate only upon the Convention as a guarantee of rights. As the amendment makes clear, the common law will continue to develop in a creative way and no doubt the Convention will be used, as the Bill makes clear, in the course of developing the common law.

SECTION 12: FREEDOM OF EXPRESSION

For the full debate which led to the inclusion of this section, see pages 217–230 below concerning Articles 8 and 10.

12. - (1) This section applies if a court is considering whether to grant any relief which, if granted, might affect the exercise of the Convention right to freedom of expression.

(2) If the person against whom the application for relief is made ("the respondent") is neither present nor represented, no such relief is to be granted unless the court is satisfied-

(a) that the applicant has taken all practicable steps to notify the respondent; or

(b) that there are compelling reasons why the respondent should not be notified.

(3) No such relief is to be granted so as to restrain publication before trial unless the court is satisfied that the applicant is likely to establish that publication should not be allowed.

(4) The court must have particular regard to the importance of the Convention right to freedom of expression and, where the proceedings relate to material which the respondent claims, or which appears to the court, to be journalistic, literary or artistic material (or to conduct connected with such material), to-

(a) the extent to which-

(i) the material has, or is about to, become available to the public; or

(ii) it is, or would be, in the public interest for the material to be published;

(b) any relevant privacy code.

(5) In this section-

"court" includes a tribunal; and

"relief" includes any remedy or order (other than in criminal proceedings).

Background

House of Commons, Committee Stage

Official Report, House of Commons, 17 June 1998, vol. 314, col. 406

The Secretary of State for the Home Department (Mr. Jack Straw): ... Let me now deal briefly with the issue of the press. It is an important issue, but we shall have an opportunity to return to it when we debate the result of the consultations and considerations on the question of protection of press freedoms—which, as I told the House on 16 February, I have undertaken with Lord Wakeham and, through him, the Press Complaints Commission. On 16 February, I told the House:

> "Lord Williams and I have been involved in detailed discussions with Lord Wakeham. In particular, we have considered whether safeguards similar in framework to those set out in Clause 31 of the Data Protection Bill"—

which was satisfactory to all parties—

> "could be brought into this Bill, without compromising its essential purpose.
> I am pleased to tell the House that these discussions have borne fruit, and we have reached an understanding with Lord Wakeham . . . on a framework for amendments to the Bill".

I then said:

> "The precise wording of the amendments has not yet been agreed".—[*Official Report*, 16 February 1998; Vol. 306, c. 776-77.]

They will be brought before the House in due course.

There has been a series of discussions with Lord Wakeham and, through him, those whom he represents. They have almost reached a satisfactory conclusion. I shall table those amendments and, as the usual channels are well aware, they will be properly debated. It will ultimately be a matter for the courts, but our considered view is that the Press Complaints Commission undertakes public functions but the press does not, which is crucial. We shall seek in the amendments to give the press further protection and reassurance.

Sir Norman Fowler: Where does that leave broadcasting organisations? Will the treatment that is applied to the press be extended to broadcasting organisations, so that they work in the same way and are subject to the same rules as the press?

Mr. Straw: The amendment as currently drafted does not mention the Press Complaints Commission specifically. It refers to a privacy code. The protection would be available to any broadcaster or publisher. For example, if someone feared that he was about to be exposed, he may seek an interlocutory action. In such a case, broadcasters would be treated similarly, but not the same, because they are not in the same position as the press. The BBC has its own charter and a separate code, which is different from that of the PCC. We are not working on an ad hominem basis in respect of the Press Complaints Commission code. [. . .][c. 415]

Sir Norman Fowler: [. . .] Does it mean that, for all media organisations, freedom of expression and the right to report takes precedence over some rights of privacy?

Mr. Straw: . . . This is not a consequence merely of the incorporation of the European Convention: having signed up to it, we cannot assert, as a contracting party, that one part of it wholly trumps another part . . . . [T]he whole point about the Convention is that it balances one article with another. What we did in respect of the Churches was to suggest to the courts that they pay particular regard to freedom of religion. That is the essence of what we are seeking to do for the press: we want to provide important procedural safeguards.

The press are most anxious about the procedural safeguards. I understand and share their concern. Someone may be worried, not that an untruth will be told, which would lead to an action for defamation, but that the truth will be told about them. The press are concerned that that person will be able to prevent that truth from being told about them by obtaining an interlocutory injunction. That shows the complexity and intellectual challenge of the law of privacy. We are entitled to keep truths about us private, but the law of privacy is complex. The law of defamation is about preventing the press or anyone else from uttering untruths or punishing them for doing so and forcing them to correct the untruth.

Mr. Garnier: It is not to punish them.

Mr. Straw: Sometimes exemplary damages are awarded as compensation for an untruth, and it has to be shown publicly that it is untrue. [. . .] The problem with privacy law is that it does not deal with the publication or the unearthing of an untruth, but with the publication or unearthing of a truth. The difficulty is that once a truth has been told, it cannot be untold, unlike an untruth. That is the problem with which we have been wrestling.

Effect of section 12
House of Commons, Committee Stage
Official Report, 2 July 1998, vol. 314, col. 535

The Secretary of State for the Home Department (Mr. Jack Straw): . . . Subsection (1) provides for the new clause to apply in any case where a court is considering granting relief—for example, an injunction restraining a threatened breach of confidence; but it could be any relief apart from that [c. 536] relating to criminal proceedings—which might affect the exercise of the Article 10 right to freedom of expression. It applies to the press, broadcasters or anyone whose right to freedom of expression might be affected. It is not limited to cases to which a public authority is a party. We have taken the opportunity to enhance press freedom in a wider way than would arise simply from the incorporation of the Convention into our domestic law.

Subsection (2) provides that no relief is to be granted if the person against whom it is sought—the respondent—is not present or represented, unless the applicant has taken all practicable steps to notify the respondent or there are compelling reasons why the respondent should not be notified. The courts are well able to deal with the first limb of that exception relating to whether all practical steps have been taken to notify the respondent, and in the case of broadcasting authorities and the press, rarely would an applicant not be able to serve notice of the proceedings on the respondent.

The latter circumstance—compelling reasons—might arise in a case raising issues of national security where the mere knowledge that an injunction was being sought might cause the respondent to publish the material immediately. We do not anticipate that that limb would be used often. In the past, such applications have been rare, but there has been at least one recent case involving the Ministry of Defence.

As I made clear on Second Reading, the provision is intended overall to ensure that ex parte injunctions are granted only in exceptional circumstances. Even where both parties are represented, we expect that injunctions will continue to be rare, as they are at present.

Subsection (3) provides that no relief is to be granted to restrain publication pending a full trial of the issues unless the court is satisfied that the applicant is likely to succeed at trial. Among concerns expressed about the Bill's possible impact on freedom of the press, there was concern that interim injunctions—known in the trade as Friday night injunctions, as the hon. and learned Member for Harborough (Mr. Garnier) will confirm; I do not doubt that he has been present in the courts on many Friday nights earning an honest crust—might be granted simply to preserve the status quo, with a view to a full hearing of the application later. However, by that time the story that was to be published might no longer be newsworthy. As I said earlier, time and again the Convention jurisprudence reinforces the freedom of the press against, for example, the assertion of rights under Article 8. One example of that is part of the judgment of the European Court of Human Rights in the 1991 "Spycatcher" case. Dealing with the issue of interlocutory relief, the court said:

> "news is a perishable commodity and to delay its publication for even a short period may well deprive it of all its value and interest."

Given that, we believe that the courts should consider the merits of an application when it is made and should not grant an interim injunction simply to preserve the status quo ante between the parties.
[. . .] [c. 538]

Subsection (4) requires the court to have particular regard to the importance of the Article 10 right to freedom of expression. Where the proceedings concern journalistic, literary or artistic material, the court must also have particular regard to the extent to which the material has or is about to become available to the public—in other words, a question of prior publication—and the extent to which publication would be in the public interest. If the court and the parties to the proceedings know that a story will shortly be published anyway, for example, in another country or on the internet, that must affect the decision whether it is appropriate to restrain publication by the print or broadcast media in this country.

Under subsection (4), the court must also have particular regard to any relevant privacy code. Depending on the circumstances, that could be the newspaper industry code of practice operated by the Press Complaints Commission, the Broadcasting Standards Commission code, the Independent Television Commission code, or a broadcaster's internal code such as that operated by the BBC. The fact that a newspaper has complied with the terms of the code operated by the [c. 539] PCC—or conversely, that it has breached the code—is one of the factors that we believe the courts should take into account in considering whether to grant relief.

Government believe that section 12 will protect publishers from legalised intimidation

House of Commons, Committee Stage

Official Report, 2 July 1998, vol. 314, col. 537

Mr. Peter Bottomley (Worthing, West): I support the Home Secretary in what he is saying, but can he confirm that the provision will deal with the Maxwell abuse, where someone who has—or seems to have—a lot of money can intimidate others by the threat of interlocutory applications? Secondly, can he confirm that if there is a way for a potential plaintiff to serve notice on a publisher that what he is about to publish is untrue or in part untrue, it will be taken into account in post-publication action?

The Secretary of State for the Home Department (Mr. Jack Straw): On the hon. Gentleman's first point about Maxwell intimidation, we believe that the new clause would protect a respondent potential publisher from what amounts to legal or legalised intimidation. We have already discussed the difficulty of getting interlocutory relief. It will be very difficult to get it unless the applicant can satisfy the court that the applicant is likely to establish that publication should not be allowed. That is a much higher test than that there should simply be a prima facie case to get the matter into court.

Definition of public interest

House of Commons, Committee Stage

Official Report, House of Commons, 2 July 1998, vol. 314, col. 539

Mr. Dominic Grieve (Beaconsfield): I am sorry to take the right hon. Gentleman back slightly, but would he care to amplify on the definition of "the public interest", which is a critical phrase in subsection (4)(a)(ii) of the new clause?

The Secretary of State for the Home Department (Mr. Jack Straw): ...
The courts are well versed in making judgments about the balance between a private interest of an applicant before them and the wider public interest. That is inherent in any case in a clash between Article 10 and Article 8. It is also inherent in the way in which the courts until now have dealt with many issues surrounding proceedings for defamation. The European Convention and the European Court of Human Rights have devoted quite a lot of time and effort to developing the concept of the public interest. Without being too tautologous, one of the points of the public interest is, to quote the words of the Strasbourg court in Handyside *v.* the United Kingdom in 1976, that

> "freedom of expression constitutes one of the essential foundations of a democratic society, one of the basic conditions for its progress, and for the development of every man"—

and these days, I have no doubt, every woman. That is a brief sketch of a subject on which I have every confidence in the courts' ability to make good judgments in particular cases.
[...]

Mr. Martin Linton (Battersea): While my right hon. Friend is still on the subject of subsection (4)(a)(i), I should be grateful if he clarified the exact meaning of the material that is or is about to become available to the public; and whether that word "public" would have a geographical limitation. This is a "Spycatcher" clause and the argument used in the "Spycatcher" case was that the material was available to the public in any country other than the United Kingdom. In the only similar case—the one involving my right hon. Friend, to which he referred—the argument used was that the material was available to newspaper readers in Scotland. However, if the term "public" was interpreted in a very narrow way, such arguments might fail.

Mr. Straw: There is no direct qualification to the word "public" in the new clause. Ultimately, it would be a matter for the courts to decide, based on common sense and proportionality. The fact that the information was available across the globe in very narrow circumstances would not be weighed in the balance. The fact that, in the situation in which I was involved at Christmas, the information was fully public in newspapers in Scotland and, by virtue of that fact, available in newspapers on sale at every London railway terminus and airport, made the notion of protection by an injunction issued in courts covering only England and Wales rather risible. The courts would be bound to take such facts into account. As I said earlier, they would also take into account the extent to which the information was available in another country or on the internet, but in each case, the courts would have to apply balance and proportionality.

House of Commons, Committee Stage
Official Report, House of Commons, 2 July 1998, vol. 314, col. 562

The Parliamentary Under-Secretary of State for the Home Department (Mr. Mike O'Brien): . . . I am perhaps tempting further interventions by going into the issue of what the public interest is, but the basic question is whether the public should have particular information. For example, information might have an effect on proper political discourse, or a matter of public policy. It might also affect individual behaviour. For example, information about BSE might have affected decisions on whether to eat beef. Those are areas in which there is a proper public interest in the press revealing information. The judge would have to ask the same question put by the hon. and learned Member for Harborough: is a matter only of interest to the public, or is it a matter of public interest? There should be some good reason why the public should know. [c. 563] It is arguable whether there should be a good reason for the public not to know something. That takes us into realms of philosophy and jurisprudence, and I do not want to go too far into them. However, judges will debate that matter among themselves as they reach their decisions.

Subsection (4): 'conduct connected with such material'

House of Commons, Committee Stage
Official Report, House of Commons, 2 July 1998, vol. 314, col. 539

The Secretary of State for the Home Department (Mr. Jack Straw): . . . The reference in the new clause to

> "conduct connected with such material"

is intended for cases where journalistic inquiries suggest the presence of a story, but no actual material yet exists—perhaps because the story has not yet been written.

Subsection (5)

House of Commons, Committee Stage

Official Report, House of Commons, 2 July 1998, vol. 314, col. 539

The Secretary of State for the Home Department (Mr. Jack Straw): . . . Subsection (5) provides that references to a court include references to a tribunal, and that references to relief include references to any remedy or order, other than in criminal proceedings. We drafted the amendment with civil, rather than criminal, proceedings against the media in mind. Without such an exclusion, judges wanting to impose reporting restrictions in a criminal trial would, for example, have to consider any relevant privacy code, although plainly it would not be appropriate in that context.

Nevertheless, as public authorities, the criminal courts will of course, in the same way as other courts, be required not to act in a way that is incompatible with Articles 8 and 10 and other Convention rights. The special provision that we are making in new Clause 13 does not therefore exempt criminal courts from the general obligations imposed by other provisions of the Bill. However, had we included criminal proceedings under new Clause 13, we would have made the running of criminal trials very complicated.

Newspapers cannot be proceeded against directly under the Act

House of Commons, Committee Stage

Official Report, House of Commons, 2 July 1998, vol. 314, col. 561

The Parliamentary Under-Secretary of State for the Home Department (Mr. Mike O'Brien): . . . An important point that has, to some extent, been overlooked is that newspapers will not be public authorities and could not be proceeded against directly under the Bill, but an Article 8 point could be raised in proceedings for harassment or a libel action, for example.

Concerning the example of the expenditure at the tuck shop of an inmate of a special hospital, there are arguments either way about whether publication should be considered to be in the public interest, and the courts would have to decide the case on its merits. The new clause simply requires them to have regard to whether publication would be in the public interest.

SECTION 13: FREEDOM OF THOUGHT, CONSCIENCE AND RELIGION

Following concerns about the impact of the Bill on religious organisations, the following section was added to the Bill.

13. - (1) If a court's determination of any question arising under this Act might affect the exercise by a religious organisation (itself or its members collectively) of the Convention right to freedom of thought, conscience and religion, it must have particular regard to the importance of that right.

(2) In this section "court" includes a tribunal.

Effect of, meaning of and motivation behind section 13

House of Commons, Committee Stage

Official Report, House of Commons, 20 May 1998, vol. 312, col. 1020

The Secretary of State for the Home Department (Mr. Jack Straw): ... [Clause 13] would come into play in any case in which a court's determination of any question arising out of the Bill might affect the exercise by a religious organisation of the Convention right of freedom of thought, conscience and religion. In such a case, it provides for the court to have particular regard—not [c. **1021**] just to have regard, going back to the earlier debate, but to have particular regard—to the importance of that right. Its purpose is not to exempt Churches and other religious organisations from the scope of the Bill—they have not sought that—any more than from that of the Convention. It is to reassure them against the Bill being used to intrude upon genuinely religious beliefs or practices based on their beliefs. I emphasise the word "practices", as well as "beliefs".

There is ample reassurance available on this point from Convention jurisprudence. Apart from stating the importance of the courts having due regard to Article 9, [Clause 13] is designed to bring out the point that Article 9 rights attach not only to individuals but to the Churches. The idea that Convention rights typically attach only to individuals and not the Churches caused considerable anxiety. I understood that, and that is why the new clause has been phrased so that the Churches have its protection as well as individuals.

There is Convention jurisprudence to the effect that a Church body or other association with religious objectives is capable of possessing and exercising the rights in Article 9 as a representative of its members. The new clause will emphasise that point to our courts. The intention is to focus the courts' attention in any proceedings on the view generally held by the Church in question, and on its interest in protecting the integrity of the common faith of its members against attack, whether by outsiders or by individual dissidents. That is a significant protection.

The Committee will note that the new clause refers to the exercise of the right to freedom of thought, conscience and religion by a "religious organisation", but leaves that expression undefined. Some hon. Members may wonder why we describe Churches in that way. The answer is partly that no definition is readily available, at home or in Strasbourg.

We considered the issue with great care, and took the advice of parliamentary counsel. I have already referred to the difficulty arising from this point in the amendments made in another place in discriminating between some religions and others. We are seeking to reflect precisely the Strasbourg case law. The Convention institutions have not offered a definition, but we are confident that the term "religious organisation" is recognisable in terms of the Convention.
[. . .] [c. 1022]

One of the advantages of Government [Clause 13] is that it is flexible enough to cover cases involving religious charities where Church issues form a backdrop to the case. I say this because it applies to a court's determination of any question arising under the Human Rights Bill that might affect the exercise by a religious organisation of the rights guaranteed by Article 9. It is therefore not tied to circumstances in which a religious organisation is directly involved, as a body, in the court proceedings.

If a case is brought against a charity, and the charity can show that what it is doing is to maintain and practise the religious beliefs which it shares with its parent Church, we consider that [clause 13] would come into play so as to ensure that due consideration was given to those beliefs.
[. . .]

The Government's new clause will not provide absolute protection for Churches or other religious organisations as against any claim that might possibly be made against them. [...]
We could not possibly do that without violating the Convention or undermining the objects of the Bill. There has never been any dubiety about that, but the new clause will send a clear signal to the courts that they must pay due regard to the rights guaranteed by Article 9, including, where relevant, the right of a Church to act in accordance with religious belief.
[...] [c. 1023]

Mr. Maclennan: For the avoidance of doubt, I want to ask the Home Secretary about the wording of [Clause 13], which I welcome, but which clearly refers in its own language to the provisions of Article 9. I assume that he does not seek to give a priori priority to Article 9 over other provisions of the Convention that are equally applicable, and would also have to be considered by the court if issues touched by the new clause were raised.

Mr. Straw: The difficulty with the amendments that are now contained in the Bill is that they give absolute precedence to Article 9 over all other Convention rights. It is our judgment, and I do not think that there is a great deal of argument about it, that that would put the Bill outwith the Convention. [Clause 13] seeks to do exactly what it says. The language is straightforward. It gives particular regard to the importance of Article 9 rights, but it applies, as I have explained, to the exercise of those rights by a religious organisation or its members collectively. That is an important protection in addition to the Churches as bodies.

Intention to protect Article 9 rights of religious organisations but placing them beyond the Convention would put the Act in breach of it – European Court of Human Rights jurisprudence provides reassurance – section goes as far as possible consistent with the Convention – extent to which churches are public authorities

House of Commons, Report Stage
Official Report, House of Commons, 21 October 1998, vol. 317, col. 1240
The Secretary of State for the Home Department (Mr. Straw): . . .

The matter was debated at considerable length on 20 May[10] when I spoke for almost 40 minutes. Let me reassure the Whips that I do not intend to do so this evening. However, I hope that the hon. Gentleman will take as read some of the arguments that I made on that occasion.

We never had the least intention of bringing forward a Bill that threatened religious freedom. [. . .] We did not believe that the Bill as originally drafted would have threatened religious freedom. However, concerns were expressed in the other place and here on the subject. [. . .] I live in hope that there may be a broad consensus behind the Bill, so I thought it very important not to insist that the Bill as originally drafted represented the last word and the best judgment, but to take action on any serious concerns raised about the drafting. We did that for the Churches.

For reasons that I explained at considerable length, we were not able to accept the amendments passed in the other place earlier in the year. We came forward with a new clause, which now stands as Clause 13 . . . It says:

> "If a court's determination of any question arising under this Act might affect the exercise by a religious organisation (itself or its members collectively) of the Convention right to freedom of thought, conscience and religion, it must have particular regard to the importance of that right."

The hon. Member for Hertsmere made a point about the relative strength of the clause. Similarly worded clauses often say that a court "may" have regard to a particular factor. We have gone as far as we can to make the provision as strong as possible, saying not that the court may have regard, but that

> "it must have particular regard to the importance of that right."

We believe that that is a strong provision.

The amendment would replace those words with an alternative provision that would mean that when such an issue arose, the court would not be able to make a determination that might infringe the Article 9 right. As the hon. Gentleman has explained, the intention of the amendment is to protect the Article 9 rights of religious organisations, even if other parties to the proceedings are asserting different and

---

[10] *Official Report*, House of Commons, 20 May 1998, vol. 312, col. 1014ff

competing Convention rights, such as the right to respect for private and family life under Article 8 or the right to freedom of expression under Article 10.

The hon. Gentleman has asked me to explain why we are not willing to accept the amendment. If it had the effect that I have described—we believe that it would because of how the words are used—it would be contrary to the Convention.

Mr. Clappison: Before the Home Secretary comes to the next stage of his argument, does he accept that under [c. 1341] the Bill, it will be possible for a Church or religious organisation to be found in breach of the Convention, but that the amendment would prevent that by giving them a guaranteed defence?

Mr. Straw: The answer is yes. The hon. Gentleman is seeking to place the Churches beyond the Convention, so that even if they were exercising the functions of a public authority and were plainly in breach of the Convention, they could not be found to be in breach. If we accepted the amendment, the Act would be in breach of the Convention. Instead of matters being resolved here, they would go off to Strasbourg and the Court would eventually declare that part of the Act in breach of the Convention. I understand the purpose behind the amendment, but it would be self-defeating.

The right to freedom of thought, conscience and religion guaranteed by Article 9.1 is not absolute. It is important to make that clear. Under Article 9.2, it may be subject to such limitations as are prescribed by law and are necessary in a democratic society, in the interests of various factors, including the protection of rights and freedoms of others. In that respect, Article 9 is similar to Articles 8, 10 and 11. The court must weigh the competing interests and come to a decision. It is not open to a court to give automatic priority in all cases to one Convention right over another.

Having said that, I want to reassure the Opposition on two points. The hon. Gentleman said that a Church will act as a public authority not just when standing in place of the state, but when it carries out functions of a public nature. That is not correct. To the extent that the second part of what he said was accurate, he was simply tautologically making the same point as the first. Churches will be subject to the Act only when standing in the stead of the state and exercising functions of a public nature. I explained that at considerable length at column 1015 of the *Official Report* of 20 May. I should also like to reassure the hon. Gentleman on Strasbourg jurisprudence.

Mr. Clappison: . . . [T]here is nothing in the Bill to say that Churches are public authorities only when they are standing in the place of the state. They are subject to the same definition in Clause 6 as everybody else. They are public authorities when they are carrying out functions of a public nature. [. . .]

Mr. Straw: The Convention exists to protect individuals from abuse by the state or by people standing in the stead of the state. That is the point of the Convention. It is not there to deal with the abuse of rights by bodies acting in a private capacity. That is spelt out in the relevant clause. For the avoidance of doubt, I shall repeat what I said on 20 May about how we think that the Bill will operate in relation to Churches:

> "Much of what the Churches do is, in the legal context and in the context of the European Convention on Human Rights, essentially private in nature . . . For example, the regulation of divine worship, [c. 1342] the administration of the sacrament, admission to Church membership or to the priesthood and decisions of parochial church councils about the running of the parish church are, in our judgment, all private matters.
>
> In such matters, Churches will not be public authorities; the requirement to comply with Convention rights will not bite on them. We do not believe that, for example, the Church of England, the Church of Scotland or the Roman Catholic Church, as bodies, would be public authorities under the Bill. I was asked to clarify that by many people, not least the Cardinal Archbishop.
>
> On the occasions when Churches stand in place of the state, Convention rights are relevant to what they do. The two most obvious examples relate to marriages and to the provision of education in Church schools."—[*Official Report*, 20 May 1998; Vol. 312, c. 1015.]

Having dealt with that, I should like to reassure the hon. Gentleman on his second point. There is good Strasbourg case law to suggest that, in practice, Article 9 rights are afforded considerable protection from attack. I should like to quote from page 359 of the text book "Law of the European Convention on Human Rights" by Harris, O'Boyle and Warbrick. It states:

> "Where there is a conflict between protected rights, the judgment of the Court in Otto-Preminger-Institut *v*. Austria speaks in favour of the

strong regard to be had for religious beliefs (and therefore, Article 9 rights) in deciding priority between the competing rights. In that case, the state had interfered with the applicants' Article 10 right to freedom of expression by seizing and ordering forfeit of a film found likely to offend the religious feelings of the Catholics who constituted the large majority of people in the region where the applicant proposed to show it. The Court upheld the interferences with the applicant's right as being necessary for the protection of 'the [religious] rights and freedoms of others.' In confirming that the interference had a legitimate aim, the Court said: '. . . the manner in which religious beliefs and doctrines are opposed or denied is a matter which may engage the responsibility of the state, notably its responsibility to ensure the peaceful enjoyment of the right guaranteed under Article 9 to the holders of those beliefs and doctrines'".

The passage went on:

"—in the context of religious opinions and beliefs—may legitimately be included an obligation [on individuals] to avoid as far as possible expressions which are gratuitously offensive to others".

The authors conclude:

"This is a strong affirmation of the power and even the duty of states to protect manifestations of religious belief."

[. . .]

On the whole, the best guide to the future—indeed, in many ways the only guide—is the past. The Court's record provides substantial reassurance. So should the history of Europe, which was written in blood until 1945. Much of that blood was spilt in the alleged cause of religious belief and religious conflict. Many of the states of Europe which now form the core of the European Union and the Council of Europe have had peacefully to accommodate conflict between Churches—between the Lutheran Church and the Catholic Church in Germany and the Catholic and other Protestant Churches in other states—just as we have in this country, and just as we at [c. 1343] long last are seeking to do in the north of Ireland. Against that background, our courts and the European Court in Strasbourg have been and will continue to be alive to the need to respect the exercise of religious freedom. They have clearly done so in the jurisprudence that has been laid down in Strasbourg.

The provisions of Clause 13, which we introduced in May, require the Court to have particular regard to the importance of the right to freedom of thought, conscience and religion. That is as far—honestly—as we think that we can go consistent with the Convention. We believe that that has also been recognised by the Churches.

I do not argue with the hon. Member for Hertsmere for seeking to revisit the issue, although the debate on the subject in Committee on 20 May followed the most intense period of discussion that I have had with representatives of the Churches. I was not able to meet their every request, but I can give a flavour of their response by quoting, as I did in Committee, from a letter that I received from Cardinal Archbishop Basil Hume, which said:

> "I have sought the best legal advice and my initial assessment is that the amendment in the form tabled by the Government"—

which now appears in the Bill as Clause 13—

> "may be the best that can be reasonably be achieved to reinforce the protection given by the Convention to the churches and other faiths under Article 9."

I was very grateful to the cardinal archbishop for saying that. I happen to believe that the legal advice that he received is accurate.

Since that debate—this should provide a further reassurance for the hon. Member for Hertsmere—we have received hardly any representations from religious organisations about the potential impact of the Bill on them. We received many beforehand. I understood them, took them on board and went as far as we could with them. It is interesting that, although they have since had five months fully to consider the matter, we have not received representations from them. If they thought that Clause 13 was insufficient or capable of improvement, I am sure that they would have told us so.

Background: Position of the Churches

Much of what churches do 'private in nature' – Convention relevant where Churches 'stand in place of the state' eg. marriages and educational provision – right that people should be able to raise Convention points against Church actions in those areas – Ministers of Religion will not be required to act contrary to their doctrine or belief

House of Commons, Committee Stage
Official Report, House of Commons, 20 May 1998, vol. 312, col. 1015
The Secretary of State for the Home Department (Mr. Jack Straw): ...
[I]t may be helpful if I say how the Government think that the Bill will operate in relation to the Churches. Much of what the Churches do is, in the legal context and in the context of the European Convention on Human Rights, essentially private in nature, and would not be affected by the Bill even as originally drafted. For example, the regulation of divine worship, the administration of the sacrament, admission to Church membership or to the priesthood and decisions of parochial church councils about the running of the parish church are, in our judgment, all private matters.

In such matters, Churches will not be public authorities; the requirement to comply with Convention rights will not bite on them. We do not believe that, for example, the Church of England, the Church of Scotland or the Roman Catholic Church, as bodies, would be public authorities under the Bill. I was asked to clarify that by many people, not least the Cardinal Archbishop.

On the occasions when Churches stand in place of the state, Convention rights are relevant to what they do. The two most obvious examples relate to marriages and to the provision of education in Church schools. In both areas, the Churches are engaged, through the actions of the minister or of the governing body of a school, in an activity which is also carried out by the state, and which, if the Churches were not engaged in it, would be carried out directly by the state.

We think it right in principle—there was no real argument about it on Second Reading—that people should be able to raise Convention points in respect of the actions of the Churches in those areas on the same basis as they will be able to in respect of the actions of other public authorities, however rarely such occasions may arise.

If that were not the case, the situation could arise, for example, in which teachers in most schools were required to comply with Convention rights, but teachers in Church schools, which are wholly or mainly funded by the local education authorities, were not. Abuses of Convention rights in one school would be amenable to correction in the domestic courts, whereas abuses in another school could be dealt with only at Strasbourg.
[. . .]

There was a time when one could get married only in church but, these days, marriage is a matter of civil law—it is the exercise of a public right. The Churches are standing in the stead of the state in arranging the [c. 1016] ceremony of marriage, which is recognised not only in canon law, but in civil law. In that instance, the Church is performing a function not only for itself, but for civil society.

Rev. Martin Smyth (Belfast, South): In the context of education in Northern Ireland, Church schools—which are primarily under the management of Roman Catholic authorities—are not subject to equal rights and fair employment legislation in the appointment of teachers. Is the Home Secretary saying that, under the Bill, those Church schools will be subject to the Convention? Moreover, although I understand that, in society, marriage may now be a civil matter, is the Home Secretary saying that an officiating minister of whatever denomination will have no right of conscience if he believes that a person has come to him for what are, in the Church's view, improper reasons?

Mr. Straw: On the second point, I say entirely the reverse. Of course a minister has a right of conscience—his duty to marry people is, first and foremost, a matter relating to the Church to which he belongs. If he conducts a marriage ceremony, that has an effect not only in canonical law, but in civil law. At that point, as I explained, the minister is exercising powers in the stead of the state.

If the hon. Gentleman will bear with me, I shall explain how we propose in the School Standards and Framework Bill, rather than in this Bill, fully to satisfy the anxieties that have been expressed in the House of Commons and in another place about the right of Church schools of whatever denomination to ensure that those they appoint are those who accept the faith.

Concern was expressed that the Bill would require ministers of religion to do things that were contrary to their doctrine or belief, such as to conduct marriages between same-sex couples or divorced persons. We have never believed that the consequences of applying the Bill to Church representatives in those matters in their capacity as public authorities would be as adverse as has been predicted. Even without the amendments made in another place and the further proposals that are before the Committee today, the Bill provides two kinds of protection against such an occurrence—I make this point to emphasise that we were not careless of the issue before it was raised in the other place.

The first protection is that, under Clause 2, the domestic courts will be required to have regard to the jurisprudence of Convention institutions. Strasbourg case law is clearly to the effect that, under Article 12 of the Convention, the right to marry does not extend to persons of the same biological sex. Moreover, Article 12 does not include the right to marry according to a particular ceremony of one's choice. The availability of a civil marriage is sufficient to meet the requirements of the article.

The second protection is that the courts will be required to give priority to domestic primary legislation over the Convention rights in the event of a conflict that cannot be reconciled by judicial interpretation. Domestic primary legislation specifically provides that same-sex marriages are void, and although Church of England priests have a statutory duty to conduct marriages—the Church of [c. 1017] England is, by law, the established Church—they are specifically granted a discretion to refuse to marry divorced persons.

Miss Ann Widdecombe (Maidstone and The Weald): The Home Secretary has described a situation in which primary law would have precedence over the Convention. If primary law says that same-sex marriages are void, as it does at the moment, that takes priority. However, if primary law were to be changed and same-sex marriages were to become valid, where would that leave Churches in the interpretation of the Convention?

Mr. Straw: We are talking about the application of the Convention. In the domestic jurisdiction of Parliament, it would be open to the House of Commons, if it wanted, to say that same-sex marriages could apply. The right hon. Lady is asking me to speculate whether that would be outwith the Convention.

Miss Widdecombe: My question is straightforward: if our civil law were to say at any stage that same-sex marriages were valid, and the teaching of the Church remained that they were not, where would that leave the Church?

Mr. Straw: I think that I understand the right hon. Lady's point. It would be open to Parliament to say that civil marriages could apply to same-sex couples, but that would palpably not apply to Churches.

There is a parallel with divorced couples. Since we allow divorce, we have to allow divorced people to remarry—well, we do not have to, but we do, and some of us have taken advantage of the facility and have been married more than once; in my experience, it saves living over the brush, as they say in Blackburn—but that applies to civil registrars and does not in any way affect the right of the Church of England to refuse to marry divorced people. The right of any Church, which we intend to strengthen, to refuse to marry divorced people remains protected by the Convention.

Sir Brian Mawhinney (North-West Cambridgeshire): The fundamental problem is the Government's unwillingness to define what constitutes a public authority. I do not want to be aggressive or offensive, but in a sense it does not matter what the Home Secretary says he believes or does not believe, because he has already said that the courts will decide. Given what he is asking the Committee to believe regarding his intention, the simplest way of dealing with the matter would be to write into the Bill the prohibitions to which he referred, to take away any ambiguity and provide clarity. Will he explain to the Committee why he refuses to do that?

Mr. Straw: . . . I am seeking to explain why I do not find the amendments made in another place acceptable. I have sent him a detailed letter and had conversations with him, explaining that I am setting out an alternative that strengthens the law and goes a long way towards meeting the Churches' concerns, as the Cardinal Archbishop and the Archbishop of Canterbury have made clear, and as Baroness Young, who tabled those amendments, was generous enough to say in an article in *The Daily Telegraph*.
[. . .][c. 1018]

There will be occasions—it is the nature of British society—on which various institutions that are private in terms of their legal personality carry out public functions. That includes the Churches in the narrow circumstances that I have described. I would suggest that it also includes the Jockey Club.

Other countries have public bodies to regulate racing; in this country, we do it in a different way. That is how we have always done it, and I know of no proposals to change the system. The Jockey Club is a curious body; it is entirely private, but exercises public functions in some respects, and to those extents, but to no other, it would be regarded as falling within Clause 6.

SECTIONS 14 TO 17: DEROGATIONS, RESERVATIONS, PERIOD FOR WHICH DESIGNATED RESERVATIONS TO HAVE EFFECT, PERIODIC REVIEW OF DESIGNATED RESERVATIONS

These clauses, providing for mechanisms for derogating from and reservations to the Convention aroused little controversy. They were therefore little discussed or explained.

Derogations.

14. - (1) In this Act "designated derogation" means-

(a) the United Kingdom's derogation from Article 5(3) of the Convention; and

(b) any derogation by the United Kingdom from an Article of the Convention, or of any Protocol to the Convention, which is designated for the purposes of this Act in an order made by the Secretary of State.

(2) The derogation referred to in subsection (1)(a) is set out in Part I of Schedule 3.

(3) If a designated derogation is amended or replaced it ceases to be a designated derogation.

(4) But subsection (3) does not prevent the Secretary of State from exercising his power under subsection (1)(b) to make a fresh designation order in respect of the Article concerned.

(5) The Secretary of State must by order make such amendments to Schedule 3 as he considers appropriate to reflect-

(a) any designation order; or
(b) the effect of subsection (3).

(6) A designation order may be made in anticipation of the making by the United Kingdom of a proposed derogation.

Reservations.

15. - (1) In this Act "designated reservation" means-

(a) the United Kingdom's reservation to Article 2 of the First

Protocol to the Convention; and

(b) any other reservation by the United Kingdom to an Article of the Convention, or of any Protocol to the Convention, which is designated for the purposes of this Act in an order made by the Secretary of State.

(2) The text of the reservation referred to in subsection (1)(a) is set out in Part II of Schedule 3.

(3) If a designated reservation is withdrawn wholly or in part it ceases to be a designated reservation.

(4) But subsection (3) does not prevent the Secretary of State from exercising his power under subsection (1)(b) to make a fresh designation order in respect of the Article concerned.

(5) The Secretary of State must by order make such amendments to this Act as he considers appropriate to reflect-

(a) any designation order; or
(b) the effect of subsection (3).

Period for which designated derogations have effect.

16. - (1) If it has not already been withdrawn by the United Kingdom, a designated derogation ceases to have effect for the purposes of this Act-

(a) in the case of the derogation referred to in section 14(1)(a), at the end of the period of five years beginning with the date on which section 1(2) came into force;

(b) in the case of any other derogation, at the end of the period of five years beginning with the date on which the order designating it was made.

(2) At any time before the period-

(a) fixed by subsection (1)(a) or (b), or

(b) extended by an order under this subsection, comes to an end, the Secretary of State may by order extend it by a further period of five years.

(3) An order under section 14(1)(b) ceases to have effect at the end of the period for consideration, unless a resolution has been passed by each House approving the order.

(4) Subsection (3) does not affect-

(a) anything done in reliance on the order; or
(b) the power to make a fresh order under section 14(1)(b).

(5) In subsection (3) "period for consideration" means the period of forty days beginning with the day on which the order was made.

(6) In calculating the period for consideration, no account is to be taken of any time during which

(a) Parliament is dissolved or prorogued; or
(b) both Houses are adjourned for more than four days.

(7) If a designated derogation is withdrawn by the United Kingdom, the Secretary of State must by order make such amendments to this Act as he considers are required to reflect that withdrawal.

Periodic review of designated reservations.

17. - (1) The appropriate Minister must review the designated reservation referred to in section 15(1)(a)-

(a) before the end of the period of five years beginning with the date on which section 1(2) came into force; and
(b) if that designation is still in force, before the end of the period of five years beginning with the date on which the last report relating to it was laid under subsection (3).

(2) The appropriate Minister must review each of the other designated reservations (if any)-

(a) before the end of the period of five years beginning with the date on which the order designating the reservation first came into force; and
(b) if the designation is still in force, before the end of the period of five years beginning with the date on which the last report relating to it was laid under subsection (3).

(3) The Minister conducting a review under this section must prepare a report on the result of the review and lay a copy of it before each House of Parliament.

Effect of sections 14 to 17

House Of Lords, Second Reading

Official Report, House of Lords, 3 November 1997, vol. 582, col. 1231

The Lord Chancellor (Lord Irvine of Lairg): . . . Clauses 14 to 17 are concerned with derogations from, and reservations to, articles of the Convention.

House of Commons, Second Reading

Official Report, House of Commons, 16 February 1998, vol. 307, col. 780

The Secretary of State for the Home Department (Mr. Jack Straw): . . . Clauses 14 to 17 cover derogations from, and reservations to, the articles of the Convention and its associated protocols.

SECTION 18: APPOINTMENT TO EUROPEAN COURT OF HUMAN RIGHTS

18. - (1) In this section "judicial office" means the office of-

(a) Lord Justice of Appeal, Justice of the High Court or Circuit judge, in England and Wales;
(b) judge of the Court of Session or sheriff, in Scotland;
(c) Lord Justice of Appeal, judge of the High Court or County Court judge, in Northern Ireland.

(2) The holder of a judicial office may become a judge of the European Court of Human Rights ("the Court") without being required to relinquish his office.

(3) But he is not required to perform the duties of his judicial office while he is a judge of the Court.

(4) In respect of any period during which he is a judge of the Court-

(a) a Lord Justice of Appeal or Justice of the High Court is not to count as a judge of the relevant court for the purposes of section 2(1) or 4(1) of the Supreme Court Act 1981 (maximum number of judges) nor as a judge of the Supreme Court for the purposes of section 12(1) to (6) of that Act (salaries etc.);
(b) a judge of the Court of Session is not to count as a judge of that court for the purposes of section 1(1) of the Court of Session Act 1988 (maximum number of judges) or of section 9(1)(c) of the Administration of Justice Act 1973 ("the 1973 Act") (salaries etc.);
(c) a Lord Justice of Appeal or judge of the High Court in Northern Ireland is not to count as a judge of the relevant court for the purposes of section 2(1) or 3(1) of the Judicature (Northern Ireland) Act 1978 (maximum number of judges) nor as a judge of the Supreme Court of Northern Ireland for the purposes of section 9(1)(d) of the 1973 Act (salaries etc.);
(d) a Circuit judge is not to count as such for the purposes of section 18 of the Courts Act 1971 (salaries etc.);
(e) a sheriff is not to count as such for the purposes of section

14 of the Sheriff Courts (Scotland) Act 1907 (salaries etc.);
(f) a County Court judge of Northern Ireland is not to count as such for the purposes of section 106 of the County Courts Act Northern Ireland) 1959 (salaries etc.).

(5) If a sheriff principal is appointed a judge of the Court, section 11(1) of the Sheriff Courts (Scotland) Act 1971 (temporary appointment of sheriff principal) applies, while he holds that appointment, as if his office is vacant.

(6) Schedule 4 makes provision about judicial pensions in relation to the holder of a judicial office who serves as a judge of the Court.

(7) The Lord Chancellor or the Secretary of State may by order make such transitional provision (including, in particular, provision for a temporary increase in the maximum number of judges) as he considers appropriate in relation to any holder of a judicial office who has completed his service as a judge of the Court.

Effect of section 18

House Of Lords, Second Reading
Official Report, House of Lords, 3 November 1997, vol. 582, col. 1233

The Lord Chancellor (Lord Irvine of Lairg): . . . Under our present law, a judge would have to resign his office here in order to take up the appointment at Strasbourg, with no guarantee of reinstatement at the end of the term of office. Clause 18 is designed to remove that obstacle, so that if a judge is appointed to the European Court he will have the right to return to the bench in the United Kingdom after his term at Strasbourg.

House of Commons, Second Reading
Official Report, House of Commons, 16 February 1998, vol. 307, col. 780

The Secretary of State for the Home Department (Mr. Jack Straw): . . . Clause 18 is concerned with the appointment of judges to the Strasbourg Court.

SECTION 19: STATEMENTS OF COMPATIBILITY

19. - (1) A Minister of the Crown in charge of a Bill in either House of Parliament must, before Second Reading of the Bill-
> (a) make a statement to the effect that in his view the provisions of the Bill are compatible with the Convention rights ("a statement of compatibility"); or
> (b) make a statement to the effect that although he is unable to make a statement of compatibility the government nevertheless wishes the House to proceed with the Bill.

(2) The statement must be in writing and be published in such manner as the Minister making it considers appropriate.

Effect of section 19

House of Lords, Second Reading
Official Report, House of Lords, 3 November 1997, vol. 582, col. 1228
The Lord Chancellor (Lord Irvine of Lairg): ... The design of the Bill is to give the courts as much space as possible to protect human rights, short of a power to set aside or ignore Acts of Parliament. In the very rare cases where the higher courts will find it impossible to read and give effect to any statute in a way which is compatible with Convention rights, they [c. 1229] will be able to make a declaration of incompatibility. Then it is for Parliament to decide whether there should be remedial legislation. Parliament may, not must, and generally will, legislate. If a Minister's prior assessment of compatibility (under Clause 19) is subsequently found by declaration of incompatibility by the courts to have been mistaken, it is hard to see how a Minister could withhold remedial action.
[. . .][c. 1233]
Clause 19 imposes a new requirement on Government Ministers when introducing legislation. In future, they will have to make a statement either that the provisions of the legislation are compatible with the Convention or that they cannot make such a statement but nevertheless wish Parliament to proceed to consider the Bill. Ministers will

obviously want to make a positive statement whenever possible. That requirement should therefore have a significant impact on the scrutiny of draft legislation within government. Where such a statement cannot be made, parliamentary scrutiny of the Bill would be intense.

House of Commons, Second Reading

Official Report, House of Commons, 16 February 1998, vol. 307, col. 780

The Secretary of State for the Home Department (Mr. Jack Straw): ... Clause 19 is a further demonstration of our determination to improve compliance with Convention rights. It places a requirement on a Minister to publish a statement in relation to any Bill that he or she introduces. The statement will either be that the provisions of the legislation are compatible with Convention rights or that he or she cannot make such a statement, but that the Government nevertheless wish to proceed with the Bill.

I am sure that Ministers will want to make a positive statement whenever possible. The requirement to make a statement will have a significant impact on the scrutiny of draft legislation within Government and by Parliament. In my judgment, it will greatly assist Parliament's consideration of Bills by highlighting the potential implications for human rights.

Section 19 invites the courts to work on the assumption that the legislature has applied itself to ensure that legislation is compatible with the Convention

House of Commons, Committee Stage

Official Report, House of Commons, 3 June 1998, vol. 313, col. 420

Mr. Hogg: Is it the right hon. Gentleman's view that the British courts should be very slow to find that where Parliament has expressly dealt with an issue involving Convention rights, the decision of Parliament is a derogation, a departure or a diminution of Convention rights? The working assumption should be that, when Parliament has addressed a matter, it has not derogated [c. 425] from Convention rights. If that is the approach that the courts should adopt, would it not be helpful to put that concept—perhaps differently expressed—in the Bill?

The Secretary of State for the Home Office (Mr. Jack Straw): We are working that matter into not only the drafting of future legislation, but into the presentation of Bills by Ministers. That is the purpose of Clause 19. When a Bill comes before Parliament, the Minister will give Parliament his best view, based on advice from officials and, above all, parliamentary counsel, on whether it is compatible with the Convention.

That was the practice for some time under the previous Conservative Administration. I think that it would be impossible to say that all legislation, of whatever antiquity, was passed in a manner compatible with the Convention. It is, by definition, impossible to say that of legislation passed before the Convention was even a gleam in the eye of a former Conservative Lord Chancellor. It took some decades before the House, our courts and the parliamentary draftsmen became sensitised to the need to ensure compatibility. It was not until the changes of 1966, allowing individual petition to the European Commission, that Governments began to take on board the need for compatibility in the way in which they went about their daily business and in the drafting of Bills. That is my answer to the right hon. and learned Member for Sleaford and North Hykeham.

Mr. Hogg: It is an historical answer.

Mr. Straw: It is. As far as the future is concerned, we are of course inviting the courts to work on the assumption that the House has applied itself to ensure that legislation is compatible with the Convention, except where a Minister comes to the House to say that there are overriding reasons why it is not, to give those reasons and to ask the House to agree the legislation in any case.

Nature of section 19 – Debate in Parliament more appropriate place for reasons for Statement to be given than on the face of a Bill

House of Lords, Second Reading

Official Report, House of Lords, 27 November 1997, vol. 583, col. 1163

Baroness Williams of Crosby: . . . We wish [the Minister] to give the reasons for his statement of compatibility or non-compatibility as the case may be.

In doing so, we reflect recent recommendations stemming back as far as the Franks Committee of 1957 and the Justice All Souls Report under the distinguished chairmanship of Sir Patrick Neill, both of

which strongly recommended the advantages of giving reasons in the making of law and in the administration of law.
[...]

The Lord Chancellor (Lord Irvine of Lairg): The Committee will appreciate that this Bill could have gone through without any Clause 19 at all. In its present form, Clause 19 is a demonstration of the Government's commitment to human rights. I appreciate that the amendment provides that a statement is not enough and it must be a statement backed by reasons. I shall address that on its merits but I suggest that Clause 19 in itself is a very large gesture, as well as being a point of substance, in favour of the development of a culture of awareness of what the Convention requires in relation to domestic legislation. And so, by requiring the Minister in charge of a Bill to give a statement about its compatibility, we are underlining our commitment to undertaking further pre-legislative scrutiny of all new policy measures.[...] Also, where the Minister states that he is unable to make a positive statement about the Bill's compatibility, that will be a very early signal to Parliament that the possible human rights implications of the Bill will need and will receive very careful consideration. Therefore, a statement giving the Government's conclusions, whether positive or negative, on the status of the Bill will go a long way towards the achievement of those aims. Therefore I ask the Committee not to underestimate the significance of what is already there.

Of course, Parliament will wish to know the reasons why the Government have taken whatever view they have taken. Therefore, I can understand why these amendments have been put forward. But the reasoning behind a statement of compatibility or the inability to make such a statement will inevitably be discussed by Parliament during the passage of the Bill. Of course it will be; and it will be discussed thoroughly.

I believe that a debate in Parliament provides the best forum in which the Government's thinking can be fully explained. In those circumstances, therefore, I require a great deal of persuasion that a written statement on the face of a Bill, setting out the Minister's reasons, would add anything of real value.

In principle, the idea of the equivalent of written argumentative essays on the face of Bills does not appeal to me. Debate in the Chamber on such issues will inevitably take place and that, surely, is the natural forum for ascertaining the Minister's reasons and having him develop them so that Members of this Chamber can test by question and debate the sufficiency of the [c. 1164] reasons. Is there any real need to clutter up the face of the Bill with a statement of reasons? I beg leave to doubt it.

Preferable that responsibility placed on individual Ministers, not Government – Ministers answering on behalf of the Government

House of Lords, Committee Stage

Official Report, House of Lords, 27 November 1997, vol. 583, col. 1164

Lord Mackay of Drumadoon: . . . The first point to make is that, when, in the future, Parliament comes to discuss a new Bill, it will, with the greatest respect to individual Ministers, not really be concerned with the view of that individual Minister; it will be concerned with the view of the Government as to whether the provisions of the Bill which are to be debated are compatible with Convention rights. That issue is essentially a question of law. It is inconceivable that, in most cases, the view will be the personal view of the Minister concerned. It will be the view of the Government informed by such legal advice as they will have taken, whether from Law Officers or from any other quarter. In effect, it will be the duty of the Minister to adopt that view and incorporate it in the statement which is [c. 1165] to be given. If Amendment No. 103 were accepted, the suggested wording would then be incorporated into the statement which the Minister would then be required to repeat in this Chamber on Second Reading.

[. . .]

The Parliamentary Under-Secretary of State, Home Office (Lord Williams of Mostyn): . . . Our scheme plainly puts responsibility upon the individual Minister who has charge of the Bill in either relevant place. He is given the particular responsibility of enuring that the policy accords with Convention rights. His is the duty and his is the responsibility to answer to this Chamber or the other place. We believe that to be the correct focus and that is where it presently stands. Of course, the Minister would be answering on behalf of Her Majesty's Government as, by Convention, Ministers answer questions not on behalf of their own [c. 1166] departments but on behalf of the Government generally. We believe that the responsibility is so particular that it ought to be left as it is.

Giving an oral statement would not enhance debate – written report in addition would be pointless

House of Commons, Report Stage

Official Report, House of Commons, 21 October 1998, vol. 317, col.1350

The Parliamentary Under-Secretary of State for the Home Department (Mr. Mike O'Brien): The three amendments relate to statements of compatibility, or incompatibility, made under Clause 19. The Clause is a demonstration of the Government's commitment to human rights. It is one which we need not have included in the Bill, but we have chosen to include it because of the importance we attach to these rights. The added responsibilities placed on a Minister are justified on that basis.

By requiring a Minister in charge of a Bill to give a statement on its compatibility, we are underlining our commitment to pre-legislative scrutiny of all new policy measures. Also, where the Minister states that he is unable to make a positive statement about the Bill's compatibility, that will be an early signal to Parliament that the possible human rights implications of the Bill will need to be given careful consideration by the House—especially, no doubt, in Committee.

[. . .] [c. 1351]

A debate would provide the best forum in which the Government's thinking could be fully explained. I cannot imagine how the mere giving of such a statement could enhance the debate that would normally take place on Second Reading or in Committee, which would usually elicit the required answers.

In such circumstances, a written report would not provide much added value. In some cases, a requirement to provide such a full report might also be odd—for example when the terms of a Bill meant that there was no connection with the Convention and no Convention rights were affected. Then it would merely be a pointless exercise.

[. . .] Acts of Parliament do not usually regulate what a Minister will or will not say in the Chamber. A written statement would be readily available to whoever wanted to read it. As I said, anything in that statement and any other aspect of the human rights implications of a Bill could be debated under the normal proceedings of the House.

What might be of assistance would be any report made on the Bill, for example, by a human rights committee of the House, if it decided to set one up. In due course, that might certainly be a way of informing the debate, whether in Committee or elsewhere, and looking into the detail of why such a statement was made by the Government. Obviously, such a committee of the House could discuss the detail.

[. . .] The hon. Gentleman asked for some examples of when the Government might want to proceed with a Bill that was not compatible with the Convention. One example would be if we were legislating on the length of time for which the Secretary of State might authorise the detention of terrorist suspects under the Prevention of Terrorism (Temporary Provisions) Acts. The Strasbourg Court found our court in breach of Article 5 of the Convention some years ago, but we have maintained the arrangements because of the situation in Northern Ireland through a derogation as set out in schedule 3 of the Bill.

We already know that we may want to proceed with certain Bills even though there is some incompatibility. It is difficult to predict all the situations that might arise as they are exceptional, as is the example that I gave.

SECTION 20: ORDERS ETC. UNDER THIS ACT

20. - (1) Any power of a Minister of the Crown to make an order under this Act is exercisable by statutory instrument.

(2) The power of the Lord Chancellor or the Secretary of State to make rules (other than rules of court) under section 2(3) or 7(9) is exercisable by statutory instrument.

(3) Any statutory instrument made under section 14, 15 or 16(7) must be laid before Parliament.

(4) No order may be made by the Lord Chancellor or the Secretary of State under section 1(4), 7(11) or 16(2) unless a draft of the order has been laid before, and approved by, each House of Parliament.

(5) Any statutory instrument made under section 18(7) or Schedule 4, or to which subsection (2) applies, shall be subject to annulment in pursuance of a resolution of either House of Parliament.

(6) The power of a Northern Ireland department to make-
(a) rules under section 2(3)(c) or 7(9)(c), or

(b) an order under section 7(11),

is exercisable by statutory rule for the purposes of the Statutory Rules (Northern Ireland) Order 1979.

(7) Any rules made under section 2(3)(c) or 7(9)(c) shall be subject to negative resolution; and section 41(6) of the Interpretation Act Northern Ireland) 1954 (meaning of "subject to negative resolution") shall apply as if the power to make the rules were conferred by an Act of the Northern Ireland Assembly.

(8) No order may be made by a Northern Ireland department under section 7(11) unless a draft of the order has been laid before, and approved by, the Northern Ireland Assembly.

SECTION 21: INTERPRETATION, ETC

21. - (1) In this Act-
"amend" includes repeal and apply (with or without modifications);
"the appropriate Minister" means the Minister of the Crown having charge of the appropriate authorised government department (within the meaning of the Crown Proceedings Act 1947);
"the Commission" means the European Commission of Human Rights;
"the Convention" means the Convention for the Protection of Human Rights and Fundamental Freedoms, agreed by the Council of Europe at Rome on 4th November 1950 as it has effect for the time being in relation to the United Kingdom;
"declaration of incompatibility" means a declaration under section 4;
"Minister of the Crown" has the same meaning as in the Ministers of the Crown Act 1975;
"Northern Ireland Minister" includes the First Minister and the deputy First Minister in Northern Ireland;
"primary legislation" means any-
- (a) public general Act;
- (b) local and personal Act;
- (c) private Act;
- (d) Measure of the Church Assembly;
- (e) Measure of the General Synod of the Church of England;
- (f) Order in Council-
   - (i) made in exercise of Her Majesty's Royal Prerogative;
   - (ii) made under section 38(1)(a) of the Northern Ireland Constitution Act 1973 or the corresponding provision of the Northern Ireland Act 1998; or
   - (iii) amending an Act of a kind mentioned in paragraph (a), (b) or (c);

and includes an order or other instrument made under primary legislation (otherwise than by the National Assembly for Wales, a member of the Scottish Executive, a Northern Ireland Minister or a Northern Ireland department) to the extent to which it operates to bring one or more provisions of that legislation into force or amends any primary legislation;

"the First Protocol" means the protocol to the Convention agreed at Paris on 20th March 1952;

"the Sixth Protocol" means the protocol to the Convention agreed at Strasbourg on 28th April 1983;

"the Eleventh Protocol" means the protocol to the Convention (restructuring the control machinery established by the Convention) agreed at Strasbourg on 11th May 1994;

"remedial order" means an order under section 10;

"subordinate legislation" means any-

    (a) Order in Council other than one-

        (i) made in exercise of Her Majesty's Royal Prerogative;

        (ii) made under section 38(1)(a) of the Northern Ireland Constitution Act 1973 or the corresponding provision of the Northern Ireland Act 1998; or

        (iii) amending an Act of a kind mentioned in the definition of primary legislation;

    (b) Act of the Scottish Parliament;

    (c) Act of the Parliament of Northern Ireland;

    (d) Measure of the Assembly established under section 1 of the Northern Ireland Assembly Act 1973;

    (e) Act of the Northern Ireland Assembly;

    (f) order, rules, regulations, scheme, warrant, byelaw or other instrument made under primary legislation (except to the extent to which it operates to bring one or more provisions of that legislation into force or amends any primary legislation);

    (g) order, rules, regulations, scheme, warrant, byelaw or other instrument made under legislation mentioned in paragraph (b), (c), (d) or (e) or made under an Order in Council applying only to Northern Ireland;

    (h) order, rules, regulations, scheme, warrant, byelaw or other instrument made by a member of the Scottish Executive, a Northern Ireland Minister or a Northern Ireland department in exercise of prerogative or other executive functions of Her Majesty which are exercisable by such a person on behalf of Her Majesty;

"transferred matters" has the same meaning as in the Northern Ireland Act 1998; and

"tribunal" means any tribunal in which legal proceedings may be brought.

(2) The references in paragraphs (b) and (c) of section 2(1) to Articles are to Articles of the Convention as they had effect immediately before the coming into force of the Eleventh Protocol.

(3) The reference in paragraph (d) of section 2(1) to Article 46 includes a reference to Articles 32 and 54 of the Convention as they had effect immediately before the coming into force of the Eleventh Protocol.

(4) The references in section 2(1) to a report or decision of the Commission or a decision of the Committee of Ministers include references to a report or decision made as provided by paragraphs 3, 4 and 6 of Article 5 of the Eleventh Protocol (transitional provisions).

(5) Any liability under the Army Act 1955, the Air Force Act 1955 or the Naval Discipline Act 1957 to suffer death for an offence is replaced by a liability to imprisonment for life or any less punishment authorised by those Acts; and those Acts shall accordingly have effect with the necessary modifications.

SECTION 22: SHORT TITLE, COMMENCEMENT, APPLICATION AND EXTENT

22. - (1) This Act may be cited as the Human Rights Act 1998.

(2) Sections 18, 20 and 21(5) and this section come into force on the passing of this Act.

(3) The other provisions of this Act come into force on such day as the Secretary of State may by order appoint; and different days may be appointed for different purposes.

(4) Paragraph (b) of subsection (1) of section 7 applies to proceedings brought by or at the instigation of a public authority whenever the act in question took place; but otherwise that subsection does not apply to an act taking place before the coming into force of that section.

(5) This Act binds the Crown.

(6) This Act extends to Northern Ireland.

(7) Section 21(5), so far as it relates to any provision contained in the Army Act 1955, the Air Force Act 1955 or the Naval Discipline Act 1957, extends to any place to which that provision extends.

Effect of sub-section 22(3)

House of Commons,

Official Report, House of Commons, 21 October 1998, vol. 317, col. 1320

The Parliamentary Under-Secretary of State for the Home Department (Mr. Mike O'Brien): . . . Clause 22(3) provides for most of the Bill's provisions to be brought into force on such day as the Secretary of State may by order appoint. [. . .]

Effect of sub-section 22(4)

On Question, Motion agreed to.

House of Lords, Committee Stage

Official Report, House of Lords, 27 November 1997, vol. 583, col. 1104

The Parliamentary Under-Secretary of State, Home Office (Lord Williams of Mostyn): On the second point, we think that it is implicit that the power to make a remedial order does not extend to cases where the Court finding pre-dates the coming into force of Clause 10. Clause 22 makes express provision for the circumstances in which another provision of the Bill—Clause 7(1)(b)—may apply to acts committed before it comes into force, and that implies that, in the absence of express provision to the contrary, the Bill should not have retrospective effect. However, as we said at the outset of our deliberations on this Bill, we are eager to see whether it can be improved consistent with the scheme of the Bill, as the noble and learned Lord the Lord Chancellor said. I am perfectly content to consider before the next stage whether this measure should be made clear on the face of the Bill. I hope the noble Lord will find that response helpful.

SCHEDULE 2: REMEDIAL ORDERS

Orders

1. - (1) A remedial order may-

(a) contain such incidental, supplemental, consequential or transitional provision as the person making it considers appropriate;
(b) be made so as to have effect from a date earlier than that on which it is made;
(c) make provision for the delegation of specific functions;
(d) make different provision for different cases.

(2) The power conferred by sub-paragraph (1)(a) includes-

(a) power to amend primary legislation (including primary legislation other than that which contains the incompatible provision); and
(b) power to amend or revoke subordinate legislation (including subordinate legislation other than that which contains the incompatible provision).

(3) A remedial order may be made so as to have the same extent as the legislation which it affects.

(4) No person is to be guilty of an offence solely as a result of the retrospective effect of a remedial order.

Procedure

2. No remedial order may be made unless-

(a) a draft of the order has been approved by a resolution of each House of Parliament made after the end of the period of 60 days beginning with the day on which the draft was laid; or
(b) it is declared in the order that it appears to the person making it that, because of the urgency of the matter, it is necessary to make the order without a draft being so approved.

Orders laid in draft

3. - (1) No draft may be laid under paragraph 2(a) unless-
(a) the person proposing to make the order has laid before Parliament a document which contains a draft of the proposed order and the required information; and
(b) the period of 60 days, beginning with the day on which the document required by this sub-paragraph was laid, has ended.

(2) If representations have been made during that period, the draft laid under paragraph 2(a) must be accompanied by a statement containing-

(a) a summary of the representations; and
(b) if, as a result of the representations, the proposed order has been changed, details of the changes.

Urgent cases

4. - (1) If a remedial order ("the original order") is made without being approved in draft, the person making it must lay it before Parliament, accompanied by the required information, after it is made.

(2) If representations have been made during the period of 60 days beginning with the day on which the original order was made, the person making it must (after the end of that period) lay before Parliament a statement containing-

(a) a summary of the representations; and
(b) if, as a result of the representations, he considers it appropriate to make changes to the original order, details of the changes.

(3) If sub-paragraph (2)(b) applies, the person making the statement must-

(a) make a further remedial order replacing the original order; and
(b) lay the replacement order before Parliament.

(4) If, at the end of the period of 120 days beginning with the day on which the original order was made, a resolution has not been passed by each House approving the original or replacement order,

the order ceases to have effect (but without that affecting anything previously done under either order or the power to make a fresh remedial order).

Definitions

5. In this Schedule-

"representations" means representations about a remedial order (or proposed remedial order) made to the person making (or proposing to make) it and includes any relevant Parliamentary report or resolution; and

"required information" means-

(a) an explanation of the incompatibility which the order (or proposed order) seeks to remove, including particulars of the relevant declaration, finding or order; and

(b) a statement of the reasons for proceeding under section 10 and for making an order in those terms.

Calculating periods

6. In calculating any period for the purposes of this Schedule, no account is to be taken of any time during which-

(a) Parliament is dissolved or prorogued; or

(b) both Houses are adjourned for more than four days.

Extent of powers to make Remedial Orders and consequential amendments – adequate safeguards in place

House of Lords, Committee Stage

Official Report, House of Lords, 27 November 1997, vol. 583, col. 1141

Lord Simon of Glaisdale: . . . I can see why the power [to make consequential amendments] is desired. The declaration of incompatibility may have repercussions in other parts of the statute book. However, subsection (2) goes well beyond consequential provisions and is far too wide. We cannot have Henry VIII trampling through the statute book in this way.

Baroness Williams of Crosby: . . . [M]any of us in this Chamber, and for that matter in another place also, have been concerned about the gradual spread of what are sometimes called "Henry VIII powers". It is noticeable in this Bill.

In the powerful report from the Delegated Powers and Deregulation Committee, paragraph 23 said explicitly,

> "This is a Henry VIII power of the utmost importance, which the Committee wishes to draw to the House's attention. . . . We have noted the Lord Chancellor's statement to the House at Second Reading that the power can only be used under strictly limited circumstances. Without strict limitations, a secondary power of such potential width would be unacceptable".

[. . .][I]t is sometimes necessary to amend primary legislation or to amend primary legislation in consequence of subordinate legislation resting upon primary legislation. We would not wish to prevent the Government from exercising such powers.

On the face of the Bill it seems to many of us that the constraints that the Government have to bear in mind in using these powers are not sufficiently explicitly brought out.

[. . .] But I want to say that all Henry VIII powers are troubling precedents. In a parliamentary democracy Henry VIII powers are the route towards an executive power unconstrained by adequate discussion and debate in Parliament. It is with a view to balancing those two necessary interests—that of the Executive and that of Parliament—
[. . .][c. 1143]

The Parliamentary Under-Secretary of State, Home Office (Lord Williams of Mostyn): It is clear from Clause 10(2) that a Minister will be empowered to make only such changes (apart from any consequential changes) as are appropriate to remove the incompatibility. As the Lord Chancellor said during the Second Reading debate,

> "the power to make a remedial order may be used only to remove an incompatibility or a possible incompatibility between legislation and the Convention."—[Official Report, 3/11/97; col. 1231.]

The Select Committee on Delegated Powers and Deregulation noted the Lord Chancellor's remarks about the strictly limited circumstances under which the order-making powers will be used, and did not express any need for the amendments being proposed.

The Government's intention therefore is perfectly plain.
[. . .][W]e do not at present believe that there are inadequate safe-

guards. If reflection shows that there may be a case for a further safeguard, we will reconsider and return at a later stage.

Procedure

House of Lords, Committee Stage
Official Report, House of Lords, 27 November 1997, vol. 583, col. 1144

Lord Henley: We come back to the Henry VIII power.... We have put forward an amendment here which I hope will to some extent allow the Committee to consider whether a new procedure should be developed, as the Delegated Powers Scrutiny Committee suggested, to scrutinise such orders, modelled on that for the Second stage of parliamentary scrutiny of deregulation orders.

I appreciate that it is not the same as that for those deregulation orders, but it is similar in effect in that the draft of any remedial order will be laid before Parliament for a period of 60 days. During that time anyone can make representations to the Minister about the order. When the order then comes into effect... it would be for the Minister to make clear what representations he had received and also what changes he had made to the order as a result of those representations. [...]

It is important that the House should have an opportunity to consider some process whereby amendments can be made to the orders before Parliament, as suggested by the Delegated Powers Scrutiny Committee.
[...]

What I can say to the noble and learned Lord the Lord Chancellor is that we always took very seriously indeed the advice given by the Delegated Powers Scrutiny Committee. The House was pleased that we did take that advice seriously.... [c. 1145]

The Lord Chancellor (Lord Irvine of Lairg): The effect of this group of amendments would be to alter the parliamentary scrutiny procedures for remedial orders.... The noble Lord referred to the report of the Select Committee on Delegated Powers and Deregulation. He used that as the basis for the amendments because they are modelled on the first stage procedure for considering draft deregulation orders under the Deregulation and Contracting Out Act 1994. In paragraph 24 of the report the committee states:

"the House may wish to consider whether there is a case for developing a new procedure to scrutinise such orders modelled on that for the second stage parliamentary scrutiny of deregulation orders".

There, if I may say so, I think the committee slipped. For "second", it should have said "first". The second stage parliamentary scrutiny of deregulation orders does not provide for the amendment of draft orders. It is the first stage that does.

We have considered that paragraph and the whole report with great care. The conclusion we have come to thus far is that Clause 12 of the Bill is adequate. In the present Bill remedial orders are limited specifically to amendments to legislation which are necessary to remove an incompatibility with the Convention. The incompatibility will have been identified very, very precisely by a higher court or it will have emerged plainly from a judgment of the European Court of Human Rights. The cause of the incompatibility will have been very precisely identified. The remedial order will have the sole purpose of improving human rights by removing a closely defined incompatibility. We have therefore thought thus far that there is no need for an amendment-making mechanism.

In the last resort, if the proposed method of dealing with the incompatibility was considered by Parliament to be unacceptable, it would be able, under the existing terms of Clause 12, to withhold its approval to the order being made, or, in the case of an order made under Clause 12(1)(b), ensure that it ceases to have effect after 40 days. In practice, that would oblige the Government to make a fresh order. [c. 1146]

This does, as at present advised, seem to us to be a sufficiently strong form of parliamentary control and one tailored to the needs of the Bill. On the other hand, we will ponder what has been said on the basis that, although it is possible to get the remedial order wrong, the scope for error in the circumstances I have described is really so little that we took the view that the provision for amendment was not necessary in the particular situation we were addressing. Similarly, I doubt whether inserting a minimum period of 60 days before remedial orders can be made under Clause 12(1)(a) would have any beneficial effect. There might well be occasions when a much shorter period for considering a draft order would suffice. What we have in mind is that an unnecessarily long fixed minimum period would unnecessarily delay the making of a remedial order and, accordingly, the removal of incompatible provisions of legislation for the purpose of enhancing human rights.

Amendments made to increase scope for Parliamentary scrutiny of remedial orders – establishment of Parliamentary Committee on Human Rights

House of Lords, Report Stage

Official Report, House of Lords, 29 January 1998, vol. 585, col. 407

The Lord Chancellor (Lord Irvine of Lairg): [. . .] In Committee your Lordships discussed in some detail the procedure for making a [section 10] remedial order. There was undoubtedly feeling that the procedure should be amended to make it easier for [**c. 407**] Parliament to exercise its scrutinising role. [. . .] In Committee, we undertook to reflect on the concerns that had been expressed. As your Lordships will see, we have responded and we have concluded that some changes to the procedure should be made, although we have not adopted all the suggestions made in Committee. Nonetheless, we hope that the Government amendments will give a measure of satisfaction.

The first change we propose relates to the period for consideration of draft remedial orders. Under [paragraph 2(a) of Schedule 2], no remedial order may be made unless a draft has been approved by Parliament. No period of time is prescribed for this procedure, so it would be possible for a draft to be approved, and an order made, very soon after the draft was laid before Parliament. The effect of government Amendments Nos. 51, 57 and 58 is to provide a minimum period of 60 days' consideration before a draft of the order may be approved by Parliament. The noble Baroness, Lady Williams of Crosby, was good enough to call attention to that. This is designed to allow interested parties an adequate period of time in which to comment upon a draft remedial order. It responds to amendments tabled in Committee by the noble Lord, Lord Meston, and to one aspect of the amendments tabled by the Opposition.

I ought to point out that the government amendments depart from those tabled in Committee in not providing a 60-day period for the consideration of urgent remedial orders made under [paragraph 2(b) of Schedule 2 then set out in Clause 12(1)(b)]. In these cases the order will expire after 40 days unless approved by Parliament. These orders are to be made without prior parliamentary approval, and we do not want to extend the time in which they may have effect without such approval. A 60-day period for consideration of these orders would simply delay the point at which Parliament could, if it chose, express its disapproval of the order.

The other change that we propose is in the government Amendment No. 56. It would require a remedial order, or draft, to be accompanied by an explanatory statement. This would contain particulars of the court case in which the declaration of incompatibility had been made, and would seek to explain what the incompatibility was. It is designed, therefore, to facilitate the consideration of remedial orders by Parliament.

We think this would be helpful because we still believe, as we said in Committee, that it would not be appropriate to create a statutory, and I emphasise statutory, requirement for the scrutiny of remedial orders by a parliamentary committee, as the amendments in the name of the noble Baroness and others would do. We assume that this will be the parliamentary committee on human rights, and we have said before, and I say again, that we would welcome the establishment of such a committee, but it is a matter for Parliament. We do not want to anticipate what the functions of that Committee might be. As we said in Committee, it is not normal practice for provisions of this kind to be set out in statute, and I have to say that I do not think there is a case for departing from [c. 408] the normal practice on this occasion. But I made perfectly plain what the position of the Government is in relation to the establishment of a parliamentary committee on human rights. Nor do we think it necessary to provide for the amendment of remedial orders once made or laid in draft, as proposed in the Opposition amendments. Statutory instruments cannot be amended. An instrument has to be revoked, remade or another amending instrument made, and remedial orders are no different. The advantage of the draft affirmative resolution procedure in [Schedule 2] is that Parliament can decline to approve so the order cannot be made and a further order would then have to be prepared to meet Parliament's concerns; otherwise the incompatibility desired to be removed would simply continue. The explanatory document that we propose will make it possible for Parliament to have an informed debate about the incompatibility which has been exactly identified by a court and what the Government's proposals are for removing it.

In proposing these changes I can say that I am conscious of looking ahead to the possible establishment of a parliamentary committee on human rights. Such a committee, I can readily say, would be able to look afresh at the issue of procedure in the light of the experience gained in operating these provisions. If it recommended that a closer Parliamentary scrutiny of remedial orders was needed, I am sure that the Government would be very much influenced by that. But for the present, although we cannot accept the Opposition amendments or those in the name of the noble Baroness, and others, I hope the House will accept, particularly in the light of the explanations that I have given, that we do offer the Government amendments for approval by your Lordships' House in a spirit of conciliation and as improvements which go some considerable way towards meeting the concerns expressed in committee.

Part 3: Specific Issues Arising out of the Human Rights Act

ARTICLES 8 & 10: PRESS FREEDOM, SELF REGULATION AND THE RIGHT TO RESPECT FOR PRIVATE LIFE

Free press is the foundation of a democratic society –Press freedom will be safe in the hands of UK judges and European Court of Human Rights after incorporation – Judges likely to develop a common law of privacy

House of Lords, Second Reading
Official Report, House of Lords, 3 November 1997, vol. 582, col. 1229

The Lord Chancellor (Lord Irvine of Lairg): . . . Before I turn to the detail of the Bill, I am determined to address concerns that have recently been expressed by the press. First, the Government are not introducing a privacy statute. They have resisted demands that they should. They believe that strong and effective self-regulation is the best way forward in the interests of both the press and the public. It is well known, and deserves to be better known, that the noble Lord, Lord Wakeham, the Chairman of the Press Complaints Commission, with which I was myself associated until May as a member of the Appointments Commission which appoints its members, has begun the necessary work of strengthening self-regulation. Although much remains to be done, there have already been significant improvements which are as welcome to Government as to the wider public. We look forward to the noble Lord's good work continuing and prospering. It is strong and effective self-regulation if it—and I emphasise the "if"—provides adequate remedies which will keep these cases away from the courts.

I want, however, to address directly the concerns of the press about how the courts will deal with Article 10 (freedom of expression, a central part of which is freedom of the press) and Article 8 (privacy) once the Convention is incorporated. I am a strong upholder of the freedom of the press; and I am a member of a Government who, as a whole, give the highest value to upholding the freedom of the press. The European Court has in terms declared that Article 10, "constitutes one of the essential foundations of a democratic society".

The Court is hostile to any attempt to restrict press freedom when the complainant is a public figure. Our highest courts have said the same. In 1990 the noble and learned Lord, Lord Bridge, said:

> "In a free democratic society it is almost too obvious to need stating that those who hold office in Government and who are responsible for public administration must always be open to criticism. Any attempt to stifle or fetter such criticism amounts to political censorship".

In 1990 the noble and learned Lord, Lord Goff, declared that in the field of freedom of speech there was no difference in principle between English law and Article 10. In 1993 the noble and learned Lord, Lord Keith, stated uncompromisingly:

> "It is of the highest—I emphasise—the highest—public importance that . . . any Governmental body should be open to uninhibited public criticism".[c. 1230]

The European Court in 1991 in Sunday Times *v.* The UK (No 2)—the Spycatcher case—declared:

> "the dangers inherent in prior restraints are such that they call for the most careful scrutiny on the part of the Court. This is especially so as far as the press is concerned for news is a perishable commodity and to delay its publication even for a short period—and I emphasise 'even for a short period'—may well deprive it of all its value and interests".

I agree with that and so, I believe, does every British judge.

I say as strongly as I can to the press: "I understand your concerns, but let me assure you that press freedom will be in safe hands with our British judges and with the judges of the European Court". I add this, "You know that, regardless of incorporation, the judges are very likely to develop a common law right of privacy themselves. What I say is that any law of privacy will be a better law after incorporation, because the judges will have to balance Article 10 and Article 8, giving Article 10 its due high value".

More practically, I do not envisage the press going down to late Friday or Saturday privacy injunctions, disruptive of publishing timetables, if the press has solid grounds for maintaining that there is a public interest in publishing.

Coverage of section 6 – right in principle for courts to be covered – Press Complaints Commission covered – Judges will now develop common law in conformity with Articles 8 and 10 of the Convention and may develop common law of privacy- insert

House of Lords, Committee Stage

Official Report, House of Lords, 24 November 1997, vol. 583, col. 771

Lord Wakeham: As the Committee will know, it is right for me to declare an interest as chairman of the Press Complaints Commission. The Commission's job is to protect the legitimate expectation of privacy on the part of individuals—but to do so through self-regulation rather than statutory control.

Let me begin by saying that I have no great problem with the principles of the Convention. My problem is not with the principle, but with the method. In short, the detail of the Bill and the consequences of that detail seem to do something which I profoundly do not want to happen; nor I believe do the Government.

[. . .][c. 773]

I had intended to pose a rhetorical question about whether the PCC was a public authority in terms of the Bill in order to demonstrate that uncertainty existed on this point. [. . .] However, an article in The Times last week by David Pannick QC asserted . . . that the PCC is caught by the definition. In addition, during the Second Reading debate the noble Lord, Lord Williams of Mostyn, suggested that this was a matter for the courts to determine. [. . .]

However, I can now answer my own question—and I am most grateful to the noble and learned Lord the Lord Chancellor for assisting me in this. He wrote to me this morning to confirm that, in his view, the PCC is a public authority within the terms of the Bill. He also confirmed the point that in privacy matters newspapers would be subject to interim as well as final injunctions under its terms. His letter confirms that, despite what had been said to the contrary, newspapers and magazines are within the terms of the legislation. In other words, we have a de facto privacy law on our hands.

[. . .] [c. 774]

[. . .] I know that [the Lord Chancellor] feels neither that my fears are justified nor that there will be established a convenient law for the rich to avoid publicity or the corrupt to escape the spotlight of investigation. I know he thinks that a free press will be safe in the hands of the judiciary.

I am sure that he will tell us that the courts will interpret these matters in a sensible and reasonable way by giving due weight to Article 10 of the Convention on freedom of expression. We may be told—as David Pannick set out in the article I mentioned earlier—that the courts may seek to leave delicate judgments on privacy matters to specialist bodies such as the PCC.
[...][c. 783]

The Lord Chancellor (Lord Irvine of Lairg)[11]: I hope that I can persuade the noble Lord, Lord Wakeham, and the Committee that it is neither necessary nor right to go down the road proposed. ...

We believe that it is right as a matter of principle that organisations which are, on a reasonable view and as decided by the courts, exercising a public function should be so treated under the Bill and should have the duty, alongside other organisations having public functions, to act compatibly with the Convention rights in respect of those functions. That means (among other things) that, in doing what they do, they should pay due regard to Article 8 (on privacy) as well as to Article 10 (on freedom of expression, which includes also the freedom of the press).

We also believe that it is right as a matter of principle for the courts to have the duty of acting compatibly with the Convention not only in cases involving other public authorities but also in developing the common law in deciding cases between individuals. Why should they not? In preparing this Bill, we have taken the view that it is the other course, that of excluding Convention considerations altogether from cases between individuals, which would have to be justified. We do not think that that would be justifiable; nor, indeed, do we think it would be practicable. As the noble and learned Lord, Lord Wilderforce, recognised, the courts already bring Convention considerations to bear and I have no doubt that they will continue to do so in developing the common law and that they have the support of the noble and learned Lord in making that use of the Convention. Clause 3 requires the courts to interpret legislation compatibly with the Convention rights and to the fullest extent possible in all cases coming before them. [c. 784] The noble Lord, Lord Wakeham, properly referred to my letter to him of this morning. I think it preferable, and for the assistance of the Committee since it has already been referred to, that I should read it

---

[11] See above under Section 6 for earlier excerpt

out in full. The first paragraph refers to the relevant paragraph from counsel's opinion, with which the noble Lord, Lord Wakeham, supplied me, and after referring to that, my letter states:

"I have been giving further thought to whether the Press Complaints Commission (PCC) is a 'public authority' under the Human Rights Bill.

The authorities which [counsel] cites are not, as I said, precisely in point because they are judicial review cases. But I do agree that they show a disposition on the part of the Courts to regard the PCC as a 'public authority'. On reconsideration, therefore, of the relevant provision of the Bill: is the PCC a 'person certain of whose functions are functions of a public nature'? (Clause 6 (3)(c)). I now tend to think that . . . the press might well be held to be a 'function of a public nature', so that the PCC would be a 'public authority' under the Human Rights Act.

I do, however, think that, for the reasons I gave when we met, this possibility is an opportunity, not a burden, for the PCC. The opportunity is that the courts would look to the PCC as the pre-eminently appropriate public authority to deliver effective self-regulation, fairly balancing Articles 8 and 10. The Courts, therefore, would only themselves intervene if self-regulation did not adequately secure compliance with the Convention.

I repeat that when the press has solid grounds, in the public interest, for publication, even where an individual's privacy is invaded, it will not go down to interim injunctions; in just the same way as it does not go down to injunctions, in libel cases, when it says that it will justify.

I look forward to the debate in Committee on Monday".

[. . .]

. . . I want to tackle the concerns of the press directly. They are essentially twofold. First, will the courts develop a law of privacy, and, secondly, is the PCC itself to be regarded as a public authority which should act consistently with the Convention? First, as I have often said, the judges are pen-poised regardless of incorporation of the Convention to develop a right to privacy to be protected by the common law. This is not me saying so; they have said so. It must be emphasised that the judges are free to develop the common law in their own independent judicial sphere. What I say positively is that it will be a better law if the judges develop it after incorporation because they will have regard to Articles 8 and 10, giving Article 10 its due high value . . .

I believe it to be well recognised, including by the press, that Parliament, if invited to do so, might well pass a tougher statute outlawing invasion of privacy than the judges are likely to develop having regard to Articles 8 and 10, balancing them and giving each its due value and giving Article 10 its due high value. [. . .] This Bill does not impose any statutory controls on the press by a back-door privacy law. [. . .][c. 785]

I would not agree with any proposition that the courts as public authorities will be obliged to fashion a law on privacy because of the terms of the Bill. That is simply not so. If it were so, whenever a law cannot be found either in the statute book or as a rule of common law to protect a Convention right, the courts would in effect be obliged to legislate by way of judicial decision and to make one. That is not the true position. If it were—in my view, it is not—the courts would also have in effect to legislate where Parliament had acted, but incompatibly with the Convention. Let us suppose that an Act of Parliament provides for detention on suspicion of drug trafficking but that the legislation goes too far and conflicts with Article 5. The court would so hold and would make a declaration of incompatibility. The scheme of the Bill is that Parliament may act to remedy a failure where the judges cannot.

In my opinion, the court is not obliged to remedy the failure by legislating via the common law either where a Convention right is infringed by incompatible legislation or where, because of the absence of legislation—say, privacy legislation—a Convention right is left unprotected. In my view, the courts may not act as legislators and grant new remedies for infringement of Convention rights unless the common law itself enables them to develop new rights or remedies. I believe that the true view is that the courts will be able to adapt and develop the common law by relying on existing domestic principles in the laws of trespass, nuisance, copyright, confidence and the like, to fashion a common law right to privacy. That was more or less what the noble and learned Lord, Lord Hoffmann, said in an important public lecture. They may have regard to the Convention in developing the common law, as they do today and as the noble and learned Lord, Lord Wilberforce, says it is right that they should.

The experience of continental countries shows that their cautious development of privacy law has been based on domestic law, case by case, although they have also had regard to the Convention. I repeat my view that any privacy law developed by the judges will be a better law after incorporation of the Convention because the judges will have to balance and have regard to Articles 10 and 8, giving Article 10 its due high value. What I have said is in accord with European jurisprudence.

In Winer v. United Kingdom in 1986 the European Commission on Human Rights concluded that because of Article 10 it did not consider that the absence of an actionable right to privacy under English law was a lack of respect for the applicant's private life.

I believe that effective self-regulation is the way forward. [. . .] The PCC should embrace and welcome the possibility that it may come to be regarded as a public authority under the Bill and expected to deliver Convention rights. A beefed-up PCC . . . perhaps with the [c. 786] power to award compensation in appropriate cases—a power that the PCC lacks today—could become the general arbitrator in practice in these cases provided it did its job strongly and well.

The courts may well develop a law of privacy, not because the Government require them to do so but because they will be exercising their freedom to do so in their own independent sphere. But if there were effective self-regulation a law of privacy developed by the judges would hardly ever have to be invoked against the press.

It is wrong for noble Lords to allow this debate to focus exclusively upon a privacy law that applies only to the media. I emphasise to the noble Lord, Lord Wakeham, that the right to privacy is a basic human right. That right can be infringed by a neighbour, an intrusive commercial agency, private investigators, the police and all manner of other people. The little man needs protection against these bodies. It is primarily these malpractices without a shred of public interest to justify them that will be in the sights of the courts if they move to develop a right to privacy as part of the common law. A well regulated press which is essential to a free society has nothing to fear and everything to gain.

I tend to believe that the important function of the PCC to adjudicate on complaints from the public about the press may well be held to be a function of a public nature, so that, as I said in my letter, the PCC might well be held to be a public authority under the Human Rights Bill. But I believe that this is an opportunity, not a burden on the PCC. The opportunity is that the courts would look to the PCC as the pre-eminently appropriate public authority to deliver effective self-regulation fairly balancing Articles 8 and 10. The courts therefore would have to intervene only if self-regulation did not adequately secure compliance with the Convention. The message for the press is plain: strengthen self-regulation and strengthen the PCC under its eminent chairmanship.

I do not believe that the courts will grant temporary injunctions where there are solid grounds for the press to maintain that they have public interest grounds to publish something, just as the courts do not restrain libels where the press intends to justify them. I say to the press that its salvation as it sees it can be in its own hands.

[. . .] [T]he door is really open to the PCC, which the noble Lord chairs, to strengthen self-regulation so that the courts will be satisfied in all cases concerning the press that effective remedies are [c. 787] provided by the PCC and they amount to compliance by the United Kingdom with its obligations under the Convention without any need for intervention.

[. . .] [c. 840]

The Lord Chancellor (Lord Irvine of Lairg): . . . Another issue of concern to some noble Lords was the possible impact of the Bill on the freedom of the press and, in particular, on the Press Complaints Commission. The noble Lord, Lord Wakeham, made a number of points to which I should like to come . . .

The noble Lord, Lord Wakeham, commented on the idea of the Press Complaints Commission awarding compensation; not fining newspapers, I emphasise—"fine" is an abuse of language—but awarding compensation to individuals who have been wronged in terms of the PCC's own code but who at present have [c. 841] no entitlement to compensation under that code. He was opposed to the PCC having a power to award compensation. In our view, if the PCC had a power to award compensation against a newspaper for unjustifiably invading someone's privacy—unjustifiably because the newspaper is serving no public interest in doing so—that individual is more likely to seek a resolution from the PCC than if no such power is available. So a power to award compensation would reduce the likelihood of an aggrieved person seeking redress from the courts. To the extent that a person might go to court because he is not satisfied with the remedy he has been given, or because he does not think the PCC is capable of giving a sufficient remedy, then the existence of a power on the part of the PCC to award compensation would, for the reasons the noble Lord, Lord Lester, gave, be highly relevant to the court's discretionary considerations.

That said, we have engaged in a dialogue, and we will continue to do so, about the likely effect of the Bill on the PCC or on newspapers generally. The issues have been debated in Committee and both the Secretary of State for Culture, Media and Sport and my noble friend Lord Williams of Mostyn have had meetings with the noble Lord, Lord Wakeham. Both I and my noble friend Lord Williams of Mostyn have stressed our readiness to meet media organisations to deal with the Bill. Finally, the noble Lord, Lord Wakeham, was concerned at what he saw as the increased likelihood of injunctions against the press. I have said before—and I repeat again—that if the domestic courts develop a law of privacy, we have little doubt that they will carefully balance the Article 10 interest in freedom of expression and the Article 8 interest in private and family life, not least at the pre-publication stage if any injunction was being sought. If the PCC develops and strengthens its code, in my view, the granting of injunctions would rarely, if ever, occur.

It may be worth reminding your Lordships— I certainly remind the noble Lord, Lord Wakeham—of the remarks of the European Court of Human Rights in the Spycatcher case in 1991, and I agree with every word of this:

> "the dangers inherent in prior restraints are such that they call for the most careful scrutiny on the part of the Court. This is especially so as far as the press is concerned for news is a perishable commodity and to delay its publication even for a short period"—

I emphasise "even for a short period"—

> "may well deprive it of all its value and interests".

I have to say that this Government do give a very, very high value indeed to freedom of the press, in just the same way as our courts do and as the European Court of Human Rights does.

I have always made it absolutely clear that the Government want to see the Press Complaints Commission take greater powers for itself. The point is that the weaker the self-regulation, the more exposed the press is to judicial action by judges in their own independent sphere. So the point about the PCC taking greater powers is that that would keep these cases out of the courts and within a strong and balanced system of self-regulation, where they ought to be. [c. **842**]

As I have said many times before, I hope that the press itself will lay down proper standards and procedures to protect the public from illegitimate intrusions into their privacy. A press properly regulating itself is the best protection of freedom of expression. If you can trust the press to judge its own failings responsibly there should be no need for the intervention of the courts. I therefore welcome a good deal of what the noble Lord, Lord Wakeham, said. Of course, all these issues remain under active consideration by Government. Final decisions have not yet been reached. I can say that the Government eagerly await what we hope will come from the noble Lord's proposals for the improvement of self-regulation of the press by the PCC.

Strasbourg jurisprudence upholds press freedom – Act will not inhibit press investigations into matters of public interest or lead to pre-publications injunctions – Incorporation will require UK courts to develop more positive concepts of freedom of expression – understanding reached with the PCC – components of the provision now in section 12

House of Commons, Second Reading
Official Report, House of Lords, 16 February 1998, vol. 307, col. 776

The Secretary of State for the Home Department (Mr. Jack Straw): . . . I shall now deal with the position of the media under the Bill. The Convention contains two articles of particular concern to them: Article 10, the right to freedom of expression, and Article 8, the right to respect for private and family life. Given the concerns of the press and the Press Complaints Commission about the possible implications of incorporation for a law of privacy, it is worth pointing out that, in practice, the Convention has already been extensively used to buttress and uphold the freedom of the press against efforts by the state to restrict it. There are at least four leading United Kingdom cases in which the Strasbourg Court has done that—and not one on privacy has detracted from such a line.

I am placing in the Library a paper prepared by my Department that contains details of cases on freedom of expression. Among others, there is the 1979 case concerning *The Sunday Times*, where the European Court found that an injunction preventing publication by the newspaper of material on the thalidomide disaster amounted to a violation of Article 10. In its judgment, the Court referred to

"a principle of freedom of expression that is subject to a number of exceptions which must be narrowly interpreted."

There was the 1991 "Spycatcher" case, where the European Court held that the continuation of an injunction preventing newspapers from printing excerpts from the book was contrary to Article 10. In that case, the Court used the following words, with which I agree, and which I think the media would also endorse:

> "the dangers inherent in prior restraints are such that they call for the most careful scrutiny on the part of the Court. This is especially so as far as the press is concerned, for news is a perishable commodity and to delay its publication for even a short period may well deprive it of all its value and interests." [c. 776]

I could also quote from other United Kingdom cases where Article 10 has been successfully invoked—for example, the 1995 Tolstoy libel case on the amount of damages awarded in defamation actions, and the 1996 Goodwin case concerning the anonymity of press sources. There is also Strasbourg case law involving other Convention countries, all supporting the view that the European Court of Human Rights accords a high value to the right to freedom of expression and recognises the crucial role of the press to a healthy democracy.

One benefit of incorporation for the press is that United Kingdom courts will be required to take account of European Court judgments and will thereby develop more positive concepts about the right to freedom of expression.

I emphasise that point with good reason. We have repeatedly stated our support for the freedom of the media and our opposition to a statutory law of privacy. We do not believe that the Bill is contrary to that position. We do not believe that it will lead to the courts developing the common law in a way that will inhibit legitimate press investigations into matters of public interest. Nor do we believe that it will lead the courts to issue injunctions in respect of stories in which there is a public interest in publication.

Despite all that, I recognise that the press are bound to be alive to any possibility that their freedoms might be eroded gratuitously by legislation before the House. In turn, the Government and Parliament have a corresponding duty to seek to assuage those anxieties if we possibly can. That is precisely what we have done in respect of data protection. We have proposed legislation on data protection, not because of any manifesto commitment but because of the imperative of an EU directive passed by the previous Administration.

The press—through the chairman of the Press Complaints Commission, Lord Wakeham—raised serious concerns about the impact of the data protection directive in the Bill on investigative journalism. I therefore readily agreed that the Under-Secretary of State for the Home Department, my noble Friend Lord Williams of Mostyn, should hold discussions about those concerns with Lord Wakeham. The outcome of those discussions was fruitful and satisfactory, and is now to be found in clause 31 of the Data Protection Bill.

Under that clause, the duty that would otherwise be placed on the press to disclose data that they held on those they were investigating is abrogated if the data are being processed for a journalistic, literary or artistic purpose, and

> "having regard to the special importance of freedom of expression publication would be in the public interest".

One key test of public interest in practice is whether there has been compliance with the Press Complaints Commission code—thus preserving the self-regulation of the press.

The Human Rights Bill is, of course, different from the Data Protection Bill, but, at their root, the anxieties expressed by the media about both Bills are the same: whether they will interfere with freedom of expression; whether they will lead to much greater use of injunctions that halt publication in advance; and, in the case of the Human Rights Bill, whether the Bill itself will encourage the development of a privacy law.

To try to allay these anxieties, Lord Williams and I have been involved in detailed discussions with Lord Wakeham. In particular, we have considered whether [c. 777] safeguards similar in framework to those set out in clause 31 of the Data Protection Bill could be brought into this Bill, without compromising its essential purpose.

I am pleased to tell the House that these discussions have borne fruit, and we have reached an understanding with Lord Wakeham, on behalf of the Press Complaints Commission, on a framework for amendments to the Bill which we believe would satisfactorily safeguard the position of the press in a way that is more comprehensive than providing an exemption for the Press Complaints Commission under Clause 6.
[. . .]

The components of such an amendment would be, first, an explicit provision that no relief or remedy is to be granted regarding Article 8 on respect for private life unless the respondent is either present or represented, or the applicant has taken all practicable steps to alert the newspaper against whom the application is brought. That would virtually rule out pre-publication injunctions being granted ex parte; secondly, an explicit provision that in any case in which a person applies for relief or a remedy on Article 8 grounds related to respect for private life, and the granting of a remedy would raise issues concerning an Article 10 Convention right, the court must have particular regard to freedom of expression—this would be consistent with the jurisprudence of the European Court, which already lays great emphasis on Article 10 rights, but it could also constitute a useful signal and reminder to the United Kingdom courts; thirdly, a requirement for the court—in the case of an application involving journalistic, literary or artistic material—also to take into account the extent of the public interest in the publication in question, whether the newspaper had acted fairly and reasonably, and whether it had complied with the provisions of the Press Complaints Commission's code.

Provisions along those lines, modelled broadly on clause 31 of the Data Protection Bill, would not be inconsistent with the Convention, but would send a powerful signal to the United Kingdom courts that they should be at least as circumspect as judgments of the European Court of Human Rights have been about any action that would give the Article 8 rights any supremacy over the freedom of expression rights in Article 10. I hope and believe that an amendment along those lines will deal satisfactorily with the concerns of the press.

Mr. Gerald Kaufman (Manchester, Gorton): Many of us will want to see the text of that amendment before coming to a judgment on it. I hope for a positive and clear answer to the following question: if my right hon. Friend seeks to make an amendment to ensure that Article 8 does not have supremacy over Article 10, will that amendment also ensure that Article 10 does not have supremacy over Article 8?

Mr. Straw: I cannot satisfy my right hon. Friend on that matter, because to do so would plainly make the [c. 778] safeguards entirely circular, and we do not want to do that. I acknowledge that he has not had the opportunity to see our amendments, and I shall be happy to show them to him in due course.

Mr. Hogg: I welcome what the Home Secretary is saying, but does he acknowledge that through the amendments that he wants to agree with my noble Friend Lord Wakeham he is in reality seeking to amend the circumstances in which the courts can address the two articles? Has he asked himself whether those amendments, which would change the circumstances in which a right could be asserted under the Convention, would be upheld by the Strasbourg Court, which is not bound by what he has just told the House? The judges there may well conclude that what he has just said is in itself a derogation from the Convention.

Mr. Straw: The answer is yes: we have indeed asked ourselves that question, and I said only a moment ago that we were certain that provisions along those lines would not be inconsistent with the Convention and would be fully consistent with the jurisprudence of the Strasbourg Court. As I explained, that fact was well set out in several judgments, including those on "Spycatcher" and on *The Sunday Times* and thalidomide. In those judgments, the European Court itself gives precedence to Article 10 over Article 8 when the freedom of the press and other media is involved.

[. . .]

Mr. Gerald Howarth (Aldershot): I am grateful to the Home Secretary for giving way. Obviously, we need to see the detail of his proposals on how to reconcile Articles 8 and 10. However, I am not clear about his proposals on injunctions that are sought ex parte in advance of publication. As he knows, once something defamatory has appeared in print, it is difficult to undo any damage that may have been caused. Does he intend, in effect, to abolish a citizen's right to seek an injunction in advance of publication?

Mr. Straw: The hon. Gentleman is talking about ex parte injunctions in cases of defamation, but the Bill does not deal with the law on defamation; it deals with Convention rights. It will ensure that it is extremely difficult to gain an ex parte injunction without notice in cases concerning Convention rights. That is entirely right and proper in the circumstances that we have laid out, and it is also entirely consistent with the jurisprudence of the Strasbourg Court in the case that I have already cited.

ARTICLE 13: OF THE EUROPEAN CONVENTION ON HUMAN RIGHTS

Concern about exclusion of Article 13

House of Lords, Second Reading

Official Report, House of Lords, 3 November 1997, vol. 582, col. 1243

Lord Lester of Herne Hill: . . . I have a few points of concern about some details of the Bill. First, I understand the Government's reasons for excluding Article 13 of the Convention from the provisions to be incorporated; that is the provision which obliges public authorities—judicial as well as legislative and executive—to provide effective remedies for breaches of Convention rights. The Government rightly consider that the Bill gives effect to Article 13 by obliging the courts, as public authorities, to comply with Convention rights. Perhaps there is also anxiety within the Government that incorporation of Article 13 might lead the courts to fashion remedies beyond those specifically prescribed by the Bill.

I do not believe that there is such a danger in fact because the Bill is quite clear as to the jurisdiction of the courts and tribunals and as to the remedies which they are and are not empowered to grant. Even in the absence of incorporation, the House of Lords and the Court of Appeal have treated Article 13 as relevant to their functions in cases such as Ex parte Khan; and Brind; and Esther Rantzen. It would be a strange legal solecism if Parliament were now to exclude Article 13 altogether from being considered by the courts when acting in accordance with the functions vested in them by the Bill.

My point would be met either by including a purpose clause stating that the Bill's object is to secure Convention rights and to provide effective remedies for their breach, or by amending Clause 1(1) so that the substantive rights may be read with Article 13 as well as with Articles 16 to 18 of the Convention. I should be grateful if that point could be further considered before Committee.

Importance of Article 13 rights

House of Lords, Second Reading

Official Report, House of Lords, 3 November 1997, vol. 582, col. 1284

Lord Ackner: . . . The particular point I make is that rights are valueless unless there exists the means to enforce or protect them. No doubt that is the reason for Article 13, which provides:

> "Anyone whose rights and freedoms as set forth in this Convention are violated shall have an effective remedy before a national authority notwithstanding that the violation has been committed by persons acting in an official capacity". [c. 1285]

Like the noble Lord, Lord Lester, I was surprised that Clause 1 of the Bill, while referring to the articles to be grafted onto English law, expressly omitted Article 13. There is no doubt an innocent explanation for it, although noble Lords were not provided with one when the noble and learned Lord the Lord Chancellor opened the debate. This is a matter which concerns me.

Article 13 is met by the passage of the Bill – Remedies provided by section 8 – nothing further is needed – Courts may have regard to Article 13

House Of Lords, Second Reading

Official Report, House of Lords, 3 November 1997, vol. 582, col. 1308

The Parliamentary Under-Secretary of State, Home Office (Lord Williams of Mostyn): Article 13 was mentioned by a number of your Lordships. Our view is, quite unambiguously, that Article 13 is met by the passage of the Bill. The answer to the question is as plain and simple as that.

House of Lords, Committee Stage

Official Report, House of Lords, 18 November 1997, vol. 583, col. 475

The Lord Chancellor (Lord Irvine of Lairg):
[. . .]
The Bill gives effect to Article 1 by securing to people in the United Kingdom the rights and freedoms of the Convention. It gives effect to Article 13 by establishing a scheme under which Convention rights can be raised before our domestic courts. To that end, remedies are provided in Clause 8. If the concern is to ensure that the Bill provides an exhaustive code of remedies for those whose Convention rights have been violated, we believe that Clause 8 already achieves that and that nothing further is needed.

We have set out in the Bill a scheme to provide remedies for violation of Convention rights and we do not believe that it is necessary to add to it. We also believe that it is undesirable to provide for Articles 1 and 13 in the Bill in this way. The courts would be bound to ask themselves what was intended beyond the existing scheme of remedies set out in the Bill. It might lead them to fashion remedies other than the Clause 8 remedies, which we regard as sufficient and clear. We believe that Clause 8 provides effective remedies before our courts. It is noteworthy that those who have supported these amendments have not suggested any respect in which Clause 8 is deficient.

When one comes to Article 13, it provides that:

> "Everyone whose rights and freedoms as set forth in this Convention are violated shall have an effective remedy before a national authority"—

that is exactly what Clause 8 provides—

> "notwithstanding that the violation has been committed by persons acting in an official capacity".

The very ample definition of public authority in Clause 6 makes it plain that there is no intention to protect persons acting in an official capacity. On the contrary, our definition of public authority in that clause could not be wider. The noble and learned Lord, Lord Ackner, may nourish suspicions, but I assure him that there is nothing to be suspicious about. [c. 476] At Second Reading I informed your Lordships that if Parliament chose to establish a committee on human rights the Government would welcome it. I said that one of the functions of that body might be to keep the protection of human rights under review. If for any reason which escapes me—none has been pointed to—it appeared to that committee in the light of the operation of this Bill that the remedial provisions of Clause 8 should be strengthened in some way, the Government would give serious consideration to that. But we would expect that committee to set out clearly the effect that its proposed amendments was designed to have. That is what we have sought to do in the Bill. It is noteworthy by its absence that the arguments put before the Committee by those who propose these amendments fail to state any respect in which Clause 8 is deficient.

Lord Lester of Herne Hill: . . . Is it the intention of the Government that the courts should not be entitled to have regard to Article 13 and the case law of the Strasbourg Court on that article in cases where it would otherwise be relevant? I give an example. In recent cases brought against Turkey, where there has been torture without adequate police investigations, the European Court has said that regard must be had to Article 13 rather than Article 6 because it is the former that requires an effective post mortem. Is it the intention of the Government that in cases where the European Court has said that the right provision is Article 13 and not Article 6 our courts should wear blinkers and are not allowed to look at Article 13 or the Court's case law? I am not clear from the speech of the noble and learned Lord so far whether that is the intention. If so, how can it possibly comply with our Convention obligations?

The Lord Chancellor: One always has in mind Pepper *v.* Hart when one is asked questions of that kind. I shall reply as candidly as I may. Clause 2(1) provides:

> "A court or tribunal determining a question which has arisen under this Act in connection with a Convention right must take into account any... judgment, decision, declaration or advisory opinion of the European Court of Human Rights".

That means what it says. The court must take into account such material.

I shall deal now with the question of whether the court may have regard to Article 13.
[...][c. 477]

My response to the second part of the question posed by the noble Lord, Lord Lester, is that the courts may have regard to Article 13. In particular, they may wish to do so when considering the very ample provisions of Clause 8(1). I remind your Lordships of the terms of that provision:

> "In relation to any Act (or proposed Act) of a public authority which the court finds is (or would be) unlawful, it may grant such relief or remedy, or make such order, within its jurisdiction as it considers just and appropriate".

Knowing the remedial amplitude of the law of the United Kingdom, I cannot see any scope for the argument that English or Scots law is incapable within domestic adjectival law of providing effective remedies.

[T]o incorporate expressly Article 13 may lead to the courts fashioning remedies about which we know nothing other than the Clause 8 remedies which we regard as sufficient and clear. Until we are told in

some specific respect how Clause 8 is or may reasonably be anticipated to be deficient we maintain our present position.
[...]

The Lord Chancellor: Clause 8(1) refers to remedies in respect of acts of public authorities because that is what the Bill is about. I do not think that it would be profitable for me to take up the time of the Committee in spelling out every remedy or relief available in English law, which is one of the most sophisticated and developed systems of law in the world.

Preferable Courts should know that they should have regard to Article 13 (Lord Lester)

House of Lords, Committee Stage

Official Report, House of Lords, 18 November 1997, vol. 583, col. 480

Lord Lester of Herne Hill: ... The noble and learned Lord the Lord Chancellor agrees that under the Bill the courts are fully entitled to have regard to Article 13, even though it is not to be incorporated. He also agrees that the courts are obliged to have regard to the Strasbourg case-law on Article 13 to the extent that it is relevant. The issue which remains is whether ... it is sensible for Clause 1(1) to allow the judges to look at Articles 16, 17 and 18 in construing the substantive articles of the Convention, but not to look at Article 13.

I can think of several practical examples where in real cases it will help the courts to know that they can have regard to Article 13, even if it is not directly incorporated. Perhaps I may give two examples. First, the Turkish cases in which there is no proper post-mortem or police investigation into a suspicious murder. I am not suggesting that in practice such circumstances are likely to arise in this country, but in those cases the Strasbourg court stated that Article 6, which is to be incorporated into UK law, is not the right article. It stated that Article 13 is the right article and it is the one to which domestic courts should have regard. [c. 481]

Perhaps I may take an example closer to home, which is the case of Chahal. The noble Lord, Lord Williams of Mostyn, will be particularly familiar with the case because Parliament had to enact special legislation on immigration appeals to give effect to the European Court's judgment in Chahal. The vice was a breach of Article 13. That breach arose because there was no proper judicial procedure where a suspected terrorist was facing deportation to a country where he would face torture or inhuman or degrading treatment or punishment. Therefore, we had to spend time enacting a new Bill.

If there were no clear inconsistency in the primary legislation and the courts could have regard to Article 13 when construing their remedial powers under Clause 8 of the Bill that would greatly assist them in fashioning the effective remedy. There is nothing between the noble and learned Lord the Lord Chancellor and myself about the aim. We are concerned only about making the Bill clear on its face so that legal scholars, publishers, barristers, solicitors and, in the end, judges are not troubled by having to read this debate in order to arrive at the simple conclusion that it was the intention of Parliament that the courts would have regard to Article 13 of the Convention.

House of Lords, Report Stage
Official Report, House of Lords, 19 Jan 1998, vol. 584, col. 1266

The Lord Chancellor (Lord Irvine of Lairg): My Lords, I am grateful . . . to consider . . . Article 13 and the provision of remedies. All of this was debated in some detail in Committee. . . . [O]n the decision not expressly to include Article 13. . . . I would refer also to Clause 8, which provides:

> "In relation to any act (or proposed act) of a public authority which the court finds is (or would be) unlawful, it may grant such relief or remedy, or make such order, within its jurisdiction as it considers just and appropriate".

Our courts are rich in remedies and have every freedom under Clause 8

No one . . . has suggested any respect in which the Bill is deficient in providing effective remedies to those who have been victims of an unlawful act. That is what determines it for me. The noble Lord, Lord Lester of Herne Hill, said that there may be some elsewhere who harbour suspicions that the Government must have some secret or hidden motive . . . If they do, I do not know what they are. The Bill has been constructed in a way that affords ample protection for individuals' rights under the Convention. We have adopted an intentionally wide definition of public authority under Clause 6, and Clause 8(1), which I have already read, gives the courts ample scope for doing justice when unlawful acts are committed. I would say that these are measures of a government determined to deliver a strong form of incorporation, not a government fighting shy of enhancing our citizens' rights.

Bill gives effect to Article 13 – inclusion of Article 13 undesirable – could cause courts to act in ways not intended by the Act – Courts bound to take judicial notice of Article 13 without being bound by it – Government concerned about the strain on the public purse and that the Courts do not develop a law of damages beyond the Convention – best way of applying Article 13 is through a specific section, i.e. section 8

House of Commons, Committee Stage
Official Report, House of Commons, 20 May 1998, vol. 312, col. 975
The Secretary of State for the Home Department (Mr. Jack Straw):
[. . .]
I hope to explain, fully consistently with what my learned Friend the Lord Chancellor said, why we thought that, on balance, it would be better to omit Article 13 than to include it.

In response to the first three general points made by the right hon. and learned Gentleman, of course we support him. The case for incorporation, among others, is that British judges can be involved in the development of jurisprudence. I happen to think that that will be extremely helpful, both because they obviously have a better understanding of circumstances in this country than judges from other jurisdictions, and because we have a body of people in the higher judiciary with a degree of skill and professionalism that is in some ways unrivalled throughout the world. It is important that that skill should be utilised in the interpretation of a profoundly important Convention and a profoundly important Bill.

Secondly, the right hon. and learned Gentleman felt that it was right that we should incorporate the Convention in a way that fashioned the law through the combined efforts of the judiciary and Parliament. In opposition, when we first looked into the matter, we certainly tried to achieve that.

On the third point, we did not want to incorporate the Convention in a way that challenged the supremacy of Parliament and its sovereignty. I have noticed some correspondence and articles in the newspapers suggesting that we should have gone down that route, and that, if we did not, it would be a milk-and-water version of incorporation.

When reference is made to Bills of Rights not only in the United States but in jurisdictions such as Canada, what is forgotten is that those jurisdictions have written constitutions and that there is what amounts to a superior law, which is brought into effect by the procedures for change in the constitution itself. We do not have that facility, and I do not suggest that we should. As an alternative, we have the sovereignty of Parliament, and therefore it is of profound importance that the ultimate judge of what should or should not be a right and a responsibility in the United Kingdom must be this Parliament and no other body.

In the discussions that took place among ministerial colleagues, we thought about this matter long and hard. If the right hon. and learned Gentleman does not mind me saying so, I was pleased and to some extent amused that, despite his hesitancy about the overall principle of [c. 979] incorporation, he is now proposing a purer form of it than some would say we have put in the Bill. We decided it was inappropriate to include Article 13, for the following reasons.

First and foremost, it is the Bill that gives effect to Article 13, so there was an issue of duplication. The Bill sets out clearly how the Convention rights will be given further effect in our domestic law, and what remedies are to be available when a court or tribunal finds that a person has been the victim of an unlawful act. We will be discussing those clauses in more detail later, but I will briefly summarise the relevant provisions.

Clause 3 requires legislation to be read and given effect, as far as possible, in accordance with Convention rights. Clause 6 makes it unlawful for a public authority to act in a way that is incompatible with a Convention right. Clause 7 enables the victim of an unlawful act to rely on his or her Convention rights in any legal proceedings, or to bring proceedings on Convention grounds. Clause 8 provides that a court or tribunal, when it finds that a public authority has acted unlawfully, may grant the victim such relief or remedy, or make such order, within its jurisdiction as it considers just and appropriate.

Those are powerful provisions, as is acknowledged. In our judgment, they afford ample protection for individuals' rights under the Convention. In particular, clause 8(1) gives the courts considerable scope for doing justice when unlawful acts have been committed. Indeed, no one has been able to suggest any respect in which the Bill is deficient in providing effective remedies to those who have been victims of an unlawful act.

[. . .]

Mr. Garnier: Will the right hon. Gentleman give one or two examples of the remedies he envisages that would go beyond those set out in Clause 8?

Mr. Straw: In considering Article 13, the courts could decide to grant damages in more circumstances than we had envisaged. We had to consider that matter carefully, because of the effect on the public purse. We are dealing with breaches of rights by public bodies, some of which are financed by Government—whose purse is, apparently, endless and seamless—whereas others do not have access to the full resources of Her Majesty's Government and the Bank of England printing works in my home town of Loughton in Essex. We had to think carefully about the scope of the remedies that we should provide. [c. 980] Our overall judgment is that the amendment, which would incorporate Article 13, would not add anything much, but might create uncertainties. We see no particular reason to accept it.

Mr. Garnier: Does not that argument fly in the face of the terms of Article 13, which concerns everyone's right under the Convention to an effective remedy? The right hon. Gentleman's point about the public purse and defendants or respondents to complaints who do not have such a deep pocket suggests that some people will be denied an effective remedy. If Article 13 is not incorporated, an effective remedy will be denied those who are not, for example, taking action against a Government or public body with a huge purse.

Mr. Straw: We do not believe that those people will be denied an effective remedy. Indeed, as I said, very few people have suggested that the remedies we are providing will be ineffective—however, they must be balanced and proportionate. Ultimately, as the right hon. and learned Member for North-East Bedfordshire rightly said, courts will have to take account of jurisprudence laid down by the court in Strasbourg.

I accept that we are arguing a fine point, but I suspect that, if the right hon. and learned Member for North-East Bedfordshire had been pursuing the Bill in government, as easily he could have been, he would have come to the same judgment as we did—that there is little point including in a Bill additional wording whose probable effect would be not to make any difference, but whose possible effect would be to add uncertainty.

That is our judgment on a fine point, and I accept that the right hon. and learned Member for North-East Bedfordshire may consider it a moot point. No doubt I have spoken less eloquently than the Lord Chancellor and others in the Lords.

Sir Nicholas Lyell: I am most grateful to the Home Secretary, who is speaking most clearly. I entirely agree that, with regard to damages, the Bill is perfectly straightforward, and that Clause 8(4) expressly states that principles applied by the European Court of Human Rights should be taken into account.

What is to be made of the Lord Chancellor's statement in which he said:

> "My response to the second part of the question posed by the noble Lord, Lord Lester, is that the courts may have regard to Article 13."— [*Official Report, House of Lords*, 18 November 1997; Vol. 583, c. 477.]?

Lord Lester has taken that as Pepper *v.* Harting—if I may create a new verb—the result that he wants, allowing the courts to do what they could not otherwise do. The Home Secretary, not the Lord Chancellor, is in charge of the Bill. Will he clarify whether the courts are to be able to use the Lord Chancellor's words to have regard to Article 13, or whether they should simply read the Bill, which makes no such reference? Of course, I mean no disrespect to the Lord Chancellor. [**c. 981**]

Mr. Straw: Me neither. I shall certainly talk to the Lord Chancellor, but I think that he had in mind no more but no less than the fact that the courts would apply clause 2(1), which says:

> "A court or tribunal determining a question which has arisen under this Act in connection with a Convention right must take into account"—

not "have regard to"—

> "any . . . judgment, decision, declaration or advisory opinion of the European Court of Human Rights . . . whenever made or given, so far as, in the opinion of the court or tribunal, it is relevant to the proceedings in which that question has arisen."

Of course, there is Convention jurisprudence on Article 13, as on other articles. Lord Lester made that point in respect of the Chahal case, which turned on Article 13, and said that it would be taken into account and that regard would be had to it. That point is as much in our favour—suggesting that the specific inclusion of Article 13 is unnecessary—as it is in the favour of the right hon. and learned Member for North-East Bedfordshire.

Sir Nicholas Lyell: I do not want to be tedious, but the Home Secretary will recognise that clause 2(1) concerns

> "any . . . judgment, decision, declaration or advisory opinion",

while my question concerns whether the courts should have regard to Article 13. I think that he is saying that he does not agree that the courts should have regard to Article 13, as Lord Lester would have wished.

Mr. Straw: Let me try again to answer the point. The Convention has been international law for 50 years, and any tribunal will consider the bare text of any original Convention by considering the way in which its application has developed—there is, indeed, a requirement to do so—so, in practice, the courts must take account of the large body of Convention jurisprudence when considering remedies. Obviously, in doing so, they are bound to take judicial notice of Article 13, without specifically being bound by it.

That is my judgment about the way in which the law will work. I wish future Judicial Committees of the House of Lords luck in working through these debates. One sometimes wonders about the wisdom of the Pepper v. Hart judgment in terms of the work that it has given the higher judiciary. It is a fine point, but since we saw that there was no purpose, and indeed that there were some dangers, in including Article 13, we thought that it was best omitted.

Mr. Robert Maclennan (Caithness, Sutherland and Easter Ross): Surely, if the Government had wished no consideration to be given to the jurisprudence that has developed on article 13, it would have been necessary to include a specific derogation from the provisions of clause 2(1). Without that derogation, it seems inevitable that how the courts have developed Article 13 rights will be a matter that the court not only may consider, but ought to consider.

Mr. Straw: With respect, that is the point that I sought to make. The distance between us is small.

Mr. Garnier: If the Home Secretary agrees with the point just made by the right hon. Member for Caithness, Sutherland and Easter Ross (Mr.

Maclennan), why not [**c. 982**] include Article 13 so that there is no doubt? Then the House of Lords Judicial Committee would not have a *Pepper v. Hart* problem.

Mr. Straw: We think that it would create doubt. We believe that we are adequately covering the issue of remedies in Clauses 3, 6, 7 and 8. We are specifically providing remedies that are understandable in English and Scots law. In determining whether a particular remedy is to be granted in respect of any action, the courts must interpret Convention rights as laid down in Clause 2.

If I may labour the point, we do not believe that incorporating Article 13 adds anything positive to the Bill that is not already there; that covers the point about the courts having to take judicial notice of Article 13 as a basic text without being bound by it. We believe that it could create unnecessary doubt, and that is why it is not sensible to accept the amendment, which I respectfully invite the right hon. and learned Member for North-East Bedfordshire to withdraw.

[. . .][**c. 983**]

Mr. Dominic Grieve (Beaconsfield): I find a lack of logic behind the decision to [**c. 984**] exclude Article 13 from the Bill. I listened carefully to what the Home Secretary had to say, and I understand the thrust of it. If it is the case, which it must be, that the courts will have to have regard to Article 13, to exclude it from the text of the Bill but to infer that the courts will still have to have regard to it, must be a fertile field for argument and money for lawyers when human rights cases come to court.

I do not see how the Article will cause exceptional problems if it is included in the Bill. It will be clear that where no domestic remedy may exist in damages, one will have to be created. That is something that the common law has been rather adept at doing for a long time.

I am bound to say that when I was first contemplating how best to incorporate the European Convention, it struck me that one way was simply to say that it was part of our common law, full stop, and leave it to the judiciary to formulate the remedies. That is what is being done—the Home Secretary may agree—with Article 13. It is being left up in the air for the judiciary to make a formulation in so far as one may be required. It is in fact going to be part of our common law, but in a furtive way, as the right hon. Member for Llanelli said.

I find a lack of logic. It is perhaps an exercise in semantics, because the Article will be included anyway when the time comes. However, when something is left out, we can rely on the fact that lawyers in court will latch on to it and formulate an argument that damages cannot be awarded. I can foresee a circumstance wherein the domestic remedy cannot be found in damages. Some court or other will say that it cannot award them. Then there will be the problem of going to appeal and possibly ending up in Strasbourg, when it is abundantly clear in the Convention that an effective remedy of damages must be found. I question why Article 13 is not included. I accept that at the end of the day it will be included by one means or another, but as we are trying to draft sensible legislation, I must raise a question mark.

Mr. Garnier: I wish briefly to pose a question or two to the Home Secretary. I could not agree more with what my hon. Friend the Member for Beaconsfield (Mr. Grieve) just said. I hope that the Home Secretary will allow us another opportunity to revisit this subject. We do not want to overdo the dancing on a pin, be it a stately saraband or a rock and roll, depending on which side of the argument one happens to be on.

The Home Secretary gave us two reasons for not incorporating article 13 in the Bill. First, he said that it would be duplication. Secondly, he said that it would create confusion and perhaps additional remedies that were not intended. I draw his attention to the terms of Article 13:

> "Everyone whose rights and freedoms as set forth in this Convention are violated shall have an effective remedy before a national authority notwithstanding that the violation has been committed by persons acting in an official capacity." [c. 985]

The right hon. Member for Llanelli (Mr. Davies) asked about the jurisprudence on the word "effective" and we could sit here all night discussing what "effective" means, but I should like to bring the Home Secretary home—if I may use that expression—to Clause 8(4), which deals with the way in which a court should determine whether to award damages. It states that, in doing so,

> "the court must take into account the principles applied by the European Court of Human Rights in relation to the award of compensation under Article 41".

One can revolve around that for ever, but marry it up with the words "effective remedy" and envisage a case in which a citizen wishes to recover damages from a Government institution—in this country, the Crown.

I am sure that I shall be corrected if I am wrong, but as I understand the common law of England it is not possible to get exemplary damages against the Crown; one can get exemplary damages against a chief officer of police or in other circumstances, but one is not entitled to exemplary damages against the Crown. Article 13, whether or not it appears in the Bill, suggests that we should all be entitled to an effective remedy, but if that remedy involves an application for exemplary or punitive damages against the Crown to compensate, the complainant in such cases will be denied. It may be that I am completely wrong on that point, but I should be most grateful if the Home Secretary could either remove my confusion or, as my hon. Friend the Member for Beaconsfield said, allow us to return to the issue on another occasion.

Mr. Straw: Let me answer—I hope to their satisfaction, but perhaps not—the points that right hon. and hon. Members have raised. My right hon. Friend the Member for Llanelli (Mr. Davies) asked what the problem is and raised the issue of uncertainty. It was that uncertainty that concerned us when we sat down and came to a finely balanced judgment as to whether Article 13 should or should not be omitted.

I should say that I am recommending that the Committee should not accept the amendment. I shall reflect on the arguments that have been advanced, because the point is needle fine—everybody is agreed on the objective; the question is merely one of how to achieve that objective. We have come to one judgment, but I would not for a moment suggest that that is because we on the Treasury Bench are possessed of better judgment on such matters than other right hon. and hon. Members, who have far greater experience of the law than I have.

My right hon. Friend the Member for Llanelli asked whether damages would ever be available. In paragraph 2.6 of the White Paper, we said:

> "In some cases, the right course may be for the decision of the public authority in the particular case to be quashed. In other cases, the only appropriate remedy may be an award of damages."

The White Paper went on to make the point that the hon. and learned Member for Harborough (Mr. Garnier) made, which is that in considering an award of damages on Conventional grounds, the courts are to take account of the principles applied, not so much by the Convention, but by the European Court of Human Rights. In that way, people will be able to receive compensation from a [c. 986] domestic court equivalent to that which they would have received in Strasbourg. My right hon. Friend will know from the explanatory and financial memorandum to the Bill, on page iii, that the awards at Strasbourg

> "tend to range from £5,000 to £15,000 and are not made simply because the Court finds a violation of the Convention."

Mr. Denzil Davies: I understand that, but it was my right hon. Friend who, quite properly, muttered about the public purse. What has the public purse got to do with the incorporation of Article 13 if all those damages can be issued anyway? My impression is that he was saying that the Government were worried that, if they put Article 13 in the Bill, it would cost far more money. My question is, how?

Mr. Straw: We might have been overworrying, but we did worry about the matter. My right hon. Friend was a Treasury Minister, so he will know that there is always concern about the financial effects of Bills, and quite right too. It is far more difficult to predict the financial effect of this Bill than of almost any other Bill coming before the House, because we are charting new waters and do not know exactly how it will develop. Our concern was to ensure that the courts applied themselves to the jurisprudence of the Convention and that they did not, for example, develop awards of damages that exceeded the Convention. It was for that reason that we took the view that the best way of applying Article 13 in the context of incorporating the Convention was to spell out in specific clauses how those remedies should be made available. Therefore, we take from Article 13 that

> "Everyone whose rights and freedoms . . . are violated shall have an effective remedy"

and then set out in the Bill what those effective remedies should be and how they can be accessed.

The hon. Member for Beaconsfield (Mr. Grieve) is to some extent right to say that the argument is about semantics and that it is probable that, at the end of the day, we shall have been arguing about a distinction without a difference. On balance, we came to the view that it was better and created more certainty to omit the precise text of Article 13 from the Bill, but to apply it in the ways set out, not only in the clauses that provide for remedies, but through the force of Clause 2. As I said, it is a finely balanced judgment.

[. . .]

As far as I am concerned, we are indeed legislating by black-letter law on the face of the Bill. [c. 987] We could have a separate debate about the wisdom of the decision in Pepper *v.* Hart: I know why the Judicial Committee made that decision and, to some extent, there is common sense in seeking to tease out the meaning of words where they are ambiguous, but I have always taken the view that what Parliament passes is not what Ministers say, but what is on the face of a Bill. That is of profound importance to the manner in which we make legislation.

If there turns out to be some gap in the remedies, it will be possible for litigants to go to Strasbourg

House of Commons, Third Reading

Official Report, House of Commons, 21 October 1998, vol. 317, col. 1367

The Secretary of State for the Home Department (Mr. Jack Straw): . . . My hon. Friend the Member for Slough (Fiona Mactaggart) asked a question about Article 13. Article 13 states:

> "Everyone whose rights and freedoms as set forth in this Convention are violated shall have an effective remedy before a national authority notwithstanding that the violation has been committed by persons acting in an official capacity."

Although Article 13 mentions a national authority, the truth is that it is there to provide a remedy for the international Court at Strasbourg. For that reason, the Government thought that it would be inappropriate to include Article 13 in the Bill to incorporate the principal operational parts of the Convention that provide substantive rights.

English law and Scots law have been imaginative and innovative in developing new remedies. As proof of that, one has only to consider development of the idea of judicial review, which—from an almost standing start—has developed into a rather large industry.

[. . .]

[W]e end up being judicially reviewed more regularly than some other Departments because of the nature of our business. It is right that we should be reviewed more regularly, as we are daily dealing with crucial issues of the liberty of the subject. I personally have no difficulty about the fact that the quasi-judicial decisions that I have to make—like the decisions that the former Attorney-General had to make—have to be made with very clear application of the law and judicial review.

Judicial review and many other remedies have been developed, and the Government believe that the courts will be imaginative in developing other remedies if they are needed. If—as I do not think will happen—there turns out to be some gap in the remedies, the safeguard is that it will be possible for litigants to go to Strasbourg, where Article 13 will arise.

I do not want to go into too much detail about the Turkish case, except to say that it involved the most extraordinary allegations of failure against the Turkish [c. 1368] police, failure on a scale that no one could conceive would apply in this country. The case involved the killing of civilian by a Turkish police officer and the almost total and wilful failure of the Turkish authorities to investigate. It is impossible to conceive of such a circumstance arising in this country. We considered the matter carefully but do not believe that we lose anything by the omission of Article 13. Indeed, we think that there could be problems if we included it.

MARGIN OF APPRECIATION

Doctrine of margin of appreciation means allowing this country a margin in an international court – margin of appreciation spelt out in section 2

House of Commons, Committee Stage
Official Report, House of Commons, 3 June 1998, vol. 313, c. 424

The Secretary of State for the Home Department (Mr. Jack Straw): ... The doctrine of the margin of appreciation—it is an important one—recognises that a state is allowed a certain measure of discretion, subject to European supervision, when it takes legislative, judicial or administrative action in respect of some Convention rights. In other words, it is best placed to decide in the first place whether—and, if so, what—action is required.

My first point about the margin of appreciation is that it is more relevant to some Convention rights than to others. It is especially relevant to Articles 8 to 11, which enable restrictions to be placed on rights where that is necessary in a democratic society, for any one of a number of reasons. It is less relevant to some of the other articles, for example, Article 2 on the right to life and Article 3 on the prohibition on torture or inhuman and degrading treatment or punishment.

The doctrine of the margin of appreciation means allowing this country a margin of appreciation when it interprets our law and the actions of our Governments in an international court, perhaps the European Court of Human Rights. Through incorporation we are giving a profound margin of appreciation to British courts to interpret the Convention in accordance with British jurisprudence as well as European jurisprudence.

One of the frustrations of non-incorporation has been that our own judges—for whom I have a high regard, as, I believe, do Opposition Members—have not been able to bring their intellectual skills and our great tradition of common law to bear on the development of European Convention jurisprudence.

Mr. Grieve: I agree with every word that the right hon. Gentleman has said on this matter. It is why I favour incorporation. However, it is interesting to note that, although that is clearly the intention—and I believe will be the result—this Bill is statute, not common law. Where does it spell out to the judiciary that the margin of appreciation is available to it in the way that it interprets the Bill? This is an interesting point and I would welcome the right hon. Gentleman's comments on it. We may have inferred that that is what the courts should do, but where is that stated in the Bill?

Mr. Straw: The margin of appreciation is laid down in many commission and Court judgments. Therefore, it is spelt out in the meaning of Clause 2. That is the direct answer to the hon. Gentleman's point. In addition, and as the financial memorandum makes clear, we will spend £5 million on judicial training. I am not making a trivial point. A great deal of time, effort and money will go into the training of the judiciary. I know from my contacts with senior members of the judiciary that they are already alive to the need to bring themselves up to speed on this important development of our law.

Margin of appreciation refers to the way the Strasbourg court gives the benefit of the doubt to domestic jurisdictions

House of Commons, Third Reading

Official Report, House of Commons, 17 June 1998, vol. 314, col. 432

The Secretary of State for the Home Department (Mr. Straw): . . . The hon. Member for Beaconsfield (Mr. Grieve) asked me about the margin of appreciation, and whether our national courts will be ahead of Strasbourg in applying the Convention. He and I both use the term "margin of appreciation" in a loose way, for which I have been admonished, so I pass that admonition on to him. Technically, the term refers to the way in which the Strasbourg Court gives the benefit of the doubt to a domestic jurisdiction. It will continue to do so. Indeed, the more we can develop our own jurisprudence in connection with the Convention, the greater the margin of appreciation that will be given.

HUMAN RIGHTS COMMISSION

Human rights commission not ruled out, but premature now
House of Lords, Second Reading
Official Report, House of Lords, 3 November 1997, vol. 582, col. 1233

The Lord Chancellor (Lord Irvine of Lairg): . . . Lastly, the Bill does not provide for the establishment of a human rights commission. I appreciate that this will cause disappointment to some. It is suggested that a commission would have a useful role to play in promoting human rights and advising individuals how to proceed if they believe their rights have been infringed. Although we have given this proposal much thought, we have concluded that a human rights commission is not central to our main task today, which is to incorporate the Convention as promised in our election manifesto. There are questions to be resolved about the relationship of a new commission with other bodies in the human rights field; for example, the Equal Opportunities Commission and the Commission for Racial Equality. Would a human rights commission take over their responsibilities, or act in partnership with them, or be an independent body independent of them? We would also want to be sure that the potential benefits of a human rights commission were sufficient to justify establishing and funding for a new non-governmental organisation. We do not rule out a human rights commission in future, but our judgment is that it would be premature to provide for one now. [c. 1234] We have, however, given very positive thought to the possibility of a parliamentary committee on human rights. This is not in the Bill itself because it would not require legislation to establish and because it would in any case be the responsibility of Parliament rather than the Government. But we are attracted to the idea of a parliamentary committee on human rights, whether a separate committee of each House or a joint committee of both houses. It would be a natural focus for the increased interest in human rights issues which Parliament will inevitably take when we have brought rights home. It could, for example, not only keep the protection of human rights under review, but could also be in the forefront of public education and consultation on human rights. It could receive written submissions and hold public hearings at a number of locations across the country. It could be in the van of the promotion of a human rights culture across the country.

[...]

Government would look favourable on development of a Parliamentary Committee

House of Lords, Second Reading

Official Report, House of Lords, 3 November 1997, vol. 582, col. 1309

The Parliamentary Under-Secretary of State, Home Office (Lord Williams of Mostyn): . . . A number of your Lordships, not least the noble Baroness, Lady Amos, referred to the question of whether at this stage there should be a human rights commission.. The Government believe that Parliament has an extremely important part to play. That is why the Lord Chancellor went out of his way to indicate that the Home Secretary and he would both look favourably, if Parliament wished it, on the development of a human rights committee.

Dealing with the point about education and the dissemination of material, he said specifically that it might well be subject to the committee's views and that the committee would wish to travel within the jurisdiction in order to take evidence, hear representations and have public forums. That is a development which another place and your Lordships' House might well wish to see. What the Government have said—I hope that your Lordships will think this prudent—is that it is for Parliament to decide on the mechanisms that it wishes to adopt. We are not in any sense drawing back from our commitment.

The noble Lord, Lord Holme of Cheltenham, asked whether I could say whether there would be a Treasury veto on the human rights commission. If I may put it bluntly, all I can say is I do not readily understand that anyone would be able successfully to overrule the Lord Chancellor and the Home Secretary if they concluded that they wanted public funding, but that is a little way down the road. The question was whether there will be a Treasury veto. I shall try again: no, no, no.

The noble Lord, Lord Holme, also asked whether we would be "proactive"—I believe that that is the word nowadays—about relationships with the existing statutory commissions. Of course—we have been in regular correspondence with them in past months.

Human rights commission not ruled out

House of Lords, Committee Stage

Official Report, House of Lords, 24 November 1997, vol. 583, col. 849

The Parliamentary Under-Secretary of State, Home Office (Lord Williams of Mostyn): . . . I want to make the Government's position perfectly plain, as I tried to do at Second Reading. I turn to the White Paper, which states:

> "The Government's priority is implementation of its Manifesto commitment to give further effect to the Convention rights in domestic law so that people can enforce those rights in United Kingdom courts . . . the Government has not closed its mind to the idea of a new human rights commission at some stage in the future in the light of practical experience of the working of the new legislation". [c. 850]

[. . .]

We do not wish to bully through a human rights commission without the fullest consultation with the Equal Opportunities Commission and the Commission for Racial Equality, to name but two. I pay tribute, as we all do, to the noble Baroness, Lady Lockwood, who has great experience of the EOC. When she cautions us and says that the principle may be appropriate but that we need the most careful, intricate and informed consultation with those bodies, I respectfully believe her to be right.

As we said in Rights Brought Home, we have not ruled out the idea of a commission for the future. [. . .]

We believe that the right way forward is the one that has been proposed and that we should do our best to get the best possible Bill. If there is to be a parliamentary committee, single or joint, we welcome its involvement in scrutiny first should there be a human rights commission. Secondly, it is very important that we get the nuts and bolts and practicalities right after taking evidence and approaching the matter with care. The constitution and nature of a human rights commission, if there is to be one, is very important. It is extremely important that we get it right first time. [c. 851] We are not ruling out the idea of a human rights commission. We believe that we should have the best possible material available before we decide, first, whether to have one and, secondly, what its terms of reference and proper parameters should be.

Proposal for 'Standing Advisory Commission on Human Rights' devoid of merit

House of Lords, Committee Stage
Official Report, House of Lords, 27 November 1997, vol. 583, col. 1153

The Parliamentary Under-Secretary of State, Home Office (Lord Williams of Mostyn): [. . .]

The amendment moved by the noble Lord, Lord Molyneaux, proposes the constitution of a commission to be known as the Standing Advisory Commission on Human Rights. Its purpose is to advise the Secretary of State on any matter related to the Convention. That misses the point of the Bill. The purpose of the Bill is to enable people who believe that their Convention rights have been violated to enforce those rights in domestic courts. Its purpose is not to create a statutory source of advice for the Government on whether they are acting compatibly with the Convention. We do not believe that any such device would have any practical value or merit. It does not go beyond anything that can be done by a parliamentary committee on human rights. It would not be in the business of advising individuals; it would be limited to giving advice to the Secretary of State. The Government do not see the value or virtue of such a commission.

No consensus on issue of commission

House of Commons, Committee Stage
Official Report, House of Commons, 24 June 1998, vol. 314, col. 1987

The Parliamentary Under-Secretary of State for the Home Department (Mr. Mike O'Brien): . . . [T]he Government have considered the issue of a human rights commission very carefully and consulted various organisations about [c. 1088] it. It became clear that there was no consensus on the issue, and that if we decided to establish such a commission through the Bill, we would end up not with a discussion of how to secure access to rights at Strasbourg but with a big debate and campaign about a commission and its terms of reference.

The Government do not have a closed mind on a commission—we have made our position clear. Different interest groups—the Commission for Racial Equality, the Equal Opportunities Commission and so on—have different views on whether a human rights commission would be a good thing, so the best that we can do at the moment is to ensure that the Convention is accepted as part of our law. After that, the need for a human rights commission may be the subject of a future debate—we shall have to see how that develops.

I believe that we have framed the Bill in a way that provides individuals with effective protection of the rights under the Convention. As I have explained today and on previous occasions, the Government consider that the wording of Clause 7 is wholly consistent with our overall approach.

PARLIAMENTARY COMMITTEE

Government very positive, but does not require legislation

House of Lords, Second Reading
Official Report, House of Lords, 3 November 1997, vol. 582, col. 1234

The Lord Chancellor (Lord Irvine of Lairg): . . . We have, however, given very positive thought to the possibility of a parliamentary committee on human rights. This is not in the Bill itself because it would not require legislation to establish and because it would in any case be the responsibility of Parliament rather than the Government. But we are attracted to the idea of a parliamentary committee on human rights, whether a separate committee of each House or a joint committee of both Houses. It would be a natural focus for the increased interest in human rights issues which Parliament will inevitably take when we have brought rights home. It could, for example, not only keep the protection of human rights under review, but could also be in the forefront of public education and consultation on human rights. It could receive written submissions and hold public hearings at a number of locations across the country. It could be in the van of the promotion of a human rights culture across the country.

I have tried to explain why the Government want to bring rights home and how we propose to do it. This Bill represents a major plank in our programme for constitutional change and invigoration. I have for many years been downcast by the want of protection for human rights in the United Kingdom. In a democracy it is right that the majority should govern. But that is precisely why it is also right that the human rights of individuals and minorities should be protected by law.

Terms of reference of parliamentary committee would govern whether individual cases would be considered

House of Lords, Committee Stage
Official Report, House of Lords, 27 November 1997, vol. 583, col. 1153

Lord Hylton: Before the noble Lord sits down, can he say whether or not any parliamentary committee on human rights would be able to look at individual cases?

Lord Williams of Mostyn: As has been agreed on all sides, what any parliamentary committee looks at depends upon its terms of reference. Its terms of reference are by definition a matter for another place and this place if either or both Houses wishes to have such a committee.

Government proposes parliamentary committee

House of Commons, Second reading

Official Report, House of Commons, 16 February 1998, vol. 307, col. 857

The Parliamentary Under-Secretary of State for the Home Department (Mr. Mike O'Brien): . . . My hon. Friend the Member for Slough raised also the issue of a parliamentary Committee. The Government propose to strengthen Parliament's role by supporting the creation of a new parliamentary Committee on human rights. It could be a Joint Committee of both Houses or a Committee of each House; that is a matter for the House to decide. If the House so decides, the Committee's function could be to scrutinise proposed legislation, to ensure that human rights are respected, to assess UK compliance with various human rights codes and to keep the Act—as it will eventually undoubtedly become—under constant review.

The original proposal for a Committee was made to the previous Government by Lord Lester of Herne Hill, Lord Alexander of Weedon, Lord Simon of Glaisdale and my noble Friend the Lord Chancellor. A Committee would give Parliament the ability to consider reports that examined the overall issue of human rights in the United Kingdom context, and would advise the Government and both Houses of Parliament on how rights under the Convention were developing and how we should respond to those developments. I hope that that proposal will be welcomed by both sides of the House.

ARTICLE 14: PROTECTING AGAINST DISCRIMINATION

Relationship of rights in Human Rights Act to Convention rights – Intention to 'grant access' to Convention rights, not to 'put a gloss' on them – Intention that courts should not in geeral take a different view on issues to the European Court of Human Rights – Underlying principles behind section 13

House of Commons, Committee Stage

Official Report, House of Commons, 2 July 1998, vol. 314, col. 568

The Parliamentary Under-Secretary of State for the Home Department (Mr. Mike O'Brien): [T]he new clause[12] essentially puts a gloss on the Convention and, throughout the Bill, we have tried not to do that. We have tried to grant access rather than create a new gloss on those Convention rights. Even in new Clause 13, we were careful about that. Our concern is that, with the best of intentions, new Clause 10 would not continue that level of care.

I understand the view that may be expressed that, despite, for example, the Sutherland case, the European Court of Human Rights has been somewhat conservative in its judgments concerning Article 14, and perhaps too ready to find in favour of states on the ground that there was objective justification for some action which, on its face, might be considered discriminatory. However, whether or not that is so, it is not something we can influence by an amendment to the Bill. Nor do the Government wish to suggest that, in general, our courts should take a different view on the issue from that taken by the European Court.

The Bill is based firmly on the proposition that it is about access to the Convention rights, not their substance, and that our courts must

---

[12] The suggested new clause read as follows:

New clause 10
Guarantee of non-discrimination

'(1) If a court's determination of any question arising under this Act concerns an issue of discrimination, it must have particular regard to the guarantee in Article 14 of the Convention that the rights and freedoms set forth in the Convention shall be secured without discrimination on any ground.

(2) In this section, "court" includes a tribunal.'.—*[Mr. Maclennan.]*

It was proposed and debated after the debate in Committee on 2 July 1998 on new Clause 9 (Section 9) and new Clause 13 (Section 13) and rejected following a vote.

take into account the Strasbourg jurisprudence. We cannot honourably pick and choose which rights should be subject to those propositions and which should be open to more generous treatment from the point of view of applicants to our courts.

New Clause 10 is an attempt to go some way down that road. It might be seen as an attempt to gloss the Convention, encouraging our courts to interpret Article 14 more widely than can be justified by reference to Strasbourg jurisprudence. If it does not do that, I fail to see what it does do.

It has been pointed out that, in many ways, new Clause 10 merely tries to do for various minorities what other new clauses that the Committee has accepted do for the Churches and the press. I do not think that the parallel is appropriate. Our provision on the Churches emphasises to the UK courts how the Strasbourg institutions have consistently interpreted Article 9 rights. It directs the courts' attention to Strasbourg case law, which is to the effect that a Church body or other association with religious objects is capable of possessing and exercising rights contained in Article 9 in its capacity as a representative of its members.

Similarly, the provision on freedom of the press is grounded firmly on Strasbourg case law, which encourages the particular importance of the Article 10 right to freedom of expression. Moreover, those changes, as well as being wholly in accord with the principles of the Bill and the Convention, address concerns of the Churches and the media that the Bill might worsen their position. That consideration does not apply to Article 14.

Our reservations about new Clause 10 do not imply any lessening of our commitment to combat discrimination. I do not think that anyone has suggested that. We recognise the importance of judges being able to deal with minority groups in a way in which those groups can have confidence. The Judicial Studies Board carries out extensive training involving members of ethnic minorities, for example, in talking to judges to ensure that [c. 569] discrimination does not occur. We think that that is a better way forward. We do not think that adding glosses to the Convention at this stage is appropriate or desirable.

[. . .] However, the new clause would do something that we have been trying to avoid. It would be a change in the way that we have handled the Bill which should not be acceptable to the Committee. I accordingly invite the right hon. Member for Caithness, Sutherland and Easter Ross to withdraw his new clause, in the interests of a Bill which is about granting access to the rights that people should have access to in our courts—but for which, at present, they have to go Strasbourg—rather than about changing the substance of those rights[13].

SCOTLAND

Power to invalidate Scottish primary legislation that is not compatible with the Convention exists under the Scotland Act 1998.

House of Lords, Second Reading
Official Report, House of Lords, 3 November 1997, vol. 582, col. 1306
The Parliamentary Under-Secretary of State, Home Office (Lord Williams of Mostyn): . . . Perhaps I may deal with an obvious question because the answer is in the words read out by the noble Lord, Lord Henley. Scotland is different because it would be ultra vires for the Scottish Parliament to pass laws incompatible with the Convention. Therefore, because those are the constitutional arrangements which we have arrived at, the Scottish judges will have the powers to act as the noble Lord, Lord Henley, indicated. The United Kingdom Parliament remains sovereign. We have therefore opted, I believe prudently, rightly and in accordance with United Kingdom tradition, to limit the power of the judges to the declaration of incompatibility. It really is as simple as that.

Powers to make specific rules of court in Scotland

House of Lords, Committee Stage
Official Report, House of Lords, 24 November 1997, vol. 583, col. 852
Lord Mackay of Drumadoon: . . . It may be helpful to those in Scotland who are interested in this matter if the noble and learned Lord the Lord Advocate would confirm that the rules which are referred to in subsection (8) are limited to rules in terms of which the Secretary of State would specify which courts in Scotland could entertain proceedings as they are referred to in Clause 7(1)(a). If, at this stage, it is possible to indicate what the Secretary of State has in mind as to the courts, I am sure that would also be of interest.
[. . .][**c. 853**]

---
[13] Amendment failed on vote.

The Lord Advocate (Lord Hardie): . . . The intention is that the Secretary of State would make rules as to which court or tribunal would have jurisdiction to entertain claims.

On the other hand, I wish to record that it is entirely appropriate that the head of the judiciary in Scotland, the Lord President or the Lord Justice General, as the case may be, should have responsibility for any procedural rules within the court. I am satisfied that that can be achieved without any special provision in the Bill, under existing powers.

On the other point raised by the noble and learned Lord, Lord Mackay of Drumadoon, I am afraid that I cannot indicate at this stage what the Secretary of State has in mind.

Section 2

Rule-making powers found within Scotland Act 1998

House of Commons, Committee Stage

Official Report, House of Commons, 3 June 1998, vol. 313, col. 413

The Parliamentary Secretary, Lord Chancellor's Department (Mr. Geoffrey Hoon): The Scottish legislation provides that the Lord Advocate and the Solicitor-General for Scotland will cease to be members of the United Kingdom Government, and become members of the Scottish Executive. It is therefore necessary, in the context of references to the Lord Advocate, to ensure that the powers enjoyed are either exercised in relation to reserved matters by the Secretary of State for Scotland or such other appropriate Minister as he or she should ultimately designate, or dealt with as devolved matters through the Scottish Executive.

Section 4

Provision preventing judges of the High Court of the Justiciary from making declarators of incompatibility in criminal trials reflects overall policy that judges in criminal trials should not make such declarations

House of Lords, Committee Stage

Official Report, House of Lords, 18 November 1997, vol. 583, col. 550

Lord Mackay of Drumadoon: . . . Amendment No. 26 seeks to explore, in the context of Clause 4(5)(d) the reason why "declarators of incompatibility", as I understand them to be called in [c. 551] Scotland, can be made by a High Court judge sitting in his civil jurisdiction as a judge in a Court of Session, but not by the same High Court judge sitting in his criminal capacity as a judge in the High Court of Justiciary. In criminal matters, it is only when a case has reached the Court of Criminal Appeal that the option of a declarator will be open.

One can anticipate that in criminal cases issues will arise as to whether the statutory provision upon which a charge is based is compatible with Convention rights. One can envisage also arising situations when evidence is recovered in terms of a search warrant granted in terms of statutory provisions alleged to be incompatible with Convention rights. If those issues are to be raised, it will be the duty of counsel to address the High Court judge on the legal argument. He will undoubtedly form a view as to whether there is that alleged incompatibility with Convention rights.

The purpose of the amendment is to see why the judge is not to be given that option in criminal matters when, if similar issues arise in civil cases, he will have such an option. I beg to move.

The Lord Chancellor (Lord Irvine of Lairg): I wonder whether what lies behind the noble and learned Lord's amendment is concern that somehow or other the statutory provision may be operating as some kind of slight on the High Court of Justiciary in Scotland. Not so. The Bill does not call in question the standing of the High Court of Justiciary in Scotland and well understands that it is of equivalent rank to the High Court in England. The intention is not to confer on judges presiding over criminal trials, whatever their rank, the power to grant declarations of incompatibility. In fact, High Court judges in England who sit in crime at, say, the Old Bailey in London or anywhere in the country, sit in the Crown Court albeit that they are High Court Judges; whereas it is well understood that when Scottish judges sit as criminal judges and in the High Court of Justiciary, they do so in a rank which, for the purposes of criminal cases, is equivalent to the rank that they occupy in the Court of Session. That is well understood.

The point is different. Put simply, the policy that the Bill reflects is that judges who preside over criminal trials should not have the power to make declarations of incompatibility. However, judges sitting in the High Court in England, not as judges sitting in the Court of Session in Scotland, in a judicial review matter would be empowered to make declarations or declarators of incompatibility. But the policy that lies behind the existing statutory provision is that we do not believe that trials should be upset, or potentially upset, by declarations of incompatibility that may go to the very foundations of the prosecution.

House of Lords, Report Stage

Official Report, House of Lords, 19 January 1998, vol. 584, col. 1302

The Lord Advocate (Lord Hardie): . . . My Lords, in Committee, the noble and learned Lord, Lord Mackay of Drumadoon, tabled an amendment which would have conferred on the High Court of Justiciary, sitting as a trial court, the competence to make a declaration that a provision of primary or secondary legislation was incompatible with one or more of the Convention rights.

My noble and learned friend the Lord Chancellor explained that it was not the intention that any such power should be conferred on judges who preside over criminal trials. The noble and learned Lord's amendment, as well as concerns expressed separately by the noble and learned Lord, Lord Hope of Craighead, caused the Government to look again at the provision. As currently drafted, the provision would prevent the High Court of Justiciary from making declarations of incompatibility when considering applications to the nobile officium. That is not the Government's intention which is, as I have explained, only to prevent judges presiding over criminal trials from making such declarations. Amendment No. 17 accordingly provides that such declarations may be made by the High Court of Justiciary, except when it is sitting as a trial court.

Church of Scotland's position

Scotland Act 1998 makes acts of Scottish Government contrary to the Convention void – Courts will prevail if churches fail to observe human rights when acting as public authorities – Act does not interfere with religious freedom of Church of Scotland – Courts will not interfere in spiritual questions

Editor's note: The full debates on the impact of s.13 HRA on the Church of Scotland can be found at - Official Report, House of Commons, 20 May 1998, vol. 312, col. 1054

House of Lords, Committee Stage
Official Report, House of Lords, 19 January 1998, vol. 584, col. 1273

Lord Mackay of Drumadoon: . . . At the outset I wish to make it clear, as the Church of Scotland has already made it clear to the Government, that it is not seeking a blanket exclusion from the Bill's provisions. Neither of the amendments would have such an effect. The Church seeks to safeguard the exclusive jurisdiction of its Church courts to legislate and adjudicate upon matters spiritual which involve— I quote from the fourth Declaratory Article set out in the schedule to the 1921 Act—

> "all matters of doctrine, worship, government, and discipline in the Church, including the right to determine all questions concerning membership and office in the Church, the constitution and membership of its Courts, and the mode of election of its office-bearers, and to define the boundaries of the spheres of labour of its ministers and other office-bearers".

The Church of Scotland is content that the Bill's provisions would apply to other activities in which it is engaged as a public authority; for example, work that it does to implement care-in-the community provisions, funded by central or local government. I am informed by the principal clerk of the General Assembly that the Church has no difficulty with the Bill's general purposes, and recognises that in relation to matters which are not matters spiritual the Church should properly come under the Bill's provisions. In that respect, the Church of Scotland may be in a different position from other Churches. The Church would wish your Lordships to consider its position from a different standpoint; namely, the constitutional settlement incorporated in the 1921 Act [. . .].

[. . .] [c.1274]

In 1929, the United Free Church of Scotland and other Churches united again with the Church of Scotland. An essential precursor to that union was the enactment of the Church of Scotland Act 1921. Before the Act was presented to Parliament the General Assembly of the Church of Scotland prepared what are known as Declaratory Articles which set out the constitution of the Church in matters spiritual. Those claimed the exclusive jurisdiction of the nature I have described. The Act was then passed. Section 1 of the Act provided that Parliament recognised that those Declaratory Articles were lawful articles in which the constitution of the Church was set forth, and no limitation of the liberty, rights and powers in matters spiritual could be derived from any statute or law affecting the Church.

Parliament thus recognised that the Church of Scotland had an exclusive jurisdiction of the nature that I have described—a jurisdiction free from interference by the civil authority. A serious concern has now arisen. It is that the Bill's provisions constitute an unavoidable breach of the provisions of the 1921 Act.

[. . .] [c.1275]

I move the amendment today with the clear request that in reply the noble and learned Lord the Lord Advocate, on behalf of the Government, will acknowledge whether such a conflict exists; whether the Bill will permit the civil authorities to interfere with the way in which the Church courts conduct their business; and whether the Bill will admit the possibility of the Court of Session entertaining an application under Clause 4 to have a declarator of incompatibility granted in respect of the 1921 Act. If such acknowledgements are given, I hope that the noble and learned Lord the Lord Advocate will also be able to say that the Government will bring forward an amendment which eliminates such a conflict.

If, on the other hand, the Government's position is that having considered the matter since November last year such a conflict exists and the provisions of the Bill must and should prevail, it is incumbent upon the Minister to make that clear. The members of the General Assembly of the Church of Scotland, when they gather together in May, will then be aware of what has happened and can consider their reaction to what many in the Church will perceive as an attempt to undermine the constitutional settlement that has existed since 1921.

Successive governments since 1921 have reaffirmed their support for that settlement. I understand that the present Government did so shortly after coming to power. That is why I believe that what has happened has been unintended. I put that forward in a constructive mood because, as I indicated at the outset, I do not for one minute regard the issue as being one of party politics.

[. . .] [c. 1284]

The Lord Advocate (Lord Hardie): [. . .] Under the Scotland Bill anything done by the Scottish Parliament, or by a Minister of that Parliament, which is contrary to the European Convention will be void. In relation to the second question, namely the position of the other Churches in Scotland, all Churches in Scotland will be treated on the same basis.

I turn to the point raised the noble and learned Lord, Lord Mackay of Drumadoon; namely, whether the Bill interferes with the Church of Scotland in its dealing with matters spiritual. I confirm that that is not the case. The Bill regulates only human rights. Unless the Church courts and the Church itself, in the exercise of their public functions, wish to depart from the concept of human rights in the way in which they conduct their business, there will be no conflict between church and state. I am confident that the Church will do its best to observe the principles of human rights referred to and incorporated by the Bill into domestic law.

As noble Lords will be aware, frequently, although with the best of intentions, people fail to achieve their objectives. In the event that there is a failure to observe human rights there may well be a conflict between the Church and this provision. If there is such a conflict, it is our position that the courts will prevail. The civil courts will deal only with Convention rights and not with the spiritual government of the Church. [c. 1285]

The purpose of these amendments is to exempt the Church of Scotland Act 1921 from the provisions of the Human Rights Bill and to re-state the recognition under the 1921 Act of the separate and independent government and jurisdiction of the Church in matters spiritual.

In Committee, several noble Lords raised points about the possible impact of the Bill, not only on the Church of Scotland but on other Churches. [. . .]

So far as the Church of Scotland is concerned, I accept that the amendments are not influenced by party-political considerations. I hope that the noble Lords will accept that the position adopted by the Government is equally not influenced by such considerations, or indeed by considerations of any particular religious persuasion. In the case of the Church of Scotland we have to look carefully at the implications of this legislation for the Church of Scotland Act 1921, which the Church of Scotland very properly considers a very important legislative statement of its independence in matters spiritual.

I wish to make it clear that the Government have no intention of interfering with the Church's religious freedom. That is a repetition of a statement that was made by the Government in confirmation of statements made by previous governments in relation to the position of the Church of Scotland. However, I wish to emphasise that the Bill does not interfere with the religious freedom of the Church of Scotland, nor is it intended to do so. I cannot emphasise that point strongly enough. The Church of Scotland Act 1921, to which the Church of Scotland rightly attaches much importance, establishes clearly the independence of the Church in spiritual matters. Such issues are properly matters for the Church and the Church alone.

However, it may be that in some circumstances the authorities of the Church of Scotland could be public authorities for the purposes of the Bill. The noble and learned Lord, Lord Mackay of Drumadoon, properly recognised that certainly in performing certain functions they would come within that category. He referred to care in the community.

The question of whether a church body is a public authority in any particular circumstance will be a matter for the ordinary courts, as it is at the moment. I refer to the case of Logan in 1995 mentioned by my noble and learned friend Lord Hope of Craighead. That was a case where the Court of Session considered whether it had jurisdiction. After the Bill becomes law—if that is your Lordships' wish—the position will be that the Court of Session will consider whether the particular circumstances of an act by the Church indicate that, in performing that act, the Church can be described as a public authority. [c. 1286]

If it is a public authority, there seems to be no reason to exempt the institutions of the Church of Scotland from the public authority provisions of the Bill when it is acting in that capacity. The policy of the Government is that if a Church body is a public authority the Bill should apply to it. In this situation it seems to me that the Church would not wish to maintain that breaches of human rights committed by its institutions are purely matters of spiritual concern which should be excluded from the jurisdiction of the ordinary courts. In saying that, I wish to express confidence that the Church of Scotland, as other Churches, will do its utmost to comply with the spirit and intention of the legislation.

It is also clear to me that the civil courts will not want to involve themselves in spiritual matters, as was evidenced by the case of Logan to which the noble and learned Lord, Lord Hope of Craighead, referred. The civil courts will wish to confine themselves in any individual case to the minimum examination necessary to arrive at a decision on whether there has been any infringement of the legislation: in other words, was the Church acting as a public authority and, if so, is it in breach of the legislative provisions?

The civil courts would not want to intrude further into the business of the Church than is required to ensure proper observance of Convention rights. Nor will the Bill entitle them to do so. The courts would, I am certain, continue to respect the spiritual independence to which the Church of Scotland properly attaches great importance.

While, as I have acknowledged, there are difficult issues of jurisdiction here, I do not think it would be right to exempt the Church of Scotland Act 1921 from the provisions in the Bill in the way proposed. The policy of the Government, as expressed in the Bill, is to enable the ordinary courts to inquire into proceedings of Church bodies only so far as may be necessary to resolve human rights questions. I hope that, in the light of that explanation, the noble Lords will feel able to withdraw the amendment.

Lord Renton: My Lords, before the noble and learned Lord sits down, would he be so good as to look at page 4 of the Bill? Near the top of that page he will see subsection (3) of Clause 6, which says:

> "In this section, 'public authority' includes—
> (a) a court or tribunal, and
> (b) any person certain of whose functions are functions of a public nature".

For the removal of doubt, and to give clear guidance to the courts in deciding the matters which the noble Lord has mentioned, would it not be a good thing to add in that subsection words such as:

> "but 'public authority' does not include any kind of Church court or religious court of any kind"?

Lord Hardie: My Lords, I am grateful to the noble Lord, Lord Renton, for that intervention, but, with respect, I do not think that that would meet the point. If a Church court were performing a function which could be described as a function of a public authority and is dealing with something other than a purely spiritual [c. 1287] matter peculiar to the Church, it would not be appropriate to exempt such a body from the provisions of the legislation.

Lord Campbell of Alloway: My Lords, the noble and learned Lord says that the courts will not inquire into spiritual matters. How will one stop a court from doing so if a complaint is made before it? Is the suggestion that the Church of Scotland, the Church of England, or whichever Church, should move to strike out the pleadings? How is one to define the line between spiritual and other matters? I simply ask as a practical, knock-about lawyer. I can see tremendous difficulties in what is being proposed.

Lord Hardie: My Lords, that is precisely the kind of question that the civil courts deal with at present. They would consider the particular circumstances of the situation and decide whether the body was acting as a public authority. If it were acting in a purely spiritual capacity, the courts would decline jurisdiction.
[. . .]

Lord Mackay of Clashfern: My Lords, just before the Lord Advocate sits down finally, my question is, [c. 1288] would the definition which the Government have put into this Bill, taking the court of Scotland as an example, make a Church court which was deciding a spiritual matter, a matter of faith, a public authority within the meaning of that definition? If not, why not?

Lord Hardie: My Lords, the short answer to my noble and learned friend is, no, it would not include that situation, the reason being that the Scottish courts, as my noble and learned friend will be aware, because of the relationship between Church and state, have been slow to interfere, and indeed have refused to interfere in matters of this nature. Therefore, if the Church court were deciding a matter spiritual, the courts would not be entitled to review that.

House of Lords, Third Reading
Official Report, House of Lords, 5 February 1998, vol 585, col. 792

The Lord Advocate (Lord Hardie): . . . [. . .] The effect of the 1921 Act was to end the status of the Church as the established Church of Scotland and change it instead into a national Church. The 1921 Act recognised the independent jurisdiction of the Church of Scotland in matters spiritual. It is worth recalling exactly what was meant by that. I refer noble Lords to Article IV of the Declaratory Articles appended to the 1921 Act which provide, so far as is material for present purposes, that,

"This Church, as part of the universal Church wherein the Lord Jesus Christ has appointed a government in the hands of Church office-bearers, receives from him, its divine King and Head, and from him alone, the right and power subject to no civil authority to legislate, and to adjudicate finally, in all matters of doctrine, worship, government and discipline in the Church".

The effect of that article was considered by the Inner House of the Court of Session in the case of Ballantyne v. Presbytery of Wigtown in 1936. I shall not trouble your Lordships with the detail of that case. Suffice it to say that the court ruled that any matter contained within Article IV of the Declaratory Articles, by virtue of being so contained, was a spiritual matter in relation to which the civil authority had no jurisdiction. Since Article IV of the Declaratory Articles mentions the government and discipline of the Church, those matters are spiritual.

For the purposes of the 1921 Act, as interpreted by the Court of Session in 1936, "spiritual matters" do not include only those matters relating to doctrine and worship, which one might have thought, on an ordinary view of the question, were included in that term, but include also the practical and administrative procedures by which the government and disciplinary procedures of the Church of Scotland are carried out.

The concern of the Church of Scotland is that if this Bill is not amended it is possible that the courts of the Church of Scotland will be held to be public authorities for the purposes of Clause 6 of the Bill and, indeed, may be held to be courts within the meaning of that clause. That in turn would mean that actions by those courts which were incompatible with a Convention right would be reviewable in the Court of Session. In the Church's [c. 794] view that would amount to a reversal of the recognition by Parliament of the independence of the Church under the 1921 Act.

That is a brief summary of the background of the present legal position of the Church of Scotland and, more particularly and more importantly, of the genuine concern which the Church has in relation to this Bill. I shall now move to the second part of my remarks to consider how much of a practical, as opposed to a theoretical, problem there is. The acts, which the Bill treats as acts of a public authority, include, as your Lordships will see from Clause 6(3)(a), on the one hand, acts of a court or tribunal. On the other hand, as Clause 6(3)(b) provides, there are included acts of a person certain of whose functions are functions of a public nature. But, as is clear from Clause 6(5), acts of a private nature are not included.

The Church is concerned that its courts may be held to be public authorities within the meaning of Clause 6. As I indicated at Report, in response to a question from the noble and learned Lord, Lord Mackay of Clashfern, it is my view that the courts of the Church of Scotland are not courts for the purposes of this Bill. I should like to take a moment to explain why.

Courts of the Church of Scotland do not, as a matter either of their constitution or practice, carry out any judicial functions on behalf of the state. Nor do they adjudicate upon a citizen's legal rights or obligations, whether common law or statutory. They operate in relation to matters which are essentially of a private nature. Unlike the courts of the Church of England—this is one of the differences—they do not have the right to compel the attendance of witnesses or the production of documents.

[. . .] [T]he effect of the 1921 Act, which, as I have said, recognised the independence of the Church from regulation by Parliament, was to define the Church as a non-public or private institution in the sense that its affairs were of no concern to the state. The 1921 Act effectively disestablished the Church of Scotland. It would seem to me illogical to say that the state had no interest or jurisdiction over the affairs of the Church and its courts while at the same time saying that those courts were nevertheless courts for the purposes of a public general Act. That is the Government's view on whether the courts of the Church of Scotland are courts for the purposes of this Bill.

Clause 6, when read with Clause 2, is of course designed to invite the civil courts of the United Kingdom, as far as possible, to treat as a "public authority" those bodies which the Strasbourg institutions would treat as bodies whose acts engage the responsibility of the state. However, as I said at Report, whether or not the courts of the Church of Scotland are courts for the purposes of the Bill, it is possible that they might in some circumstances be public authorities. [c. 795]

At the meeting which the Secretary of State and I had with the Moderator, who was accompanied by the Principal Clerk to the Church of Scotland, the procurator to the Church of Scotland and the solicitor to the Church of Scotland, no one in the party from the

Church of Scotland was able to suggest a concrete example of a case in which a court of the Church of Scotland would clearly be acting as a public authority within the meaning of Clause 6. I may say that the meeting took some time. The matter was explored. The Church came prepared for the meeting. It was given plenty of time to come up with examples and it was significant that it was not able to do so.

Within government there have been extensive discussions of this point among officials from the Lord Chancellor's Office, the Home Office, the Foreign and Commonwealth Office, the Scottish Office, the Cabinet Office, parliamentary counsel's office and my own office. Therefore, to suggest that this matter has been treated lightly is not a fair comment.

[...] [c. 796]

Article 6.1 is reproduced on page 15 of the Bill. I do not think it necessary to repeat it. However, it is possible that proceedings before a kirk session considering disciplinary action against a minister may require, for the purposes of Article 6, to be,

> "a fair and public hearing by an independent and impartial tribunal established by law".

Questions might then arise—I emphasise that I am referring to a hypothetical situation—as to whether a kirk session was independent and impartial and, in particular, whether it was established by law. I would have some doubts as to whether a kirk session could be so described. As I have said, it seems to be reasonably clear that there was a period in the history of the Church when much of its administration and government was regulated by Acts of the Scottish Parliament. At that period it would have been easy to say that kirk sessions and indeed the assembly itself were "established by law".

However that may have been, it appears to me that the effect of the 1921 Act was to cut the connection between the general law of the land and the administration and government of the Church. That being so, it must be at least doubtful whether the kirk session and the general assembly could any longer be said to be "established by law". It is also possible that questions might be raised as to whether Church courts present a sufficient appearance of independence and impartiality.

It is not perhaps necessary for me to express any definitive view on any of these questions. I would only remark that in the 30 years since individual petition to Strasbourg became competent, no such point has been taken before the European Court of Human Rights by any Scottish minister.

However, I must continue to make these improbable assumptions for the purposes of the argument. Let me continue. If a Church body to which the Bill applies commits a wrong in Convention terms, it would fall to the civil courts to right it. The Convention rights are in this context part of the law of the land. The civil courts would investigate the Convention issue—in the disciplinary example I have given, the criticism of the procedural unfairness levelled against the Church—in exactly the same way in which they would address any other question arising under the law of the land; for example, a complaint that someone acting on behalf of the Church had committed a delict, or tort in English terms. That would be consistent with long-standing Strasbourg jurisprudence on these questions. The civil courts' task does not, and cannot, involve trespassing on the doctrinal or spiritual interests of the Church, any more than the European Court of Human Rights would do were a complaint to be made direct to Strasbourg before the Bill comes into force.

To sum up on this part of my remarks, neither the Church nor the Government have been able to identify a real practical problem which this Bill will cause to the courts of the Church. The least unlikely problem is one related to whether the Church courts are independent and impartial tribunals established by law, within the meaning of the Convention. If that problem exists, it exists now. The Bill will not solve it. The only [c. 797] difference the Bill will make is that questions relating to that problem will be dealt with in Edinburgh rather than in Strasbourg. In relation to an earlier group of amendments, I would simply refer to the intervention of the noble Earl, Lord Russell, who expressed this point more eloquently than I can. But the point is exactly the same.

I turn now to what I referred to as the theoretical threat to its independence which the Church perceives. The Church has repeatedly asserted that it would not wish to act inconsistently with the Convention. The Government of course accept and welcome that as a general statement of the Church's position. But by seeking to be exempted from the provisions of the Bill the Church is asserting that, in the event of its courts acting in a manner incompatible with a Convention right—perhaps because their internal organisation and procedures are inconsistent with Article 6—that matter should not be reviewable by the ordinary courts in Scotland but should only be reviewable by appeal within the system of Church courts. I would only observe that, in the case of a breach of Article 6, further consideration by other Church courts is unlikely to cure the defect.

But, as was made clear at the meeting with the Secretary of State for Scotland, the Church's position goes further than simply claiming to deal with human rights matters within its own courts. In the event of a finding by the European Court of Human Rights that the United Kingdom was in breach of its international obligations by reason of a Church court's having acted incompatibly with the Convention, the Church of Scotland asserts that the United Kingdom Parliament would have no entitlement to require the Church of Scotland to change its procedures so as to make them compatible with the Convention. According to the Church of Scotland, the most that Parliament or the Government could do would be to ask the Church to reconsider the matter. It would be for the Church to decide whether to change its procedures. The Church is claiming the right to continue to deny Convention rights to those affected by the actings of its courts.

Perhaps I may say in passing that I inquired of the Moderator and the other representatives at the meeting as to how long this procedure would take. I understood from my researches that we would be talking about two years. In fact it would be three general assemblies before the Church could bring it into line. We are talking about three years. But even then, at the end of three years the Church might decide that it was not going to come into line with the requirement, in which case Parliament would require to consider what amendments were required to the 1921 Act.

I have already said that I have not been able to imagine a case in which such a situation would arise. But if it were to arise, the responsibility of this Government, and of any future government, would be to implement the international obligations of the United Kingdom. Those obligations, in the case of the human rights Convention, consist in guaranteeing Convention rights to everyone in the United Kingdom. No exception is made in the Convention for persons who may be subject to the jurisdiction of the Church of Scotland. [c. 798]

As I have said before, the Government do not seek to subject the institutions of the Church to detailed parliamentary control. We have no wish to provoke a disruption of the kind which soured Church-state relations in the last century. We seek only to incorporate into domestic law the rights which the United Kingdom has for some 45 years undertaken to guarantee to its citizens under the European Convention on Human Rights.

I shall add one final point before I finish. Your Lordships will note that this legislation is to apply to every public authority in the United Kingdom. The Bill represents a major constitutional change in the working of institutions throughout the country. The very courts of the land are to be subject to the Bill. The only exceptions are the two Houses of Parliament acting as such.

I have tried to show that the concerns of the Church are not based on any realistic fear of interference by the civil courts with the Church courts. No one has been able to think of a real example. I have explained that, if the least unlikely example of conflict were to arise, the Bill would neither help nor hinder the arguments which the Church might present. It would enable the matter to be dealt with by a Scottish court rather than by a European court in Strasbourg. I would have thought that that would have been to the Church's advantage.

The Church's position ignores the practical implications of the United Kingdom's international obligations. It maintains that it is not for Parliament to legislate in such a way that the civil courts might be able, even in theory, to review the actions of Church courts. The logic behind these amendments is that even in the event of a finding by the European Court of Human Rights that the United Kingdom was, by reason of the actions of a Church court, in breach of its obligations under the Convention, this Parliament could not put the matter right.

The Government's object in bringing this legislation forward is to enable the citizens of the country whose human rights within the meaning of the Convention are being interfered with to raise that matter before the courts of this country rather than being required to take the matter to Strasbourg. Her Majesty's Government see no reason to make an exception to that general rule in respect of persons whose Convention rights may have been adversely affected by institutions of the Church. Therefore, in the light of that full explanation, I hope that the noble and learned Lord will withdraw his amendment.

CHANNEL ISLANDS AND THE ISLE OF MAN

Application of the Act
House of Lords, Report Stage
Official Report, House of Lords, 19 January 1998, vol. 584, col. 1307
The Parliamentary Under-Secretary of State, Home Office (Lord Williams of Mostyn): . . . I am most grateful to the noble Lord, Lord Lester of Herne Hill . . . He has correctly identified, as have other noble Lords, the constitutional position of the Channel Islands and the Isle of Man. It is a fact that there is a great reservoir of ignorance about the true constitutional arrangements between the Channel Islands, the Isle of Man and the United Kingdom. [. . .] The fact is that they are independent jurisdictions and are extremely and understandably astute that their interests be properly considered; that they be properly consulted; and that every due regard be given to their views. Dare I say, in this evening's context, that that is one of their human rights?

Generally speaking, I do not disagree with the constitutional analysis put forward by the noble Lord, Lord Lester of Herne Hill. The Crown is ultimately—and I stress the word ultimately—responsible for the good government of the islands. We have full power in principle to legislate for the islands, but it is a fact that it would be contrary to constitutional Conventions to which all governments of whatever political complexion have adhered for the power to be used in the ordinary course of events without the agreement of the island governments. [. . .] In extremis, we could take that power but we do not regard these circumstances as appropriate for the power to be taken. We prefer to work by co-operation, as did previous governments.

Enabling provisions are included in published Bills only after full consultation with the island governments. Similarly, any orders that the islands subsequently agree should be made are drafted in consultation with the island authorities. Many noble Lords asked, perfectly properly, whether Her Majesty's Government had consulted with the appropriate island governments. The answer is an unambiguous yes. All three stated categorically that they did not wish the Human Rights Bill to be extended to them. . . . All of them said no, and they were quite categoric in that respect. [c. 1308] I respectfully suggest that we ought not to force different arrangements upon them when they have expressed themselves so firmly.

However, it is right that the Isle of Man authorities have announced their intention to introduce insular legislation. I say that knowing that I might be derided but I believe it to be the correct adjective. That insular legislation—it being an island, after all—would give effect to the Convention on the island. They have taken that view. The authorities in the Channel Islands do not intend to take that step for the present, but it is not ruled out for the future.

The Government's position is quite plain. We have our obligations. We have our obligations under the Convention. We have consulted the islands fully and have our obligations to consider their views. We have done so. [. . .]

I am most grateful for the support expressed from various quarters of your Lordships' House. We are dealing with delicate matters and there are sensibilities involved which must properly be attended to and taken into consideration. We believe that the stance we have adopted is the correct one, bearing in mind the Conventional history of the relationships between the United Kingdom and three islands which have their own distinct traditions, their own separate views and their own discrete legislatures.

House of Commons, Committee Stage
Official Report, House of Commons, 3 June 1998, vol. 313, col. 471

The Secretary of State for the Home Department (Mr. Straw): I am grateful to my hon. Friend the Member for Great Grimsby (Mr. Mitchell) for tabling the amendments and raising this important issue, just as the Government were grateful in the other place for the way in which Lord Lester raised the matter there.

As we have heard, the amendments would apply the Bill's provisions in various ways to the Channel Islands and the Isle of Man. My hon. Friend has pointed out that the United Kingdom is obliged to ensure that the islands comply with the Convention and that there is a right of individual petition to the Convention institutions in Strasbourg in respect of the islands, but that the Convention does not at present have effect in their domestic law. I am happy to tell the Committee that the island authorities have made it clear that they want to bring rights home to the islands, just as we are doing in the United Kingdom.

[...]

United Kingdom laws are sometimes extended to the islands with their agreement. We consulted the island authorities about the extension of the Bill to them. All [c. 472] three said that they did not wish it to be so extended, and, as we want to maintain satisfactory relations with the islands, we paid careful attention to their views, as always.

The Committee will be glad to know that my noble Friend Lord Williams, the Minister with responsibility for the Channel Islands and the Isle of Man, has undertaken a series of visits to find out from the island authorities what plans they have in the human rights field. I am pleased to say that their responses have all been positive. Each of the island authorities has made clear its intentions with respect to the Bill and the incorporation in its domestic law of the European Convention. I have placed copies of their public statements and letters in the Library and have made them available to the official Opposition, to the Liberal Democrats and to my hon. Friend the Member for Great Grimsby.

[...]

> The Bailiff of Jersey has now made it clear that the insular authorities
> "wish to confirm their previously declared intention to progress the matter of legislation to incorporate the European Convention on Human Rights into Jersey law, having regard to the particular circumstances of the Island, once the United Kingdom Bill has completed its progress through Parliament in Westminster."

The Bailiff's letter goes on:

> "The Insular Authorities confidently expect to have a draft law with the Home Office for pre audit in the normal way by the end of this year."

The States of Guernsey issued a public statement on 22 May. The President of the Advisory and Finance Committee said:

> "The States Advisory and Finance Committee intends to recommend to the States of Guernsey that legislation be enacted"—

to incorporate the Convention—

> "having regard to the particular circumstances of the Island".

He said that once the Bill has become law, recommendations will be laid before the States of Guernsey. He added:

> "The Committee is confident that it will be possible to submit a draft law to the Home Office for pre-audit before the end of this year."

In December 1997, the Isle of Man made it clear that it intended to introduce legislation to give effect in Manx law to the Convention on human rights. It says:

> "Before any Government Bill is introduced in the House of Keys, a draft is always sent to the Home Office for their comments, if necessary after consultation with other United Kingdom Departments, and appropriate measures are taken to consult local interests."

In the light of those statements, I hope that the Committee will recognise that the Governments of each of the three islands are committed to introducing [c. 473] legislation fully to incorporate the European Convention into their own law and to consult me, my officials and the Government more widely on the precise terms of that incorporation. I believe that that is a satisfactory outcome.

[. . .] I hope that, in the light of those clear undertakings, my hon. Friend the Member for Great Grimsby will see fit to withdraw the amendment.

My hon. Friend asked whether any of the island authorities could incorporate into their domestic law the fourth Protocol of the Convention, even though it is not being incorporated into the Bill. The answer is that they cannot incorporate any part of the Convention that the United Kingdom and the Crown, as high contracting party to the Convention, have not accepted. That important part of our relationship with the islands gives the Crown and the United Kingdom Parliament ultimate authority over them: we, and not they, enter into all international obligations, which are then binding on the islands.

That said, it would none the less be open to each of the island authorities and Parliaments, should they want to, to write the terms of the fourth Protocol, or of any other protocol not incorporated into the Bill, into their domestic law.

DUTIES ON COUNSEL

Counsel must educate themselves on European Court of Human Rights jurisprudence – prosecutors should assist court on human rights matters where criminal defendants are unrepresented

House of Lords, Committee Stage

Official Report, House of Lords, 18 November 1997, vol. 583, col. 526

The Lord Chancellor: Certainly I can confirm that there are textbooks which are comparatively inexpensive and that there are comprehensive periodicals. They are readily accessible. I repeat what I said, that counsel are not to be spoon-fed but must educate themselves as part of a continuing process of self-education in developing areas of the law. It is intended that Convention rights and values shall permeate the work of the courts at all levels. It is up to counsel to get themselves up to speed in that endeavour.

As regards the unrepresented defendant, in this country it is usually a matter of choice because in the criminal courts legal aid will be available. But where a defendant insists upon defending himself, there is a well [c. 527] recognised and honourable tradition in the courts of the judge giving the defendant the maximum assistance that he can.

Lord Meston: Will the noble and learned Lord also agree that there is a tradition that prosecuting counsel should assist the court in those circumstances?

The Lord Chancellor: Yes.